The Prophets of Israel

T0337585

CRITICAL STUDIES IN THE HEBREW BIBLE

Edited by

Anselm C. Hagedorn
*Humboldt Universität
zu Berlin*

Nathan MacDonald
University of Cambridge

Stuart Weeks
Durham University

The Prophets of Israel

Reinhard G. Kratz

Translated by
Anselm C. Hagedorn and Nathan MacDonald

Winona Lake, Indiana
Eisenbrauns
2015

© Copyright 2015 Eisenbrauns

All rights reserved.
Printed in the United States of America.

www.eisenbrauns.com

Library of Congress Cataloging-in-Publication Data

Kratz, Reinhard Gregor, 1957– author.
  [Prophetenstudien. English]
  The prophets of Israel / Reinhard G. Kratz ; translated by Anselm C.
  Hagedorn and Nathan MacDonald.
      pages   cm. — (Critical studies in the Hebrew Bible ; number 2)
  Includes bibliographical references and indexes.
  ISBN 978-1-57506-317-1 (pbk. : alk. paper)
  1. Bible. Prophets—Criticism, interpretation, etc.   I. Hagedorn,
Anselm C., translator.   II. MacDonald, Nathan, 1975– translator.
III. Title.
  BS1505.52.K7313   2015
  224′.06—dc23
                                                           2015030851

The paper used in this publication meets the minimum requirements of the American
National Standard for Information Sciences—Permanence of Paper for Printed Library
Materials, ANSI Z39.48–1984. ♾™

Contents

Preface

The prophets of Israel as we encounter them in the books of the Hebrew Bible are the most distinctive representatives of Jewish religion. In looking back at the past, analyzing the present, and predicting the future, they bear witness to a God who has rejected his people but is unable to abandon them completely. At the same time, they confront a people that has forsaken its God but is unable to live without him. The rift could not be deeper, and yet God and his people belong to each other like nothing else. It goes without saying that the prophets of the Hebrew Bible are not only of central importance for Jewish tradition but also for Christianity and Islam—both in terms of theology as well as ethics. It is the God of the prophets who—despite all their differences—unites the three monotheistic world religions.

This, however, has not always been the case. The prophets of the Hebrew Bible have a history. This history goes back to the ancient Near East and to ancient Israel and Judah, to a time when Jewish religion did not yet exist. During these times, the prophets played an important role as mediators between God and people. They did not, however, write books. They did not reflect on the relationship between God and people but instead embodied it. This is one of the reasons why in biblical tradition we have to distinguish between the historical and the literary prophet. The historical prophet is a representative of ancient Israelite and Judahite religion, while the literary prophet—as presented in the biblical books—is part of the tradition of emerging Judaism.

The depiction of the prophets of Israel presented in this book takes this distinction seriously and will focus primarily on the literary tradition. This tradition needs to be recognized as such and should not be confused with the historical prophet and his words. Limited space does not permit a detailed analysis of the biblical and nonbiblical sources. Such an analysis is presupposed and only the results of the critical reconstruction of the religio-historical and literary development will be presented here. After an overview of various models for the interpretation of biblical prophecy (chap. 1), we will consider first the broader historical background and the phenomenology of prophecy in the ancient Near East, including ancient Israel and Judah (chaps. 2–3). We will then move on to the literary evidence of prophecy in biblical tradition and its historical context, including the earliest commentaries on prophetic books, the *pesharim* from Qumran (chaps. 4–10). The study concludes with an appendix that will introduce the reader to scholarship on the prophets and provide some suggestions for further reading (chap. 11).

Passages from the Hebrew Bible are quoted according to the New Revised Standard Version (NRSV), with some modifications. Because the pronunciation of the divine name is uncertain, it will be written with consonants only (Yhwh). Nonbiblical sources are quoted according to the editions listed in the abbreviations.

If the reader enjoys reading the book, this is thanks to the _Wissenschaftskolleg Berlin_, which awarded me a fellowship during the academic year 2002–2003, allowing me to write the German original of this book. For the English edition, the text was revised and expanded with chapters 9 and 11. To maintain both the introductory character and a certain reader-friendliness, additional references to secondary literature and footnotes in chapters 1–10 are avoided.

Anselm C. Hagedorn (Berlin) and Nathan MacDonald (Cambridge) translated the book, and I would like to thank them for their careful and diligent work. Further thanks are due to Franziska Ede, Peter Porzig, and Laura Victoria Schimmelpfennig, who took care of the corrections and the bibliographies as well as compiling the index. I am grateful to Anja Klein and her students at New College, University of Edinburgh, who read the first draft of the English version in her course on Hebrew Prophecy in 2014. Dr. Klein as well as Stephen M. Germany, a Fulbright scholar from Emory University (Atlanta), who kindly offered to read the final version of the manuscript, contributed many corrections and invaluable feedback. Finally, I would like to thank Jim Eisenbraun and his staff for the professional support during the production of this volume.

The following editions are referred to by an abbreviation:

ANET   Pritchard James B., ed. _Ancient Near Eastern Texts Relating to the Old Testament_. 3rd ed. Princeton: Princeton University Press, 1969.

COS   Hallo, William W., and K. Lawson Younger, eds. _The Context of Scripture_. 3 vols. Leiden: Brill, 2003.

DSS.C Charlesworth, James H., ed. _The Dead Sea Scrolls: Hebrew, Aramaic, and Greek Texts with English Translation_. Vols. 1–4 and 6B. Tübingen: Mohr Siebeck / Louisville: Westminster John Knox, 1994–2006.

DSS.SE García Martínez, Florentino and Eibert J. C. Tigchelaar, eds. _The Dead Sea Scrolls: Study Edition_. 2 vols. Leiden: Brill, 1997–1998 (Paperback ed. Leiden: Brill / Grand Rapids, Michigan: William B. Eerdmans, 2000).

OTP   Charlesworth, James H., ed. _The Old Testament Pseudepigrapha_. 2 vols. London: Darton Longman & Todd, 1983–1985.

WAW   Nissinen, Martti (with contributions by C. L. Seow, R. K. Ritner). _Prophets and Prophecy in the Ancient Near East_. SBLWAW 12. Edited by Peter Machinist. Atlanta: Society of Biblical Literature, 2003.

CHAPTER I

The Law and the Prophets

Models of Interpretation

If we open the Bible and start to read from the beginning, we need to exercise patience while we wait to encounter the Prophets. In Christian Bibles they are placed at the end of the Old Testament. Thus, it is only after the historical books and the poetic and wisdom literature that we will find the three Major Prophets: Isaiah, Jeremiah, and Ezekiel, followed by the twelve Minor Prophets: Hosea, Joel, Amos, Obadiah, Jonah, Micah, Nahum, Habakkuk, Zephaniah, Haggai, Zechariah, and Malachi. The Book of Daniel appears after the Major Prophets, and sometimes Lamentations follows the prophet Jeremiah, as do the Book of Baruch, Jeremiah's scribe, and the Letter of Jeremiah in the Bibles of the Roman Catholic church.

Editions of the Hebrew Bible differ in their ordering of the books. The prophets are placed after the Pentateuch. The prophetic corpus not only consists of the three Major and twelve Minor Prophets but also includes the books of Joshua, Judges, Samuel, and Kings that precede them. Daniel and Lamentations are placed elsewhere; Baruch and the Letter of Jeremiah are missing.

The position and extent of the prophetic books are no accident but the result of selection, reflecting the different versions of the Hebrew and Greek canon. Here we see differences in the understanding of the prophets that have influenced the history of interpretation. In what follows, I will give a few examples of different interpretive approaches.

1. The Prophets as Authors of Sacred History

The canon of the Hebrew Bible that became accepted in Jewish tradition and—as far as the content is concerned—also in the Protestant churches follows the order Law (Torah), Prophets (Nevi'im), and Writings (Ketuvim). The other version, in which the prophets are relegated to the

1

end and which also contains several so-called "hidden writings" (i.e., the Apocrypha), is the order of the Septuagint, the Greek translation of the Hebrew Bible. The Septuagint was the Bible of the Greek-speaking Jews as well as of the early Christians and has decisively influenced the tradition of the Oriental churches and also—via the Latin translation (Vulgate)—the Roman Catholic church (see chart on p. 3.

Both versions of the canon are believed to be divinely inspired, and it is claimed that the authors of the biblical books were prophets. This notion is encountered in *Contra Apionem* (I.37–41), a work of the first century Jewish author Flavius Josephus, as well as in the Babylonian Talmud (Tractate Baba Batra 14b–15a). It is an idea that is already implied in the Hebrew Bible itself. Writing around 300 B.C.E., the author of Chronicles assumes that each epoch of the sacred history had its own prophet and that each prophet authored a book about his epoch, works from which the Chronicler himself now draws (1 Chr 29:29). The sources available to the Chronicler are indeed none other than the biblical books known to us from Genesis to Kings and from Isaiah to Malachi. The Chronicler's theory about his sources grants these books canonical status.

The division of the second part of the canon into "Former" and "Latter" Prophets also raises these books to canonical dignity. In the Hebrew canon, the books of Joshua, Judges, Samuel, and Kings are called the Former Prophets, whereas the Septuagint counts them among the historical books. The books from Isaiah to Malachi are called the Latter Prophets. Their extent and order varies in the manuscript tradition, but they form the prophetic corpus that the Septuagint places at the end of the canon. One reason why the books of Joshua to Kings were subsumed under the "Prophets" is certainly that they contain narratives about prophets. The decisive reason, however, was most likely the intention to put their authors on an equal footing with Moses, the prophetic archetype (Deut 18:15; Hos 12:14), as well as with the Latter Prophets. The transfer of the spirit of prophecy from Moses to his successor Joshua is described in Num 27:18–23 and Deut 34:9.

In this way, Torah and Prophets are combined into a continuous story filled with the spirit of the prophets and written down by them. For the time of Isaiah (2 Kgs 18–20 // Isa 36–39) and Jeremiah (2 Kgs 24–25 // Jer 52) the texts of the Former and the Latter Prophets partly overlap and thus indicate the historical setting of the prophets. In the Hebrew canon, this continuous story ranges from the creation of the world to the restitution of Jerusalem under Persian rule or—in the words of Josephus and the Rabbis—from Moses to Artaxerxes. Afterward, it is said, the prophetic spirit ceased. It is the same extent of sacred history that the books of

Hebrew Bible	Greek Bible (Septuagint)
Law (Torah)	**The Five Books of Moses**
Genesis (Gen)	Genesis
Exodus (Exod)	Exodus
Leviticus (Lev)	Leviticus
Numbers (Num)	Numbers
Deuteronomy (Deut)	Deuteronomy
Prophets (*Nevi'im*)	**Historical Books**
Former Prophets	
Joshua (Josh)	Joshua
Judges (Judg)	Judges
Samuel (1–2 Sam)	1–2 Kingdoms (1–2 Kgdms =
Kings (1–2 Kgs)	1–2 Sam)
Latter Prophets	3–4 Kingdoms (3–4 Kgdms =
Isaiah (Isa)	1–2 Kgs)
Jeremiah (Jer)	1–2 Chronicles
Ezekiel (Ezek)	1 Ezra (1 Esdr)
Hosea (Hos)	2 Ezra = Ezra/ Nehemiah (2 Esdr)
Joel (Joel)	Esther (with additions = Add Esth)
Amos (Amos)	Judith (Jdt)
Obadiah (Obad)	Tobit (Tob)
Jonah (Jonah)	Maccabees (1–4 Macc)
Micah (Mic)	**The Educational Books**
Nahum (Nah)	Psalms (with Odes)
Habakkuk (Hab)	Proverbs
Zephaniah (Zeph)	Qoheleth
Haggai (Hag)	Song of Songs/Canticum
Zechariah (Zech)	Job
Malachi (Mal)	Wisdom of Solomon (Wis)
Writings (*Ketuvim*)	Sirach/Ben Sira/Ecclesiasticus
Psalms (Ps/Pss)	(Sir/Eccl)
Job (Job)	**Prophets**
Proverbs (Prov)	Hosea
Ruth (Ruth)	Amos
Song of Songs/Canticles	Micah
(Song/Cant)	Joel
Qoheleth/Ecclesiastes (Qoh/Eccl)	Obadiah
Lamentations (Lam)	Jonah
Esther (Esth)	Nahum
Daniel (Dan)	Habakkuk
Ezra (Ezra)	Zephaniah
Nehemiah (Neh)	Haggai
Chronicles (1–2 Chr)	Zechariah
	Malachi
	Isaiah
	Jeremiah
	Baruch (Bar)
	Lamentations
	Epistle of Jeremiah (Ep Jer)
	Ezekiel
	Daniel (with additions = Add Dan)

Chronicles, Ezra, and Nehemiah recapitulate; the third part of the canon, the "Writings," which originated in a collection of the psalms of David, is integrated into the same chronological framework. It is this framework of the biblical history that the "Praise of the Fathers" in the Book of Ben Sira, written in Hebrew at the beginning of the second century B.C.E. and translated into Greek around 130 B.C.E., summarizes according to the canonical order of the Hebrew Bible (Sir 44–49).

The Septuagint follows a different ordering principle. The historical books include the books of Maccabees, and thus the sacred history extends as far as the Hellenistic period. By placing the prophetic books at the end of the canon, the Septuagint indicates that the sacred history has not yet reached its destination and still awaits its eschatological fulfillment.

2. *The Prophets as Teachers of the Law*

The Prophets not only record the sacred history but also play a role in it. Their function is stated clearly in the last verses of the collection of prophetic writings in Malachi 3:

> Remember the teaching of my servant Moses, the statutes and ordinances that I commanded him at Horeb for all Israel. (Mal 3:22 [NRSV 4:4])

This verse creates an overarching collection of prophetic books by echoing YHWH's admonition of Joshua at its beginning in Josh 1:7–8. Thus, the "Prophets" are connected to the Torah of Moses. For the entire period from the conquest of the Promised Land to the exile, the Former and Latter Prophets are seen as teachers of the law who call the people of Israel to obey their God and warn of the consequences of disobedience.

The basis of the prophetic teaching is the Law of Moses, revealed at Mt. Sinai and publicly proclaimed by Moses in the plains of Moab shortly before the people's entry into the Promised Land. This law and especially its proclamation in the Book of Deuteronomy is the constant point of reference in the Former Prophets—that is, the books from Joshua to Kings. Because of this basic orientation to the Book of Deuteronomy, we speak of a Deuteronomistic History, or, more correctly, of a deuteronomistic redaction of the books of Joshua to Kings. This redaction is responsible for the perception of the prophets as teachers of the law and admonishers of the people (2 Kgs 17:13; 21:10–16; 22:14–20). It also correlates the word of God in the mouth of the prophets with the Law of Moses, taking the word of God in the prophetic books almost as a divine hypostasis that determines the course of history (Isa 9:7; 40:8; 55:10–11). The prophetic succession (Deut 18:15)—as the Apostolic one in later times—vouches for the authenticity and unbroken transmission of the teaching. Because this teaching is still valid after the actual occurrence of the disaster announced by the prophets, the admonition to obedience to the law is repeated in Mal 3. With this warning the second part of the canon, the Nevi'im, closes with what is seen as the quintessence of the Latter Prophets' proclamation (cf. Jer 7:25–26; 44:4–5).

Following Chronicles (2 Chr 36:15–16) and Daniel (Dan 9:6), the prophets became part of Jewish tradition as teachers of the law. Here, the prophets are understood and interpreted in light of the law. Accordingly, the ideal scribe who explores the wisdom of his ancestors and in doing so also struggles with the understanding of the prophecies (Sir 39:1) is identical with the righteous man of Psalm 1 who studies the law of the Most High day and night. Until today, a reading from the prophets concludes the recitation of Torah in synagogue worship. The understanding of the prophets as teachers of the law is formulated in classical fashion in the "Sayings of the Fathers":

> Moses received the Torah from Sinai and transmitted it to Joshua; Joshua to the elders; the elders to the prophets; and the prophets handed it down to the men of the Great Assembly (*Pirqei Avot* I.1a)

The idea that the prophets were teachers of the law is also found in the New Testament and in this way introduced into Christian tradition. Using a term adapted from Judaism, scripture is called "the Law" or "the Law of Moses and the Prophets" (Matt 23:34–36; Mark 12:1–12). Much later, the German reformer Martin Luther formulates it in classic fashion in his preface to the Old Testament from 1523:

> What, then, are the other books, the prophets, and the histories? I answer: They are nothing other than what Moses is (Luther's Works 35, 246).

3. The Prophets as Preachers of Christ

Opinions, however, differ about "what Moses is." Martin Luther continues in his preface to the Old Testament:

> Thus, the prophets are nothing more than agents and witnesses of Moses and his office, bringing everyone to Christ through the law (Luther's Works 35, 247).

What Martin Luther refers to here is the prophetic hope that—according to the Christian understanding—points to the revelation of God in Jesus Christ and to the New Testament. This understanding is rooted in the New Testament itself. To be sure, according to the New Testament, Jesus did not come to abolish the law and the prophets, but to fulfill them (Matt 5:17). Before heaven and earth pass away, not one jot of the law will fail (Matt 5:18). Nothing needs to be done in order to attain salvation other than to listen to Moses and the Prophets (Luke 16:29, 31). The law is holy, just, and good (Rom 7:12). However, it is the law itself, Moses and the Prophets, that contains the divine promise and thus points to John the Baptist as precursor (Matt 11:11–14) and Jesus Christ as perfecter (Luke 24:27; Acts 26:22–23; John 1:45; Rom 3:21–22, etc. "according to the scriptures").

The Christian understanding of the law and the prophets reflects the view of the Septuagint, where the prophets open an eschatological horizon of expectation. Such an eschatological anticipation is not alien to the Hebrew canon itself, as the prospect of the return of Elijah in Mal 3:23–24, immediately following the admonition to obey the law in Mal 3:22, shows. It is, however, clearly limited. In the Septuagint, as well as in other Jewish writings from the Greco-Roman period, such anticipation plays a much larger role. The Book of Daniel, as well as other apocalyptic writings that were not included in the Hebrew Bible, call for obedience to the law but also find in the law a further and deeper sense concerning the dawn of the end times. Their interpretation of the Law of Moses and the sacred history is influenced by the Prophets.

Commentaries on prophetic books found in the caves of Qumran show how the prophets, and in their light the law, were understood in the last two centuries before the Common Era. Their exegesis rests on the conviction that God gave and dictated to the prophets a message that refers to a distant time. Yet, according to these commentaries, the prophets themselves did not know to whom or to which time the prophecy referred. All this was only revealed to the Teacher of Righteousness, the highest authority in the Qumran texts. Due to this additional revelation, the commentaries' authors are able to interpret the prophecies in reference to the community of Qumran and its own time—a period when they saw the end times dawning. Other circles trace the correct interpretation of the scripture back to Daniel (Dan 9:2) or to the antediluvian sages Enoch or Noah. They have, all in their own way, interpreted and updated the word of scripture in light of their own time.

In the New Testament, the revelation of God in Jesus Christ guides the understanding and exegesis of the Holy Scriptures. The early Christians believed that Elijah had returned (Mal 3:23–24) in the person of John the Baptist (Matt 11:14). Jesus Christ, the Son of Man, follows Moses and Elijah, and with him the end of the world begins (Mark 9:2–13). Since the end of the world did not take place, Christian tradition deferred it to the second coming of Christ, as did the Jewish tradition when introducing the return of Elijah. For the time being—that is, the period between Christ's two comings—there is the Christian tradition that, like its Jewish counterpart, regards the prophets as teachers of the law, preachers of an enlightened ethics, or exceptionally gifted orators or poets.

4. The Prophets as "Men of the New"

The traditional Jewish and Christian understanding endured for a long time. During the nineteenth century, however, this tradition was called into question by historical-critical scholarship. The discovery of the personality of the prophets, their individuality and poetic force prepared the ground for a historical understanding. The decisive breakthrough was the insight that the law is younger than are the prophets. In other words, the prophets do not follow the law, as the canon suggests, but the law follows the prophets.

This reversal of the biblical chronology does not imply that during the time of the prophets there was no Israelite legal tradition. Torah already existed. In that time, however, Torah described priestly instruction or the teaching of a sage. It was not "the Law," the Torah of Moses, as preserved in the Pentateuch—namely, in the priestly-colored legislative passages of the books Genesis to Leviticus and Deuteronomy. In these passages, legal regulations, priestly instructions, and the teaching of the sages have become the will of God, and following the divine will is a matter of life and death. Only after this development is it possible to speak of "the Law" as a theological entity. Its characteristic claim is stated in the First Commandment in an abbreviated form: "I am YHWH your God; you shall have no other gods besides me" (Exod 20:2–3; Deut 5:6–7).

This notion of "the Law" is originally unknown to the prophets. Those passages within the prophetic writings that refer to the First Commandment and the Law of Moses are later literary additions. Sometimes the prophets apply standards known from ancient law, old sacrificial rituals, or ancient wisdom. These standards, of course, were regarded as divinely legitimated, since an order not endorsed by the gods was an unknown concept in the ancient Near East. The prophets, however, do not invoke the Mosaic law in support of their ethical standards. They rely on given norms, as did judges, priests, and sages. These norms had authority in

and of themselves and not because God required their fulfillment. This
changed when the institutional framework and social context in which the
norms had their validity disappeared. From this moment, according to the
prophets, the divine will demands actions that are no longer self-evident
or cannot be taken for granted anymore, as well as many other things.
However, even in this case, the prophets generally do not appeal to the
Law of Moses.

What, then, remains when one strips away the law from the prophets?
Without seeking support from tradition, the prophets speak of a transcendent God who demands justice for himself and the people and in so
doing risks the doom of his people. Because this God is the God of Israel,
and Israel is the people of God, the end of his people in the two disasters
of 722 and 587 B.C.E. could have only been decided and caused by him.
The end, however, is at the same time a new beginning: it calls for radical
change and repentance.

Nowhere else in the entire ancient Near East did prophets or other
men of God ever proclaim such a message. True, outside Israel, gods could
be angry and bring disaster upon their cities, countries, and people. Yet
the foundations on which the relationship between God and his king,
his city, or his people rested was never questioned. What the prophets of
Israel, in turn, announced was outrageous and new in the ancient world.
Quite rightly, they have been described as *Männer des ewig Neuen* "men
of the eternally new" (Bernhard Duhm). This is not contradicted by the
fact that they really did not intend "to say anything new, they are only pro-
claiming old truth" (Julius Wellhausen). But since they made this ancient
truth—namely, the relationship to God mediated by kings, judges, priests,
seers, and sages—dependent on God's desire for justice, they reversed the
traditional order. The prophets did not (yet) have the law as a foundation
but rather paved the way for it. Thus, they effectively became the "founders of the religion of the law" (Julius Wellhausen).

5. *The Prophets as Founders of Jewish Tradition*

Such a late dating of Moses and his law has consequences for the
sacred history handed down under his name and the names of Joshua
(Josh), Samuel (Judg–Sam), and Jeremiah (1–2 Kings). The historiography of the Hebrew Bible, too, is influenced by the law and, in this respect
at least, comes after the prophets.

The influence of the law is very extensive. The picture of the history of
the people of Israel offered by the biblical sources is a late construct. The

text as we have it today is the result of a literary editing that presupposes the Mosaic law. If one disregards the editorial additions, then the traditions in Judges, Samuel, and Kings fall apart into separate pieces. These pieces do not deal with the whole people of Israel but instead constitute narratives of individual regions, tribes, places, and kingdoms. They tell stories that appear to be parallel events rather than part of a historical sequence. A (reliable) historical chronology can only be found in the old annals of the two royal houses of Israel and Judah, preserved in the framing notices to the individual kings.

It is the same in the Pentateuch, to which the old narratives in Joshua connect seamlessly. Here, Israel conquers the land twice: once as the clan of Abraham, Isaac, and Jacob originating in Mesopotamia, the cradle of humanity (Gen 2–35) and once as the people of Israel coming out of Egypt under the leadership of Moses (Exod 2–15 + Num 20–25 + Josh 2–12). The current narrative is an artificial historical combination that reduces two myths of Israel's origins to a common denominator. Guided by the unity of God and his people, both originally competing legends of the origin of Israel were joined together into one sacred history. In the course of this history, God reveals himself first in the promise to Abraham (Gen 12), then through the liberation from Egypt (Exod 2–15), and in both cases through covenant and law (Gen 15 and 17; Exod 19–24; 32–34). Again, both myths of origin are based on individual traditions that were originally independent of each other.

These diverse individual traditions existed before, alongside and after the time of the prophets and their books. They offer glimpses into the lives of families, tribes, and places as well as the royal houses of both monarchies. They give an impression of how the world was imagined. The old narratives belong to the same category as the old legal, cultic, and wisdom traditions, and the Hebrew Bible only preserves fragments of them.

The combination of the individual traditions into larger narrative cycles and ultimately into a sacred history in Genesis 1 through 2 Kings 25 is not self-evident. It presupposes the loss of the traditional political, cultic, and social order that the old stories assume and provides a new theological foundation for a life under changed conditions. Before the law became the measuring rod of history, it was the direct bond between God and his people that determined the course of history in good and bad times. Later, the two monarchies were replaced by the concept of the people of God, and the cosmic and political order given by God was replaced by the history of God with his people. Thus, the traditions of ancient Israel and Judah gave way to Jewish tradition, to which we owe the Hebrew Bible.

This process can hardly be understood without the prophets. In the light of the end of the two monarchies of Israel (722 B.C.E.) and Judah (587 B.C.E.), whether threatened or already a reality, the prophets denounce the existing institutional relationship between God and the two royal houses. Consequently, the relationship was placed on a new basis. On this new basis the history of God with his people was built, and subsequently the law was integrated into this history. Thus, it is not only the law that is younger than the prophets but also the sacred history and its notion of God and the people of Israel. Both law and history were later to influence the prophetic tradition. The prophets, however, initiated both law and sacred history and thus are the founders of Jewish tradition.

CHAPTER 2

Mantic and Magic

Prophecy in the Ancient Near East

When we look at the ancient Near East, the background of the Hebrew Bible, a different picture emerges. There we do not find prophetic books but instead encounter the various practices employed by priests and prophets to ascertain the divine will. In general, scholarship on the history of religion calls this phenomenon manticism or divination. Following Cicero (*de divinatione*), scholarship distinguishes between inductive and intuitive divination.

Inductive ("artificial") divination was most widespread. The divine will was determined from omens in nature or via specially developed techniques such as extispicy (i.e., reading and interpreting the entrails of sacrificial animals). For these techniques, divine or demonic forces were needed. Magic is close to inductive divination. Assyria and Babylonia mostly used methods of inductive divination. Techniques and results were systematically compiled in written collections so that the omens could be reused at any time and applied to new situations. As such, inductive divination can be seen as a branch of ancient science.

Intuitive ("natural") divination was less widespread. Here, the deity communicates with a professional or specially gifted medium. The prophets can be numbered among this group. The word "prophet" is of Greek origin and describes all those persons who have received divine messages and made predictions. The few surviving sources that speak of prophets are spread widely in space and time. Nevertheless, as far as their form and content are concerned, they display an astonishing degree of similarity, so that one can gain from them a relatively reliable picture of the religious phenomenon of ancient Near Eastern prophecy in Syria and Mesopotamia.

1. Royal Archives

The main sources of our knowledge come from two archives: the royal archive of Mari (Tell Hariri) on the upper reaches of the Euphrates

11

(eighteenth century B.C.E.) and the archive of the royal library of Nineveh in Neo-Assyrian times (seventh century B.C.E.).

Since 1933, excavations at Mari have unearthed thousands of letters. The city was situated at the border of Syria and Mesopotamia and had many personal and diplomatic contacts in both directions. The letters allow us to view the political intrigues of the ancient Babylonian city-states during the Middle Bronze Age (first part of the second millennium B.C.E.), intrigues that also feature the famous king and lawgiver Hammurabi of Babylon. About fifty letters contain descriptions of prophetic oracles addressed to King Zimri-Lim, who was absent from time to time. Often the hem or a lock of hair of the prophet or the writer of the letter was included to authenticate the message (WAW, 13–91).

In the archive of Nineveh, around thirty oracles addressed to the Neo-Assyrian kings Esarhaddon (681–669 B.C.E.) and Ashurbanipal (669–627 B.C.E.) from the goddess Ishtar of Arbela and other gods were found (WAW, 97–175). To these we can add the references to prophets and oracles in royal inscriptions. Only a few passages allow us to discern an external motive. The oracles focus on the legitimation of the kings, who were fighting against internal enemies, as well as on tensions relating to Assyrian rule over Babylon. The mysterious death of Sennacherib, the father of Esarhaddon, and the revolt of Shamash-shumukin, son of Esarhaddon, who revolted against his brother Assurbanipal, seriously weakened the Neo-Assyrian Empire, which fell to the Babylonians in 612 B.C.E.. The last two major rulers of the Neo-Assyrian Empire hoped to compensate for political weakness by heightened religious activity and indulged in their literary proclivities. We owe the discovery of Mesopotamian culture and the knowledge of most of the cuneiform texts of the "Babylonian canon" to the library of Nineveh. Created with great effort by Assurbanipal, it was excavated in 1849.

In addition to the two royal archives are other isolated finds, among them some that are chronologically and geographically closer to Israel and Judah.

The Egyptian Wenamun, who around the year 1076 B.C.E. was sent by his king to Syria to purchase lumber from Lebanon, recounts a strange episode. Anchoring in the port of Byblos on the Syrian coast, he was asked by the king of Byblos to leave. Suddenly, a person in a frenzy, most likely an ecstatic, arose and announced that Wenamun was a messenger of the Egyptian god Amun-Ra. This message changed the mind of the king of Byblos, and he agreed to enter into negotiations about the delivery of lumber (ANET, 25–29; COS I, 89–93).

An inscription of the Aramaic king Zakkur of Hamath around the year 800 B.C.E. (ANET, 655–56; COS II, 155) reports an incident in conventional style. Zakkur is pressured by a coalition of Aramaic city-states under the command of the king of Damascus, Bar-Hadad (in Hebrew: Ben-Hadad), son of Hazael, who is also known from the Hebrew Bible (2 Kgs 13:3, 22–25). Zakkur lifts his hands to the "Lord of Heaven" and consults seers and diviners. The deity answers him with an oracle of salvation ("Do not be afraid") and promises him military victory. And indeed, Zakkur— most likely with the help of the Assyrians—rids himself of his enemies and was able to expand his territory. The "Lord of Heaven" and his prophets apparently approved of a political alliance with the Assyrian Empire.

As recently as 1967 a fragment of a wall inscription written in red and black ink was discovered at Tell Deir Alla, a hill in the eastern Jordan valley (COS II, 140–145). Despite its poor state of preservation, it soon became clear that it preserved a "Book/Writing of Balaam, son of Beor," a divine "seer" to whom the gods came at night. This seer is none other than the Balaam known to us from the Hebrew Bible (Num 22–24), whom we encounter here in his original setting and time (eighth century B.C.E.), before he was adopted by Israel and the biblical tradition. What the gods show him does not bode well. As far as the text is legible, we read of announcements of doom and curses that Balaam, weeping bitterly, recounts to his people. Balaam acts as a sort of incantation priest, perhaps with the intention of averting the imminent doom announced by the assembly of the gods. In Num 22–24 this message is transformed—much to the consternation of Balak, king of Moab—into an oracle of salvation for Israel.

Finally, a last document has to be mentioned here, even if it is not part of the ancient Near Eastern surroundings but rather from Judah itself. It is one of twenty-one potsherds found between 1935 and 1938 on Tell ed-Duweir, identified as the Judean city of Lachish. These sherds, called ostraca, were used to write letters. The letter preserved on ostracon No. 3 (ANET, 322; WAW, 212–14; COS III, 79–80) contains a reference to a prophet of Yʜᴡʜ from the time between 597 and 587 B.C.E., the period shortly before Lachish and subsequently also Jerusalem were conquered and destroyed by Nebuchadnezzar II. The author is a petty officer named Hoshayahu who calls himself a "servant" and in other letters a "dog." He writes to his commanding officer and "lord" Yaush at Lachish. In his letter, Hoshayahu defends himself against his officer's charge that he misunderstood some order. In addition, he mentions that general Konyahu, son of Elnatan, moved south to Egypt, most likely with the intention to forge a military alliance against the Babylonians. In this context, another letter that the subordinate had forwarded to his superior is mentioned. From this letter, he quotes a prophetic oracle in abbreviated form:

> (Herewith) I am also sending to my lord the letter of Tobyahu, servant of the king, which came to Shallum son of Yada from the prophet and which says: "Beware" (COS III, 79).

The expression "Be careful, beware!" is common in prophetic speech and generally introduces a warning but can also open an oracle of salvation (2 Kgs 6:9; Isa 7:4). Whether the letter of the prophet mentioned had anything to do with the actions of the general Konyahu, and what role Tobiah and his prophet played in this dangerous political situation, cannot be determined from Hoshayahu's letter. All the names of ostracon 3 also appear in the Hebrew Bible, but it is impossible to identify any of the persons mentioned in the letter with one of the biblical characters.

2. Charisma and Office

Ancient Near Eastern prophets were a fairly badly supported and low class of priests at the temple or they were employed at the royal court. Women with this occupation are also known to us. In the sources, they are called ecstatics, speakers, oracular priests/priestesses, seers, and diviners, or they are simply called by their personal names. Even the biblical word for prophet ("*navi*'") appears. Charisma and office (Max Weber) were not mutually exclusive but two sides of the same coin. Occasionally we learn of spontaneous inspirations of private persons, who then report them to the court.

The divine revelation was generally received in auditions or visions and dreams, often in an ecstatic state. The natural place for such revelations was the temple, but the written sources say little about the exact circumstances. We can only speculate about the techniques and psychological processes before and during the reception of the revelation. Even modern brain research that locates frenzy and epilepsy within the same part of the brain is of no help.

The language and genres that were used to express the message of the prophets are very similar to those found in the Hebrew Bible. We find reports in the first and third person, salvation oracles, oracles of doom, admonitions, reviews of earlier events, and oracles against foreign nations or enemies. The oracles were not only inspired, but also authored by the gods. The prophet speaks either in the name of the deity or in his own name. The formulas of the messages follow the style of contemporary epistolary correspondence.

3. Politics and Propaganda

Prophecy in the ancient Near East was a political tool of state propaganda that was used to preserve the prevailing order. Generally, the divine message of the prophets refers to the king and addresses the fate of the royal house; it has little to do with the common people. In Assyria in particular, prophecy serves to legitimate the ruling dynasty.

Sometimes, mild criticism of the king is combined with grandiose promises, when the prophets remind the king of his duties toward the gods, their temples and priests, as well as toward his subjects. This criticism, however, is very different from the fundamental doubts about the cultic system or the existing social order as we find them in the Hebrew Bible.

Otherwise, the oracles report good or bad omens to the king during times of war or other events of national significance. This implies that they warn of impending doom. In comparison with biblical prophecies, it is remarkable that the oracles never announce the final destruction of the state or the end of a dynasty. The goal of ancient Near Eastern prophecy was instead to avoid or avert disaster. This could and should be done by political maneuvering, cultic means, or moral behavior. Deity and prophets vouched for this. Whoever argued the converse and announced the downfall of the ruling king was branded a "false" prophet.

Not all oracles came true. A dramatic case is known to us from Mari. We read in two letters that Zimri-Lim, king of Mari, was assured he would defeat Hammurabi of Babylon, who had turned against the king, his former ally. Shortly after this prophecy, Hammurabi conquered Mari and forever razed it to the ground. We do not know how people came to terms with such a catastrophically incorrect prognosis.

4. Media of Communication

Most prophetic oracles from the ancient Near East are preserved in letters. Here, a third party reports the divine message that was received either from the prophet himself or via another person. In general, the authors of the letters report the prophecies in their own words. The process of communication is extremely complex, and in at least two respects it is even unpredictable: first, because of the direct or indirect transmission of the original revelation to the writer of the letter; second, because the letter writer, who would have had to employ the help of a professional scribe, reports the message. At both points, the wording probably changed. Just think of the extremely abbreviated quotation of the prophetic word in the

Lachish ostracon (see above, pp. 13–14)! Furthermore, the context, as well as the compilation of two or more oracles within a single letter, also make a difference. Thus, in these letters we do not hear the authentic voice of the prophet. Oral and especially written transmission is always accompanied by individual interpretation.

An interesting example of such an interpretive process has been found in the Mari archives. Three letters from different writers contain the same oracle: "Beneath straw, water runs." The metaphor refers to a planned alliance of the king of Mari with the king of Eshnunna, a neighboring city with which Mari was at war. The three letters quote three prophets from the temple of Dagan of Terqa who appeared at the court of Mari to advise against such an alliance. They all spoke the same watchword ("Beneath straw, water runs") but interpreted it differently. One prophet deduces from it an admonition to the king that he should consult an oracle. A prophetess gives the political advice to mistrust the king of Eshnunna and his ingratiating words. Finally, a third prophet announces outright that the king of Mari will be victorious. As far as the subject matter is concerned there are no differences: Dagan of Terqa wants peace with Eshnunna not by alliance but by conquest. The three prophets (or the letter writers), however, dressed the message of the god—with the exception of the metaphor—in different words, both their own and those of Dagan of Terqa.

The reproduction of a prophetic message in letters is a special form of communication for a unique historical moment. As such, it does not establish a prophetic tradition. The significance of the letters, however, increased when they were filed in the royal archive. Just like the collections of omens, they were now always accessible, and the prophetic oracles reported in the letters were reusable. The textual fixation of prophetic oracles as part of royal inscriptions, the plaster inscription from Deir Alla, or the cuneiform tablets comprising a collection of numerous short Neo-Assyrian prophecies served a similar purpose. As in the letters, we have to assume a certain degree of transformation of the wording and meaning on the way from the reception of the oracle via its transmission to its recording by professional scribes. Like the archiving of the letters, the textualization of oracles as part of inscriptions or on clay tablets served the intention of preserving them forever. Both recording and archiving are the first steps of tradition.

The demise of the ancient Near Eastern kingdoms, however, always entailed the demise of their archives and inscriptions too. What survived was not the literary tradition, but the religious phenomenon of ancient Near Eastern prophecy that repeatedly surfaced at different times and in different places in the Syro-Mesopotamian area. This has to do with the fact that the tradition—be it in the form of inscriptions, letters, or archives—is closely linked to the existence of institutions. This means especially the institutions of kingship and temple but also the entire nexus of communication of the persons involved. When the social and political structures collapsed, the system of transmission collapsed too. This is different in the Hebrew Bible, as the tradition of prophetic narratives and prophetic oracles adopted a form that proved resistant to the vicissitudes of history.

CHAPTER 3

Kingmakers and Miracle Workers

Prophets in Israel and Judah

The Hebrew Bible knows of two forms of prophetic tradition: (1) the stories about the prophets' ministry and (2) the collection of their utterances in books. The latter is generally labeled "classical" prophecy, while the former is called "pre-classical" prophecy. In light of ancient Near Eastern analogies, things appear to be different. Phenomenologically speaking, the "pre-classical" and "pre-literary" prophecy in the narratives, especially in Samuel and Kings, as well as in Chronicles, corresponds to classic ancient Near Eastern prophecy and is attested continuously for the whole history of Israel and Judah. In contrast, the "classical" prophets of the prophetic books constitute an exception and represent a special development, not only in the ancient Near East but also in Israel and Judah themselves. However, the narratives are not simply authentic sources for the religio-historical circumstances in ancient Israel or Judah. Like all traditions of the Hebrew Bible, they are overlaid with late additions and require critical analysis. Only the rough contours of classical prophecy in ancient Israel and Judah are still recognizable.

As we discuss the prophets of Israel and Judah in the following chapters, we have to recall that the Bible uses the term "Israel" in a double sense. On the one hand, it is a geopolitical term describing one of the two kingdoms that arose in Palestine after the year 1000 B.C.E. Of those two kingdoms, the northern kingdom—that is, Israel with its capital Samaria—existed until 722 B.C.E., while the southern kingdom—Judah with its capital Jerusalem—was conquered by the Babylonians in 587 B.C.E. On the other hand, the term "Israel" is used as a personal name and a religious cipher for the people of God from Israel *and* Judah, or the twelve tribes of Israel. The religious use of the word, transcending both political kingdoms, is a later development than the geopolitical use and presupposes, at the very least, the end of the northern kingdom.

18

1. *"True" and "False" Prophets*

We find different terms for experts in divination in the Hebrew Bible just as we do in ancient Near Eastern sources. These experts are called "man of God," "seer," "soothsayer," "sorcerer," "necromancer," or "caller" (*navi'*, fem. *nᵉvi'ah*)—the term most frequently used for a prophet or prophetess in the Hebrew Bible. Often, "priests and prophets" are mentioned in the same breath. Again, we are dealing with different classes of cultic officials. In addition to their divinatory abilities, some of these persons are said to have the rare gift of performing miracles. From this as well as from the various designations for such experts we can surmise that divination and magic were not that far apart. Already the tradition was unable to distinguish between them (1 Sam 9:9). Mosaic law forbids most divinatory and magical practices (Deut 18:9–22). Therefore, the seers and prophets of old were transformed into "false" prophets who prophesy "lies" and who lead Israel astray into idolatry (Deut 13; 1 Kgs 22; Jer 23; 27–29; Ezek 13). These prophets are superseded by the prophet like Moses, the ideal figure of biblical tradition.

The god in whose name these prophets prophesied is always called YHWH in the extant sources. YHWH was not always—as the biblical sources want us to believe—the only god beside whom no other gods existed. Originally, YHWH was the god of the two kingdoms Israel and Judah just as Baal or Hadad was the god of the Arameans, Kemosh the god of Moab, or Milcom the god of the Ammonites. As the main deity of the kingdom, YHWH was worshiped at several sanctuaries in the villages and towns of Israel and Judah and played a significant role in personal piety.

His place in prophecy can be illuminated by the example of the Zakkur inscription and the Neo-Assyrian oracles of salvation. The stele of Zakkur of Hamath is dedicated to El-Wer, a manifestation of the Syrian weather god. Toward its end we find a list of deities that protect the physical integrity of the stele. The oracle obtained from seers and soothsayers that announces the victory of the king, however, is given in the name of the "Lord of Heaven," Baal-shamayin, the main deity of the kingdom. Similarly, the Neo-Assyrian prophecies of salvation are almost exclusively given in the name of one goddess, Ishtar of Arbela, as if she were the only goddess and there were no other gods beside her. The preeminence of the main deity of a kingdom does not preclude, however, the existence and worship of other deities. The biblical tradition—that is, the books of the prophets and the redaction of the narratives—is exceptional for declaring the main deity of Israel and Judah to be the one and only god.

The prophets appeared as individuals or in groups. As is to be expected in the light of the ancient Near Eastern analogies, most of them are found in the vicinity of the royal court and the temple (2 Sam 24:11; 1 Kgs 1:8; 2 Kgs 22:14). Others were institutionalized at local sanctuaries (Judg 4:4–5; 1 Sam 9:6; 1 Kgs 13:11) or were organized in certain communities (2 Kgs 2:15). They were consulted but could also speak spontaneously, without being asked. The main addressee of their oracles was the king. Diviners in towns and villages could also be consulted by the common people.

The Israelite and Judean prophets, like their ancient Near Eastern counterparts, received their divine messages in dreams and visions (1 Kgs 22:17, 19; Isa 6:1) or by way of auditions (1 Sam 3; 9:15; 2 Sam 7:4). It is said especially of the prophetic groups that they were prone to ecstatic behavior and then acted like men who were possessed (1 Sam 10:5–6, 10–13; 19:20–21; 1 Kgs 18:25–29; 22:10–12). In Hebrew, the technical term for such a behavior is derived from the same root as the word "prophet" or "to prophesy" (*nibbāʾ*; *hit-nabbēʾ*). The strange behavior, nevertheless, gave them an ambivalent reputation (1 Sam 10:11–12). They are regarded as "crazy" (2 Kgs 9:11; Jer 29:26; Hos 9:7), the Hebrew root from which the Yiddish term *meshugge* (or *mᵉšuggāʿ*) is derived.

Among the forms of communication of prophetic messages, short or long sayings are attested, sometimes accompanied by symbolic actions such as wearing horns as a sign of imminent victory over one's enemies (1 Kgs 22:11) or removing a yoke from one's neck to symbolize the end of Babylonian oppression (Jer 28:1–4, 10–11). Previous scholarship had gone to great pains to classify the various prophetic sayings according to their form and content and to relate them to a concrete social setting (*Sitz im Leben*). Today, we know that the mode of transmission corresponds to ancient Near Eastern practice and follows the usual style. The prophet is sent directly as a messenger or conveys divine information to the king or another addressee via a third party. In the Hebrew Bible, however, the prophets normally do not deliver messages typical of their profession.

2. Prophecy and Kingship

In the Hebrew Bible, the prophetic genealogy begins in the premonarchic period. Prominent representatives are Abraham (Gen 20:7), Miriam (Exod 15:20); Moses (Num 12:6–8; Deut 18:15, 18; 34:9), the foreign seer Balaam (Num 22–24), and Deborah (Judg 4:4–5). This is hardly surprising, because every ancient society—and Israel was hardly an exception in this regard—knows of charismatic intermediaries who were entrusted with priestly and prophetic functions. The premonarchic genealogy is, however, like the epoch itself a projection of later times. Apart from the brief mention of a group of people bearing the name "Israel" on a stele of the Egyptian pharaoh Merenptah around 1200 B.C.E. (ANET, 376–78; COS II, 40–41), nothing is known about the historical origins and the history of the people of Israel before the monarchy. The historical Balaam is attested in an inscription only in the eighth century B.C.E. and not before.

Only with the origin of kingship around 1000 B.C.E. do Israel and Judah—and with them the prophets—appear. Like kingship, prophecy was not a foreign institution copied from other nations but native to Israel and Judah. Both prophecy and kingship were no different from the corresponding institutions of the Canaanite neighbors among whom both kingdoms emerged. Prophecy survived the fall of the monarchy in both biblical literature and religious practice, the latter of which is criticized by the biblical tradition (Neh 6:7, 10–14; Zech 13).

From the stories in Samuel and Kings, we can gather that the prophets during the monarchic period behaved as was expected of them. They acted as kingmakers and gave their blessing to the ruling dynasty. According to an old tradition, Saul—while looking for the escaped she-asses of his father—was anointed as king in a village in the land of Zuph by a local man of God called Samuel (1 Sam 9–10). The anointing of David by Samuel, in turn, is modeled on that of Saul (1 Sam 13:14; 16:1–13) and is further confirmed by the prophet Nathan (2 Sam 7). Nathan's actions can be identified in more detail during the intrigues surrounding the succession of David. Together with Zadok the priest and other officials he sides with the younger Solomon, the son of Bathsheba, against the older Adonijah (2 Sam 11–12; 1 Kgs 1–2).

This, however, is only half the truth. The editors of the books of Samuel and Kings were interested in something else. Through the course of tradition, Samuel, the man of God, is transformed into an anointed priest who—in the transition from the period of the Judges to the monarchy—anticipates the fall of the corrupt priesthood of the sanctuary at Shiloh (1 Sam 1–3). He also condemns and denounces the kingship that he had just established and that is now considered contrary to God's will (1 Sam 8; 12; 13:7–14; 15). In this way, the editors changed the prophetic critique of the ruling house, which is quite common in the ancient Near East, into a fundamental opposition to monarchy. This redaction presupposes the end of the monarchy in Israel and Judah and demands exclusive obedience to God's word. Earthly kingship and divine rule are in competition, and the ideal form of government is a theocracy.

Theocracy, then, is also the key that explains the hope that the Hebrew Bible sets on David. The common pattern of state legitimation does not serve political propaganda but has simply a theological purpose. For the biblical tradition, the decisive point about David and his dynasty is not the existence of an actual kingdom of Judah, which in reality had long perished. Rather, the important factors are the divine election of the king and of Jerusalem as the place of the temple planned by David and built by Solomon, which had become the hope of Judaism after the exile until the present day. The famous oracle of Nathan (2 Sam 7) that promises the eternal endurance of the house of David is a product of postexilic theology, which—following the end of the kingdom of Judah—retrojects onto its beginnings what should be valid for all time. In consequence, the parallel text in 1 Chr 17:17 (following 2 Sam 7:16) no longer speaks of the kingship and house of David but about the kingdom and house of YHWH.

The flip side of the hope in David and in the Judean dynasty is the demonization of the kings of Israel. Jeroboam I, the usurper and founder of the Israelite monarchy, is also anointed by God through a prophet, Ahijah of Shiloh, as king over the ten tribes of Israel (1 Kgs 11:26–40). According to the editors of Samuel and Kings, however, Jeroboam was not like YHWH's servant David and did not keep the divine commandments. Therefore—as God again announces via Ahijah of Shiloh—the house of Jeroboam will be annihilated completely and all of Israel will be abandoned (1 Kgs 14). The "sin of Jeroboam," the first king of Israel who erected two bull figures, one at Dan and one at Bethel, and thus led the people astray, would henceforth become the *basso continuo* intoned by the redaction of Samuel and Kings and the prophets within these books. This motif explains the frequent change of dynasties (1 Kgs 15–16; 2 Kgs 9–10) as well as the fall of the northern kingdom (2 Kgs 17) and provides a cautionary tale for the future (1 Kgs 13; 16:1–4; 21:17–29; 2 Kgs 9:7–10; 17:7–41). In the end, the kingdom of Judah is also affected by the "sin of Jeroboam" (2 Kgs 17:19; 21:10–16; 22:14–20) and additionally accused of its own faults (2 Kgs 20:12–19). David and Josiah are not so much examples of a new Judean kingship but rather of the obedience toward God and his law.

Finally, theocracy is the basis for the intervention of the Israelite prophets in the succession of foreign dynasties. In the books of Kings, Elijah and Elisha are ordered by God to install Hazael, the son of and successor to the Aramean king Ben-Hadad (1 Kgs 19:15; 2 Kgs 8:7–15). During this period, the Arameans oppressed Israel. This too, in the eyes of the biblical tradition, was the work of YHWH (2 Kgs 10:32–33).

Thus, in the biblical narrative we perceive the prophets of Israel and Judah as being involved in the investiture and deposition of kings. In addition, they speak of war and peace, give advice, and provide information on favorable and unfavorable military constellations (1 Sam 22:5; 1 Kgs 12:22–25; 20; 22; 2 Kgs 3; 6–7; 13:14–19; 18–20). They also take a stand on cultic (2 Sam 7; 1 Kgs 13), moral, and legal questions (2 Sam 11–12; 24; 1 Kgs 21). All this reminds us of the ancient Near Eastern models, except that the relationship between prophets and kingship according to the biblical tradition is troubled from the beginning, and the end of the monarchy appears to be inevitable.

3. The Miracles of the Prophets

This ambivalence also shapes the stories about Elijah and Elisha that were added to the books of Kings (1 Kgs 17–19; 21; 2 Kgs 1–2; 3:4–8:15; 9:1–10; 13:14–21). In the current context, Elisha is portrayed as Elijah's apprentice and successor (1 Kgs 19:16, 19–21). In reality, it is the other way around: the Elisha stories served as the source for the Elijah narratives. Originally, both men had nothing to do with each other; they merely represented the same type of "a man of God."

Elisha was the head of a group of prophetic disciples (literally: "sons of prophets"). He is said to have performed miracles. He purifies a polluted well so that it is possible to drink from it again (2 Kgs 2:19–22). To an impoverished widow he provides copious quantities of oil and thus saves her from destitution (2 Kgs 4:1–7). He makes bad food edible (2 Kgs 4:38–41) and multiplies bread (2 Kgs 4:42–44). An axe that has sunk into a lake he causes to resurface (2 Kgs 6:1–7). He helps a woman who had often provided lodgings for him to conceive a son; and when this son falls ill and dies, he raises him from the dead (2 Kgs 4:7–38 cf. 8:1–6). Even in death his magic powers remain (2 Kgs 13:20–21). But woe to those who mock him, against whom he unleashes bears (2 Kgs 2:23–25).

The miracle stories are a unique sociohistorical testimony of a marginal group within ancient Israelite society that knew how to help itself. The same milieu would centuries later give rise to the Jesus tradition of the Gospels. The miracles are mostly wonders of nature. They are rooted in the agricultural living conditions and in the related Canaanite religion. They lack the description of a divine assembly that we know from Ugaritic and Mesopotamian myths influenced by urban life. They presuppose the belief in hidden powers that pervade nature and count on supernatural abilities that enable these powers to be controlled. The main aim of such control is to ensure the survival of the disciples and their families. When they are in danger, the miracle worker provides assistance. This belief system based on nature is the soil in which the religion of Israel and Judah takes root. The biblical tradition that took over this subject matter and reworked it theologically is far removed from it.

Elisha's actions, however, are not limited to his circle of prophetic disciples. He seems to have cultivated contacts in the royal household and engaged in politics. On one occasion, he is portrayed as a helper in time of need when a coalition of Israel and Judah fights against Moab (2 Kgs 3:9–20). Another time he serves as military adviser, combatant, and soothsayer during the war against the Arameans (2 Kgs 6:8–7:20). His magical abilities that lend weight to his political prognosis are also applied in this area (2 Kgs 13:14–19). The literary connection of these narratives with the miracle stories—themselves a result of gradual literary growth—is the product of later times. Nevertheless, the political activities of the miracle worker seem to preserve some authentic memories. The beautiful, if enigmatic, honorary title "My father, my father! The chariots of Israel and its horsemen!" which evokes military associations, was originally connected with Elisha and his role during the wars against the Arameans (2 Kgs 13:14 cf. 6:17; 7:6). Only in 2 Kgs 2:10–12 was it transferred to Elijah. The later redaction stressed this side of Elisha and his actions, thus making him an exponent of the word of God (2 Kgs 3:12; 7:1, 16). Accordingly, he is attributed with an overarching historical and theological significance that involves him and his disciples in the dynastic and political subversions in Aram (2 Kgs 8:7–15; cf. 2 Kgs 5) and Israel (2 Kgs 9:1–10). His new role connects him further with Elijah (1 Kgs 19:15–18).

Elijah too was a miracle worker who "ran beside the wheel of the king"—an expression used in contemporary Aramaic inscriptions from Northern Syria to describe loyalty to the ruling house. The oldest tradition portrays Elijah as a rainmaker who can bring about drought and is also able to end it with magical practices, after hearing the rain approach (1 Kgs 17–18). As a prophet of YHWH, he acts just like the priests and prophets of the god Baal who were responsible in Canaanite religion for the rain and the fertility of the land. As we can glean from Psalms such as Ps 29 and Ps 93, YHWH too was originally the Israelite-Judean variant of the Syrian-Canaanite weather god.

The redaction of 1 Kings 17–19 has transformed this analogy into an antagonism. Elijah has become a champion for the god whose name he bears: "my God is YHWH." As such, he comes into conflict with the king and queen and the prophets of Baal. The scene of the sacrificial competition and Elijah's triumph on Mt. Carmel results in the massacre of 450 prophets of Baal. This slaughter serves as preparation for the bloody deed that Jehu, the usurper, fulfills in 2 Kgs 9–10 according to the prediction in 1 Kgs 19:15–18; 21:17–24. Within this compositional framework, the politically motivated coup d'état—the removal of the anti-Assyrian Omride dynasty by the pro-Assyrian dynasty of Jehu—is interpreted as a religious-political act and, more than that, as evidence for the commitment to the one and only God (cf. also 2 Kgs 1:1–8). Such a belief, however, did not exist during the time of Elijah. Tradition made him "a bird that sings before the dawn" (*ein Vogel, der vor dem Morgen singt*), as Julius Wellhausen wrote so nicely.

Just as the redaction involved Elisha in the religious-political conflict of Elijah, so also Elijah inherited in 1 Kgs 17 the miracles performed by Elisha in 2 Kgs 4. From then on, both figures represent the word of God, which they confirm by miracles (1 Kgs 17:24; 2 Kgs 4:44; cf. 2 Kgs 1:9–17) and which they strongly enforce. As a champion of the first commandment, Elijah finds his way to Mt. Horeb, the place of the revelation of the Ten Commandments (Deut 5), and gains his precedence over Elisha (1 Kgs 19; 2 Kgs 2). After his ascension into heaven, it is only understandable that the hope of the return of the prophet focuses on him as the "second Moses" (Mal 3:22–23; Sir 48:1–11).

4. The Narratives

Overall, the narratives in Samuel and Kings convey a lively impression of preexilic prophecy during the period of the monarchy in Israel and Judah. The vast majority of the old seers are correctly described as cultic prophets. This term not only applies to those who held an office at the court or the temple but also those who lived in towns and villages or in religious communities and were in contact with the court. All of them, without regard to which of the different classes of mantics they belonged, were integrated in some way or other into the day-to-day business of cultic and political life. As such, they were part of the system in which they lived and for which they—like other officials—worked for better or for worse.

The prophetic stories in Samuel and Kings are related to the narratives of the prophetic books. This is especially true for the Isaiah legends, which were first placed in 2 Kgs 18–20 and then incorporated into the Book of Isaiah (Isa 36–39). The legends portray Isaiah as a prophet of salvation and a miracle worker and tell the story of how he and his God saved Jerusalem and prevented its destruction at the hands of Sennacherib in 701 B.C.E.—an event also reported in Neo-Assyrian sources. The legends originated at a later stage than the collection of sayings of Isaiah that announce doom to Israel, Judah, Jerusalem, and several other nations. They are, however, closer, most likely unintentionally, to the historical Isaiah than many of his sayings (see chap. 5.2 below, pp. 40ff.).

Similarly, the brief episode of Amos' encounter with the priest Ama-
ziah of Bethel in Amos 7:10–17 and the extensive narratives about Jeremiah (Jer 20; 26–29; 32; 36–45) seem to put the reader directly into
the political conflicts of the prophet's time. The Amos story draws on the
old, theologically charged rivalry between the two kingdoms of Israel and
Judah in Kings and Chronicles. The narratives about Jeremiah take us to
the period of the Babylonian invasion and destruction of Jerusalem—the
same time in which the ostraca from Lachish were being written. Like the
anonymous prophet mentioned in the ostraca, so too is Jeremiah involved
in an argument about the correct way to ensure the survival of the land
and its inhabitants. The prophet Hananiah, Jeremiah's adversary in Jer
27–28, wants to rely on his own (magical) power, while Jeremiah sets his
hope on the Babylonian king. Both appeal to Yhwh.

The reader should not, however, be seduced by the historical vividness
of these stories. The narrative tradition as a whole is shaped by the past disaster—the fall of Israel and Judah—which the prophets interpret as God's
judgment. This is obvious in the prophetic books. The narratives focus on
the person of the prophet and his role as an incarnation of the word of
God. Accordingly, they pursue theological rather than political aims.

In Samuel and Kings, a deuteronomistic redaction (in the broadest
sense of the term) from exilic or postexilic times took up older narratives, reworked them, and added further stories. This redaction allows the
prophets, armed with old-style promises and warnings, to advocate the
case for Israel and Judah with the purpose of accusing king and people of
iniquity while simultaneously exculpating God. The redaction (re-)used
established ancient Near Eastern patterns that also occur in Isa 40–48.
Here, in the vision of the period of salvation after judgment, the old oracle
of salvation known from Neo-Assyrian prophecies ("Do not fear") is taken
up again. However, the addressee is no longer the king but rather the
people, who are now described with the attributes of a chosen king.

Additionally, the redaction, of course, introduced its own theological
principles: the First Commandment and the law as prophetic teaching.
These principles are the reason for the fundamental opposition to kingship. Where God alone rules as king, there can be no other—not even a
human—ruler (Judg 8:22–23; 1 Sam 8:7; 12:12). This dogma provides
the reason for the fall of kingship and at the same time it opens up a
new future for those who return to God and obey his laws. Along these
lines the Chronicler recapitulates the history of the Judean dynasty and its
prophets as an example for Judah's restoration under Persian rule.

CHAPTER 4

Inspiration and Interpretation

The Books of the Prophets

Figures such as Isaiah, Jeremiah, and Ezekiel have an aura of the heroic. We imagine powerfully eloquent preachers, filled with the spirit and word of God, poets and thinkers, at the same time scarred by their difficult task and the hard, solitary life of great men. These and similar clichés do not lack a basis in the tradition, but they mostly stem from the fantasies of readers. In other words, they are part of the Bible's reception.

What we find in the Hebrew Bible are not the biographies of the prophets but their books. In them we have the collection, literary reworking, and interpretation of oracles that the prophets originally delivered orally. They are not simply the reproduction of the speech and deeds of the prophets but rather the product of learned scribal work or, in other words, the reception of the prophetic oracles. This reception has created the classic image of the prophets within the Hebrew Bible, which itself has inspired the Bible's reception.

1. Prophetic Words and Prophetic Writing

The transition from the prophetic word to the prophetic book is fluid. Between the two lie various kinds of oral and scribal communication. As we have seen, the different types of communication and transmission alter the wording and significance of the prophetic oracles. Nowhere is the voice of the prophet preserved in its original wording. The word of God is only to be grasped in its interpretation by those who wrote it down and transmitted it. In the written sources, the scribes place *their* words in the mouth of God and his prophets.

Israel and Judah, in this respect, are no different from the rest of the ancient Near East. Here, different forms of writing are attested: letters (Lachish 3; Jer 29), inscriptions on tablets (Isa 8:1–2; 30:8; Hab 2:2), and "books"—that is, scrolls (Deir ʿAlla inscription; Isa 34:16; Jer 30:2; 36;

51:59–64; Ezek 2:8–3:3). Letters were the normal means of private communication, while tablets addressed a wider public. Both the tablet and the
book could also have a magical meaning. The written word was equivalent
to the events it announced and ensured their fulfillment. From time to
time, the magical word went hand in hand with a symbolic act that represents the events in advance (Jer 51:59–64). Finally, writing had an archival
interest. The oracle should be available for consultation to see whether it
had occurred or had not (yet) been fulfilled. Either way, the oracle continued to be true. As God's word, its validity lasted over several generations,
even eternally (Isa 8:16–18; 30:8). It could point to a distant time or suit
several situations. Deposited in an archive or written in a book, the oracle
was available for future reuse and later interpretation.

Nevertheless, there is also a significant difference between the ancient Near East on the one hand and Israel on the other. The ancient
Near Eastern archives that we know from excavations have not produced
a single prophetic book, nor are the prophetic books of the Hebrew Bible
archives, and they could scarcely have been included in one. There are
simple reasons why this is the case. The ancient Near Eastern archive was a
royal library. The prophetic books of the Hebrew Bible predict the demise
of the monarchy and similar institutions. We might say that the books are
a substitute to the royal archive and all other national and religious institutions. Although these institutions were once the material and spiritual
home of the prophets, the God they proclaimed no longer wished to be
associated with them.

We could put this a different way: the recording and interpretation of
the prophetic oracles in the Hebrew Bible entail a radical theological reori-
entation. From its very beginning, written prophecy in the Hebrew Bible
was a message of doom, even when announcing a new salvation and how
to obtain it. This distinguishes the biblical prophets from the prophets of
the ancient Near East as well as from kingmakers and wonder-workers in
ancient Israel and Judah (see chap. 3 above).

2. *The Prophetic Writings*

The difference between the Hebrew Bible on the one hand, and what
we know of prophecy in the ancient Near East or ancient Israel and Judah
on the other, becomes abundantly clear when we compare the historical
evidence already examined with the prophetic books in their present form.
Before we inquire into the historical prophets and their preaching, we
must first appreciate the prophetic books as literary productions. As is true

of the literature of the Hebrew Bible in general, we do not have authentic documents from the period or people they concern. Rather, we have the products of tradition that were composed for a later time.

Our study of the books rests upon a text we know from Hebrew manuscripts of the Middle Ages (ninth to tenth centuries C.E.). The textual tradition can, however, be traced back much earlier. The oldest evidence comes from the caves at Qumran and other places around the Dead Sea (third century B.C.E. to first century C.E.). With the exception of Isaiah, the Qumran manuscripts of biblical books are only preserved fragmentarily. The finds from the Cairo Genizah—manuscripts from the eighth to twelfth centuries C.E. preserved in the Ezra synagogue of Old Cairo—provide an insight into the history of the biblical text between Qumran and the manuscripts from the Middle Ages. In addition, the oldest surviving manuscripts containing the complete Septuagint stem from the fourth and fifth centuries C.E. The evidence from the sources is unambiguous: from the second century B.C.E., books that were more or less complete were passed on and preserved.

Within the books themselves we find a variety of evidence about their literary context and intended arrangement. Most important are the books' headings. These provide the names of the prophets, sometimes their ancestry and profession, and the historical context of their work. The headings clearly have a role not only in relation to the individual books, but also in defining the entire collection. The period from king Uzziah's reign in the eighth century B.C.E. to the rebuilding of the temple at the end of the sixth century B.C.E. is traversed twice, once through the Major and once through the Minor Prophets: from Uzziah to Hezekiah (Isa 1:1 par. Hos 1:1; Amos 1:1; Mic 1:1), then from Josiah to Zedekiah (Jer 1:1–3 par. Zeph 1:1), and, finally, exile and Second Temple (Ezekiel par. Haggai and Zechariah).

Subheadings, thematic blocks, programmatic statements, and concepts as well as an abundance of literary cross-references structure each individual book. In Isaiah, Jeremiah (according to the Septuagint), Ezekiel, as well as Zephaniah, scholarship has found the same threefold structure: judgment for Israel—judgment for the nations—salvation for Israel. This, however, is only true regarding the position of the oracles against the nations, which are placed in the middle of these books; in the Hebrew text of Jeremiah, they stand at the end, and in Amos at the beginning. Obviously, the arrangement of the words about Israel follows different conventions. The arrangement aims at producing a dramatic presentation of the prophet and his message as well as organizing the book according to certain biographical and historical phases in the life of the prophet.

The authors and ancient readers of the books assumed that the biographical details were historical and the speeches authentic. Thus, for them everything that is found in the Book of Isaiah was seen and spoken by the eighth-century prophet (Isa 1:1), even if this covered a period of more than two hundred years from the time of the Assyrians to Cyrus the Persian (Isa 45:1). The problem of differentiating between the historical and literary prophet did not trouble ancient scribes as it has troubled modern scholarship since the Enlightenment and the emergence of historical-critical research on the Bible. For the ancient scribes, the prophet and the prophetic book were one. Yet, for them the most important thing about the prophet was not his biography but rather the word of God that was present in the person of the prophet and is still present in his book. Thus, the prophet and his book give access to comprehensive knowledge about God's plan, which he had made known to his prophets (Isa 44:26; Jer 23:18; 29:11; Amos 3:7).

God's plan is what the prophetic books speak about: God's actions in history. Read in their final form as a whole, they cover the different epochs of Israel's history from the Assyrian to the Persian periods, looking backward to earlier periods from creation to the prophet's own time or gazing forward to the culmination of time and the end of the world. God's plan addresses the totality of God's people, even if it is sometimes limited to only a selection, and the totality of the nations. In the prophetic books, both are informed about God's purpose for them and about what he demands of them. Despite the many parts, the whole is always in view. Historical particularities always have a general significance; specific times and historical individuals have a universal meaning. General truths are reflected in concrete historical situations. God's unity guarantees the unity of his many-sided, sometimes contradictory actions, as well as the unity and purpose of history, which despite its vicissitudes is governed by God himself.

The prophetic books provide comprehensive knowledge about God's plan revealed in past predictions. With this awareness, they aim to give their readers affirmation, orientation, and moral guidance for their own age and, above all, for the future. Reading them demands appropriation of their message and interpretation. The word of God in the prophetic books is understood to have a potential significance that goes far beyond the time they describe. The prophetic books guide their readers so that they can recognize the signs of the times and align themselves with God's plan. Everything found in these books is valid, though not everything is significant for each historical moment or generation. Many things have already been fulfilled, others await their time, and still others can (or will) be like those events that have already happened. All of this the readers must discover and apply to themselves and the future of God's people. The outcome of such a reading of the prophetic books is visible in the commentaries from Qumran (*pesharim*), in the Jewish writings of the Greco-Roman period, and not least in the New Testament. The process has continued in Jewish and Christian interpretive literature, even into the present.

3. The Process of Prophetic Writing

This process of interpretation can also be traced in the opposite direction, for the interpretation of the prophetic books already begins within the writings themselves and goes back—as far as we can see—to the first recording of the original prophetic oracles. It is the task of the literary critic to reconstruct the compositional history of the prophetic book and to distinguish between the historical prophet and the literary tradition. Though neither task is straightforward, both are inescapable.

The scribal tradition itself requires critical analysis. In the Hebrew manuscripts as well as in ancient translations, different textual versions of one and the same book are preserved. The difference is particularly evident in the case of the Book of Jeremiah. The Greek text is considerably shorter than the Hebrew, and the two versions do not agree on the sequence of the oracles. The Greek translation is based upon a Hebrew original that deviates from the Hebrew version passed down to us. Hebrew fragments of both versions appeared at Qumran. The conclusion is inescapable: we are dealing here with two stages in the formation of the book.

While in Jeremiah the differences are unmistakable, the same issues confront us, though less obviously, in other books when the manuscripts and the ancient translations are carefully compared. Throughout we discover variations in wording, minor and major omissions or additions, and reordering. These are the final traces of a long and complicated history of composition. The books were not composed in one go but rather grew over centuries.

As a rule, their beginnings are to be found in a collection of a few oracles attributed to known or unknown prophets, as is the case in the Neo-Assyrian examples. The source could also consist of letters or inscriptions deposited in official or private archives. The isolation of the original oracles by means of literary and redaction criticism only makes sense if the standards set by the ancient Near Eastern analogies are applied to the biblical material also in terms of content. Whoever expects—for whatever reason—something different or something more from the Israelite prophets confuses the literary tradition with the historical prophet and claims that prophet and prophetic book are the same.

It was the next stage of the tradition that really set the ball rolling. The original oracles were given a new theological orientation through the interpretation of the collapse of Israel and Judah as a punishment from God. Ongoing literary reworking and gradual supplementation (*Fortschreibung*) followed this interpretation of originally independent oracles or older oracle collections. Thus, a steadily progressing, never-ending process of interpretation and actualization began, in which one word gave rise to another. Existing prophecies were augmented with additional prophecies, whether formerly independent oracles or compositions dependent on their literary context. Every addition provoked new additions. The principal task of the biblical critic is to explore the individual literary layers, place them into a relative chronology, and, wherever possible, provide an absolute date. The work is far from done and in many places remains to be tackled.

Fortschreibung within the books of the prophets came to a standstill at around the end of the third or the beginning of the second century B.C.E., with only a few exceptions. This came about for a technical reason: a scroll can only grow to a certain length. In addition, the intellectual challenge of Hellenism forced Judaism toward a fixed and circumscribed stock of authoritative books as their intellectual heritage. Nevertheless, interpretation and actualization did not end. It continued in apocalyptic literature, the *pesharim* from Qumran, and the other interpretive works of the tradition.

We have already seen that the later tradition based its interpretations of the prophetic books on the conviction that the transmitted text contained the word of God, which had significance not only for the time of the prophets but also for later times. This conviction was already the basis for the interpretations within the books themselves. We should not consider it a sign of arrogance that the scribes placed their interpretation of the word of God for their times into the text and thus upon the lips of God or his prophet. It testifies, instead, to their deep respect for the traditional text. Nothing should be taken from it and nothing should be added to it (Deut 4:2). For this reason the scribes, so far as we can see, preserved the text almost completely and extended it. Literary additions as well as omissions violate the rule only formally. The supplementation (*Fortschreibung*) of the text seeks to make explicit what can already be found in the text. According to the scribe's own understanding, the interpretation of the traditional text does not add anything new or foreign. The fusion of text and interpretation in one and the same text is rather to be understood as an expression of the unity of the word of God and the unity of God himself, despite the vicissitudes of time. In this text, the inspiration of the prophet and his interpretation are inseparable. In it, prophets interpret the prophets.

4. Scribal Prophets

It would be nice to know which circles transmitted and reworked the prophetic writings. Unfortunately, nothing is known about them directly, and so we have to rely upon conjecture.

There is widespread agreement among scholars that the prophets themselves authored the earliest written versions of their oracles, which later would become the prophetic book. This assumption takes the redactional headings that refer to the whole book at their word. However, it cannot explain why the headings should be correct for one part of a book and not for another. Even the earliest material is not an exact transcription but rather a new interpretation of the original prophetic oracle. If the prophet is the author and thus his own interpreter, it is difficult to decide which interpretations can be ascribed to him and which have to be accredited to a later scribe.

Thus, we presumably need to assume anonymous, learned scribes from the beginnings of the prophetic book as well as for all subsequent stages. Unlike the prophets, these scribes were schooled in reading and writing as well as in intellectual and theological skills. We cannot exclude with certainty that some of them were prophets. In light of what we do know about the profession of prophets from the ancient Near East, however, it seems more likely that they were professional scribes who had devoted themselves to the prophetic tradition and to the God of the prophets. Normally, such people came from the scribal schools located at the royal court or the temple. It was in this context that prophetic oracles were transmitted, though the authors of the books have moved noticeably from their origins. The form and content of the prophetic books reveal their distance from both the prophetic guild and the scribal school. The prophetic books were a literary and theological innovation. They stem from neither of the aforementioned institutions but rather from the crisis that overtook both. They did not serve political agitation or propaganda but instead the study of the sacred scriptures. In the prophetic books, the prophets have become scribes, and the scribes have become prophets.

For this reason, it is not easy to say in what institutional or sociological context the books originated. The only historical example that we have is the community of Qumran attested in the Dead Sea Scrolls. Here we can study the relationship between institutional marginalization and literary production. The idea of an exodus to a secluded place in the Judean desert probably resulted from the loss of political, economic, and religious influence at the Jerusalem temple. The loss of status was replaced by the foundation of a religious community that was characterized not only by distinctive rites but also by scriptural study, transmitting of texts, and the formation of a tradition developing in various theological directions. Whether we should imagine this community as comparable to the circles that produced and transmitted the prophetic literature is not certain. Nevertheless, these are the only conjectures that have the support of a clear historical analogy.

5. *Written Prophecy and Revelation*

Some readers will no doubt be troubled to discover that the words in the prophetic books do not stem from the prophets described in the books and that the authors were not the prophets themselves but instead anonymous scribes. This discovery appears to be in contradiction to the Bible's own claims to be the divine revelation of God's word. Not only does the pious reader of the Bible confront this problem but so does the historian, who is concerned to account for the *claims* of the prophetic books to be the word of God as a relevant historical phenomenon.

Conservative scholars do not deny the evidence and recognize the need to draw a distinction between the prophet and the prophetic book. Unfortunately, they fail to recognize the full import of this distinction. They attempt to hold on to the historicity of the prophet and the authenticity of his speeches as far as possible and only attribute to a later hand what is undeniably so. This approach fails to grasp the fundamental difference between the religio-historical phenomenon of prophecy and the literary prophetic tradition. It is this difference that requires a historical explanation.

It is equally simplistic to set the prophetic books to one side because they are not a trustworthy historical source as some radical critics are apt to do. Some such scholars, either not knowing any better or wanting to make a splash, try to make out that the issue is a huge scandal. The whole thing needs to be exposed as a fraud, which deludes contemporary readers as much as those from the past. With a pretense of scholarship they seek to frighten the pious Bible reader, though all they do is provide the tabloids with another headline.

The truly critical historians, however, take into account the fact that our contemporary ideas of historical truth were not those held by ancient writers or readers. Above all, they know that the truth of revelation cannot be verified or falsified on a historical basis, whatever its standards. They will reserve their judgment and confine themselves to the claims of the prophetic literature. The literature's claim that it is the revelation of God's word is understood and explained in its historical context where, as we have seen, the problems of historicity had not been raised.

Neither the conservative historian, nor the radical historian, nor the truly critical historian can answer the question of whether the claims of revelation can justifiably be held any longer under the current terms of the historical-critical explanation of the Bible. Only faith—be it of an individual or a community—can answer that. Were faith—God forbid—based solely on the authenticity of the tradition and the historical facts, then, as far as the Bible is concerned, it would be built on sand. If, on the other hand, it is based upon the proven and confirmed experience of people and communities with God, then it is built on rock, whatever opposition it faces. God's word can only be found in human words—that is, if we accept it and do not renounce it, as everybody is free to do.

CHAPTER 5

"The End Has Come"

The Beginnings of the Prophetic Tradition

The books of the prophets originated in the course of a period of around 500 years, from the beginning of the late eighth century until the early second century B.C.E. The lower date, which marks the completion of the books, is more or less valid for all of the books. The literary production, however, began at various times. The headings of the books, which offer a date for the prophet, give us something of a clue. However, since the headings are secondary, they cannot be relied upon. Their information must be tested by internal criteria and modified where necessary.

Three decisive events mark the main epochs. The end of the kingdom of Israel in 722 B.C.E. was the catalyst for the prophetic traditions in the books of Isaiah, Hosea, and Amos. The end of the kingdom of Judah in 587 B.C.E. gave rise to a second phase of productivity, including the beginning of the tradition in the Book of Jeremiah. The Book of Ezekiel addresses the same event. The third turning point was the rebuilding of the temple in Jerusalem during the years 520–515 B.C.E. The temple remained the cultic and spiritual center of ancient Judaism in the Persian and Greco-Roman periods until its destruction by the Roman general and future Caesar, Titus, in 70 C.E. The Second Temple was the stimulus for the formation of the traditions in the books of Haggai, Zechariah, and Malachi. This era was the time of greatest literary productivity within all the prophetic books, most notably within the Book of Isaiah. The books of Joel, Obadiah, Jonah, Micah, Nahum, Habakkuk, and Zephaniah originated between these major events. They reflect the end of the kingdoms of Israel and Judah and anticipate the end of the world. The largest parts of them, however, stem from the Second Temple period—that is, in postexilic times.

1. The End of the Kingdom of Israel

The ascent of Tiglath-pileser III (745–727 B.C.E.) to the Assyrian throne in 745 B.C.E. marked the beginning of the end for the petty kingdoms of Syria–Palestine. Soon after the start of his reign, Tiglath-pileser asserted Assyrian power in the west. He and his successors, Shalmaneser V (727–722 B.C.E.), Sargon II (722–705 B.C.E.), and Sennacherib (705–681 B.C.E.) steadily worked their way from north to south. They subjugated the Aramean city-states in Syria and, subsequently, both the kingdoms of Israel and Judah.

As a result of its anti-Assyrian activity, Israel lost most of its territory in 733/732 B.C.E. (2 Kgs 15:29) and in 722 B.C.E. it lost its independence (2 Kgs 17:3–6, 24). The kingdom was dissolved and incorporated into the Neo-Assyrian Empire. Large parts of the population were exiled, while others fled to Benjamin and Judah. Some may have even made it farther south to Egypt; their descendants may be among the Jewish colonists in Elephantine, an island on the Nile, which we know about in the Persian period. In place of the Israelites, a new population was brought in from elsewhere in the Assyrian Empire. The kingdom of Israel no longer existed; there only remained Israelites in Samerina, the Assyrian province that took its name from its principal city, Samaria. In the prophetic books and the rest of the Hebrew Bible, the name Israel was taken over as a designation for the people of YHWH, including Judah and the Judeans.

Judah willingly became a vassal of Assyria in 734/733 B.C.E. and paid tribute to the Assyrian king in order to protect itself from attack by Rezin of Damascus and Pekah of Samaria during the Syro-Ephraimite war (734–732 B.C.E.; see 2 Kgs 16:5, 7–9). Yet, the Assyrian army advanced farther south along the coastal road. They penetrated as far as Gaza, the most distant outpost of the Egyptian kingdom. Here and in other Philistine cities, there were repeated rebellions against Assyrian occupation, which were brutally suppressed. Around 705 B.C.E. Hezekiah, king of Judah, made common cause with the rebels. Shortly thereafter, in 701 B.C.E., Sennacherib marched to the gates of Jerusalem and besieged the city. For reasons that are not entirely clear, presumably because his troops were needed elsewhere, he lifted the siege without having achieved his objectives (see 2 Kgs 18:7b, 13–16; 19:36–37). Hezekiah had to pay a larger tribute in order to keep the throne of David. His domain lost most of Judah and was limited to Jerusalem and its immediate surroundings.

In the political turmoil of the second half of the eighth century B.C.E., the prophets of Israel and Judah were consulted frequently. Here and there the prophetic books preserve traces of these consultations. Thus, Isaiah 8 offers the following slogan, which the prophet *Isaiah son of Amoz* issued during the Syro-Ephraimite war:

> Then YHWH said to me, "Take a large tablet and write on it in common characters, 'Belonging to Maher-shalal-hash-baz,' and

have it attested for me by reliable witnesses, the priest Uriah, and
Zechariah son of Jeberechiah."

And I went to the prophetess, and she conceived and bore a son.
Then Y<small>HWH</small> said to me, "Name him Maher-shalal-hash-baz ('swift-
booty, speedy-prey'); for before the child knows how to call 'My
father' or 'My mother,' the wealth of Damascus and the spoil of
Samaria will be carried away by the king of Assyria." (Isa 8:1–4)

Two scenes circle around the same slogan: Maher-shalal-hash-baz, 'swift-
booty, speedy-prey'. The slogan derives from an Egyptian military expression and predicts imminent victory over enemies. Both scenes, the command to write the slogan down on a tablet before witnesses and the birth
of a child, add to the oracle a written and a living sign, both of which
serve to depict it. The former sign publicizes the oracle and conjures up
the event; the latter schedules it. Both signs probably developed from the
original slogan during the course of the tradition. They constitute a report
of the prophet. The prophetic propaganda fits well the historical facts, for
Ahaz bought the help of the Assyrian king through the payment of tribute.
Both obviously stand in harmony with the will of Y<small>HWH</small> and ensure the
maintenance of political stability. In addition, the two oracles for the king
incorporated in Isa 7:1–9 (v. 4 as well as vv. 7, 8a, 9a), the oracles against
the enemies of Judah in Isa 13–23 (esp. 17:1–3) and the legends in Isaiah
36–39, are animated by the memory of Isaiah, the prophet of salvation.
We may also have preserved in Isa 22:12–25 a divine decision about a
court intrigue.

Sayings from both front lines of the Syro-Ephraimite war appear to
have made their way into the book of the prophet *Hosea, son of Beeri*. One
slogan calls to arms three Benjaminite towns, which follow a sequence
from south to north:

Blow the horn in Gibeah, the trumpet in Ramah. Sound the alarm
at Beth-aven (Bethel); look behind you, Benjamin! (Hos 5:8)

Another slogan issues an unpromising prognosis for Ephraim (Israel),
which has found itself in a woeful situation:

Ephraim shall become a desolation in the day of punishment. . . .
Ephraim is oppressed, crushed in judgment. (Hos 5:9, 11)

Yet another saying accuses Judah of border violations:

The princes of Judah have become like those who remove the
land-mark. (Hos 5:1)

The sayings probably all relate to the political conflict over the region of Benjamin, which was often a source of tension between Israel and Judah. This is the case even if the exact circumstances cannot be identified with certainty or related exactly to individual events in the enduring conflicts of the Syro-Ephraimite war. With the exception of v. 10, it cannot even be said with certainty whether the oracles originally are spoken from a Judean or an Israelite point of view. This is a secure indication of their authenticity: they made sense in their historical context. In many respects, they resemble the authentic sayings used in Hos 6:8–9 and 7:3–7. Despite having been reworked, these reflect the chaotic internal politics of the northern kingdom, above all the many violent coups toward the end of the kingdom of Israel (see 2 Kgs 15:8–31; 17:1–6). If we assume an Israelite perspective, as the canonical Book of Hosea would have us do, then we have a despairing lament about the impending collapse of the kingdom. From a Judean perspective, the passage would read as a polemic against the northern enemy.

In the case of the Judean prophet *Amos from Tekoa*, whose prophecies are preserved in Amos 3–6, we can scarcely distinguish between lament and polemic. These prophecies also relate to the end of Israel. Since there is no earlier occasion that could have given rise to them, they appear to date from the late eighth century. Amos speaks in similes:

> As the shepherd rescues from the mouth of the lion two legs, or a piece of an ear, so shall the people of Israel be rescued. (Amos 3:12)

The oracle is based on an ancient shepherd's rule, whereby the few remains of the victim are evidence of the complete destruction of the animal. In other words, Israel will not be snatched away and saved, rather it will be consumed, skin and bones. Similarly, we have the metaphor of the town that marches out to war:

> The city that marched out a thousand shall have a hundred left, and that which marched out a hundred shall have ten left to the house of Israel. (Amos 5:3)

Downfall is inevitable; and even God, who would normally provide deliverance for Israel, appears to be powerless against it:

> As if someone fled from a lion, and was met by a bear; or went into the house and rested a hand against the wall, and was bitten by a snake. (Amos 5:19)

Consequently, the prophet raises a funeral lament, whether in an attempt to ward off the evil from his own land or as a wish for the premature death of his enemy:

> Fallen, no more to rise, is maiden Israel; forsaken on her land, with no one to raise her up. (Amos 5:2)

The formal element of the "woe oracle" also stems from the lament. The woe is uttered over those who rely upon good omens and the graciousness of God:

> Woe unto those who desire the day of YHWH! Why do you want the day of YHWH? It is darkness, not light. (Amos 5:18; cf. 5:20; 6:3).

Strikingly isolated participles, once preceded by an initial "woe," announce judgment especially to the Samarian upper class for their failure, which testifies against them:

> (Woe unto those) who live in Samaria, with the corner of a couch and part of a bed! (Amos 3:12).

> (Woe unto those) cows of Bashan who are on Mount Samaria, who say to their husbands, "Bring something to drink!" (Amos 4:1)

> (Woe to those) that turn justice to wormwood, and bring righteousness to the ground! (Amos 5:7; cf. 6:12)

With these and similar oracles, the prophets of Israel and Judah, including Isaiah, the prophet of salvation, and the warning voices of Hosea or Amos, commented on the end of the kingdom of Israel—heralded in the Syro-Ephraimite war and concluded in 722 B.C.E.—a cause of lament for some of the prophets but welcomed by others.

2. The Book of Isaiah

"Swift-booty, speedy-prey": Isaiah's slogan for the Syro-Ephraimite war, predicting the collapse of Damascus and Samaria and promising the salvation of Judah from the enemies in the north (Isa 8:1–4), takes an unexpected turn in the Book of Isaiah:

> YHWH spoke to me again: Because this people has refused the waters of Shiloah that flow gently . . . therefore, the Lord is bringing

up against it the mighty flood waters of the River . . . it will rise above all its channels and overflow all its banks; it will sweep on into Judah as a flood, and, pouring over, it will reach up to the neck. (Isa 8:5–8)

The river is the Euphrates. Its mighty waters, which overflow its banks and result in a catastrophic flood, are the Assyrian armies, which march from east to west and from north to south. After Aram (Damascus) and Israel (Samaria), they will now reach Judah. What has happened?

The text is composed with hindsight. It implies that the slogan proved true and Assyria overran Judah's northern enemies. The tribute to the Assyrian king has paid off. Thus, the king and the majority in Judah may have received notice of the end of Samaria, at least for as long as there was a kingdom of Judah.

The scribes who authored and transmitted the Book of Isaiah saw things differently. For them, the end of the kingdom of Israel meant in the main that the God of Israel, YHWH of Samaria, and his institutions had fallen under the wheels of Assyria. Yet, behind the events stood the God of Judah, YHWH of Jerusalem, in whose name Isaiah had issued the slogan "swift-booty, speedy-prey." When, after 722 and especially in 701 B.C.E., the Assyrian armies threatened to advance upon Judah, then also YHWH of Jerusalem and his institutions, including his prophets, came under threat. Instead of following the usual course of prophesying against the enemy, the scribes of Isaiah drew the conclusion that YHWH was not present in Judah and Jerusalem. He was with Assyria and was present in his judgment over both the kingdoms of Israel and Judah. The scribes adhered with conviction to the God of the prophet Isaiah, and in light of that commitment they were willing to surrender not only their northern rival but also their own people. The local differences and political rivalries lost their significance in the face of the violent consequences of the Assyrian advance. Thus, the scribes discovered in the YHWH of Samaria and the YHWH of Jerusalem the same God, and in Israel and Judah the unity of "the two houses of Israel" (Isa 8:14). At this point, they laid the foundations of the later biblical monotheism and the religious cipher "Israel." Historically, this united Israel never existed, but the concept of the one people of God is an object of faith and confession in the Bible (Martin Noth). Only on this basis is the demand for justice and righteousness understandable. God enforces his claim on the people through the many political, social, and ritual accusations of the prophets and prescribes it in the law.

The reason why the tradents of the prophetic oracles and scribes of the book concern themselves with YHWH and nothing else is obvious from the reason for the divine judgment: "because this people despises the waters of Shiloah which flow gently." The waters of Shiloah symbolize Jerusalem and the security of the capital, which no one except Yʜwʜ could guarantee. The text suggests that "this people" have lost their trust in their God. Perhaps it was the certainty of victory and the activities to secure the city politically and militarily that the scribes perceived as a lack of confidence. These attempts to strengthen Jerusalem may have been supported by the oracles of salvation from Isaiah and other cult prophets, though such an idea was far from the mind of the prophet Isaiah himself (see Isa 8:1–4). In any case, the scribes accuse the people in Isa 8:1–8 as they accuse the Judean king who received a prophecy announcing victory over the enemies in the Syro-Ephraimite war in Isa 7:1–9. Behind these verses, there might be hidden one or two original oracles of salvation. Yet, an addition in v. 9b says that even the most wonderful oracle of salvation is worthless without trust in God. The prophets of the books were not followers of an opposition party that sought improvement of conditions and democratization. They have only one motto for king and people: "If you do not stand firm in faith, you shall not stand at all." (Isa 7:9).

The new perspective is set out in a sort of memoir comprising Isa 6–8. This section of the book was originally entitled "vision of Isaiah, son of Amoz, which he saw concerning Judah and Jerusalem" (Isa 1:1). The memoir opens fittingly with a vision in Isa 6, which, like Isa 8, is delivered in the first person. It concerns the sending of the prophet to "this people." As for the sending of the prophet to the king, this is recounted in the third-person account of Isa 7, which was added secondarily between Isa 6 and Isa 8. The vision in Isa 6 dates the new perception together with the call of the prophet in the year of king Uzziah's death—that is, before the Syro-Ephraimite war (Isa 6:1). What God charges the prophet with is not the prophetic oracles that he should proclaim to the people but rather their result. The prophet is instructed to harden the hearts of the king and the people, blinding their eyes and plugging their ears, since God has willed their downfall. They should keep listening but will not understand; keep seeing, but will not recognize (Isa 6:9–10). Thus, Isaiah's oracles of salvation, which communicate security and stability, are transformed into a trap for the king and the people. Hearing and seeing, they will believe the words and so fail God (Isa 8:11–15). So that this happens and "this people" are destroyed by the will of God, the memoir itself is not made public. It is sealed up and only passed on to the disciples of the prophet Isaiah until God, who has hidden himself, again shows his true face (Isa 8:16–18).

The memoir in Isa 6–8 was the starting point for the literary history of the Book of Isaiah. In the opinion of many scholars, the prophet himself composed this memoir right after the Syro-Ephraimite war. However, it is far more likely that it is a later composition from the seventh century B.C.E. At the earliest, it stems from after the fall of Samaria reflecting theologically upon this event and relating it to Judah. Some even put Jerusalem in place of Samaria and date the memoir Isa 6–8 after the end of the kingdom of Judah. This is understandable but rather too schematic: it does not explain why the memoir speaks of Israel and Samaria as the people of God and is not just concerned exclusively with the fate of Judah and Jerusalem. The Book of Jeremiah already presupposes the identification of Israel and Judah. In the Book of Isaiah, we can observe the genesis of this identification.

Thus, we can see that the fall of Samaria initiated the formation of the prophetic tradition. The end of the kingdom of Israel was interpreted as the beginning of the end for the kingdom of Judah. This is also true for the many expansions that the memoir of Isa 6–8 experienced: the rhetorically refined song of the vineyard in Isa 5:1–7 and the impressive, remorseless responsive poem in Isa 9:7–20 (see also 5:25–30). Like everything else in the first part of Isaiah (chaps. 1–12), these texts have developed gradually in a concentric pattern. They make Isaiah's unwelcome task of hardening in Isa 6–8 comprehensible by putting the blame for the catastrophe on the people. Concrete offenses, in particular the social behavior of the aristocracy, are set out as the reasons for denunciation in the catena of woe oracles in Isa 5:8–24 (cf. 10:1–4). The charges are later rationalizations of the judgment. "Justice and righteousness" (5:7) thus become God's principal claim.

For the subsequent tradition, the focus upon "Judah and Jerusalem" in the heading of Isa 1:1 (cf. 2:1) is decisive. The siege and deliverance of the city (701 B.C.E.), the destruction of the temple and the Davidic dynasty (587 B.C.E.) and not least the rebuilding of the temple of Jerusalem (520–515 B.C.E.) have all contributed to the book. In the book's literary history, the theme was deepened and the book underwent a process of *Fortschreibung* concerning "Zion and the nations." The Zion theology that dominates the Book of Isaiah is not the starting point of scribal exegesis in the growing prophetic book but rather its outcome.

Apart from various *Fortschreibungen* in Isaiah 1–12 (chaps. 1–4 and 10–12), it is particularly the so-called Assyrian cycle in Isa 28–32 that is modeled on the Isaiah memoir of Isa 6–8 and revolves around the theme "Zion and the nations." After the "woe" uttered against Samaria in Isa 28:1–6, Jerusalem has its turn (Isa 29:1–8; 30:1; 31:1). Priests, prophets, and the entire people behave as if drunk. They are deep in a sleep that YHWH has poured over them (Isa 28:7–13; 29:9–16). They fail to understand God's counsel (Isa 28:23–29). They cannot read the revelation of the sealed book—that is, the Book of Isaiah (Isa 29:11–12). They do not want to hear God's instructions written down by the prophet (Isa 30:8–11). Instead, they enter into a covenant with death: with Egypt, from which they expected military aid against the forces in the north and east of Palestine (Isa 28:14–19; 30:1–7; 31:1–3). However, help for Zion will hardly come from Egypt but will come instead from YHWH himself. He will punish Assyria and all the other nations, for they have risen up against YHWH and his city, Mt. Zion (Isa 30:27–33; 31:4–9; cf. 10:5ff.; 14:24ff.; 36–37). The arrogance of Assyria and the nations will be judged like the haughtiness of the house of Jacob (cf. Isa 2:6ff.). After the "woe" against Samaria (Isa 28:1) and Jerusalem (Isa 29:1; 30:1; 31:1) comes the "woe" against the "destroyer" who has implemented judgment against Jerusalem (Isa 33). Only then will the eschatological salvation dawn (Isa 29:17–24; 30:18–26; 32–33) upon all those, who like the prophet Isaiah of the memoir, believed and hoped in the God of judgment (cf. Isa 28:16; 30:15). Nevertheless, before this, YHWH will perform his *opus alienum*— that is, "his strange work" (Isa 28:21; 29:14). He will bring up the nations against Zion in order to thwart the covenant with death and punish his own people.

Though crushed between Assyria and Egypt, Zion, the city of God, is the only place of hope. The historical configuration of the late eighth and seventh centuries B.C.E. hardly changed in the Babylonian, Persian, and Hellenistic periods. Initially, the Neo-Babylonian and Persian Babylon assumed the role of Assyria (cf. Isa 13–14; 21; 39), and then finally it was the turn of the Seleucids to dominate Syria and Mesopotamia. Quite a few of the "Assyrian" and "Babylonian" texts in the Book of Isaiah originate from the Seleucid period. After the death of Alexander the Great, the situation intensified, with the Seleucids contending with the Ptolemaic rulers of Egypt for the dominance of Palestine (Dan 11), and this too left its mark on the literary history of the Book of Isaiah. The judgment against Israel and Judah and the storm of the nations against Zion were transformed into one massive judgment against all the neighboring nations, whether great or small (Isa 13–23), and a torrential judgment against the entire earth that revokes creation (Isa 24–27; 34). Not only will Zion and the pious Israelites who remained emerge from judgment as innocent (Isa 4:2–6; 26:1–4) but so will all Israel and the Israelites scattered throughout the world (Isa 11:10–16; 27:12–13; 35:1–10), and even the people who convert to YHWH (Isa 2:2–4; 19:18–25; 25:6–8).

"Zion and the nations": the theme runs through the entire Book of Isaiah, not only in Isaiah 1–39, the so-called First Isaiah, but also beyond it (see chap. 7). It is played in all possible variations. Judgment and salvation come upon Israel and Judah, Zion, the pious in Zion and in Israel, the universal Jewish diaspora, individual nations or all of them together, and the entire earth. YHWH as king (Isa 6:3; 33:22) or a new David reigns over them. The latter rules with justice and righteousness, and paradise dawns under him (Isa 9:1–6; 11:1–9; 32:1). All these variations emerge from the perspective of the eighth-century prophet Isaiah. Different hands insert their experiences as well as the theological and ethical maxims of their times from this perspective. The reader is expected to extract teaching for his own present and future.

3. *The Books of Hosea and Amos*

The books of Hosea and Amos grew outward from an inner core in the same manner as the Book of Isaiah. The original oracles and their collection are found in Hos 4:1–9:9 and Amos 3–6. Both collections of sayings underwent reworking numerous times and were gradually expanded forward and backward by *Fortschreibung*. In the Book of Hosea, this occured through the addition of the scenes of a marriage in Hos 1–3 and the reminiscences of sacred history in Hos 9–14. In the Book of Amos, on the other hand, it happens through the cycle of oracles against the nations in Amos 1–2 and the cycle of visions in Amos 7–9. Just like the pages of the Talmud, the sacrosanct text stands in the middle, with the interpretation arranged around it.

With the exception of some additions, the oldest sayings of Hosea are collected in Hos 6:7–7:16. This collection is headed "The word of YHWH that came to Hosea, son of Beeri" (Hos 1:1). In it we find compiled the complaints or, depending upon the perspective, the hostile reproaches of the prophet against the untenable conditions in the kingdom of Israel. But not only this: through the compilation and literary reworking, ambiguity has been eliminated and clarity produced. Admittedly, the interpretation originates from different presuppositions than in the Book of Isaiah and has new and distinctive accents. Nevertheless, the move is in the same direction. The complaints or accusations become charges that the prophet brings forth against the kingdom of Israel (Ephraim) in the name of YHWH. However, it is not only Israel that is indicted but rather the entire people of God, whether Judah is already included as "Israel" or whether it is explicitly named only retrospectively (Hos 6:10–11). The charges explain the historical circumstances of the many regicides as well as the policy of see-sawing between the potential treaty partners of Assyria and Egypt as an offense against God (Hos 7:8–12). The political consequences—the dissolution of the kingdom of Israel by Assyria—are portrayed not as a historical accident but as an act of YHWH who is leading his people into perdition.

What the people lack most is insight and knowledge (Hos 7:9). Instead of devoting themselves to a god who steers world events, they ran after all the great powers. The section consisting of Hos 5:8–6:6 adds the accusation of forgetfulness of God in the cult to the accusation of godless politics. The charge of political maneuvering hits Israel (Ephraim) and Judah in equal measure. For this reason, the older, individual sayings in Hos 5:8–11 are brought together and commented upon in 5:12–14. Further, the well-intentioned cultic efforts to secure the help of YHWH are rejected. In addition, the worship in both kingdoms, Israel and Judah, lacks knowledge: "For I desire steadfast love and not sacrifice, the knowledge of God rather than burnt offerings"—so reads the conclusion (Hos 6:6). From here the Book of Hosea develops its critique of the cult. This is developed in chapters 4–5 and 8–9 and forms a framework around the composition Hos 4:1–9:9. Apart from the competition between the political treaties and the belief in God, the cultic critique reveals a contradiction in God himself. Israel and Judah not only pursue other nations but also false gods, the YHWH of Samaria and the YHWH of Jerusalem from whom they expect salvation, not the YHWH who punishes Israel and Judah. As the tradition developed, the perverse YHWH became the false god—namely, the Canaanite's Baal and "the other gods."

Whoever decides, like the tradents and scribes of the Book of Hosea, to abandon the ancestral deity and replace the familiar god YHWH with the alien and unknown deity YHWH must have good reason for doing so. The headings of the prophetic books, together with a proper amount of confidence in the historical reliability of the theological tradition, have caused scholars to take the reasons given by the prophetic books at their word. The emergence of the prophets in the eighth century has been attributed to a lack of trust in God in politics, a bloated, baroque cult, or social ills. However, the politics of the Israelite and Judean kings was by no means godless. Rather, it was characterized by a deep trust in the national, dynastic god, YHWH of Samaria or YHWH of Jerusalem. Priests, prophets, judges, and officials could hardly be faulted for seeing nothing awry in a flourishing cult, a functioning judiciary, and a prosperous economy, as long as the political and social system continued. In every period there were, of course, abuses and injustices. These, however, offered hardly any ground for doubting God or abandoning the conventional order in his name.

Therefore, the reason must lie elsewhere. Something must have occurred that was enormous, unprecedented. Already the old sayings of Hosea from the years between the Syro-Ephraimite war and the fall of Samaria indicate something unusual. Here, I am thinking of the prophet's complaint about the resurgent boundary dispute between Israel and Judah as well as the violent and rapid turnover of kings, which were consequences of the Assyrian presence in Palestine. The oracles of the prophet Hosea suggest that these events were eventually to lead to catastrophe. But only after this catastrophe had taken place did the scribes of Hosea explain the events as the work of YHWH against his people Israel. In the course of time, after 701 and especially 587 B.C.E., the events were identified with the fate of Judah, at first only implicitly but later even explicitly through so-called "Judah glosses" in the Book of Hosea.

Despite the book's heading and the opinions of those scholars who take it at face value, the prophet Amos and the beginnings of his book date to the end of the eighth century. The legend in Amos 7:10–17 is hardly historically reliable. It makes the prophet a preacher of judgment against the northern kingdom of Israel under a king named Jeroboam. The legend is based on the story of an anonymous prophet under Jeroboam I in 1 Kings 13 whom the heading in Amos 1:1 identifies with Jeroboam II who reigned in the first half of the eighth century. The legend interprets Amos' third vision (Amos 7:7–9) and supplies a later explanation as to why YHWH will no longer forgive but has decided to bring his people to an end. Consequently, the legend supplements the visions of Amos in chaps. 7–8 that already have developed around the collection of Amos' words in chapters 3–6. Within this older collection itself, we must again distinguish between authentic sayings from the time before 722 B.C.E. and the scribal reworking afterward.

We have observed that in the case of the Isaiah memoir and the Book of Hosea, the original metaphors, participles, and woe utterances have already been interpreted from the perspective of prophetic judgment. The same is true of the oldest collection of texts in the Book of Amos. The heading "the words of Amos from Tekoa" (Amos 1:1) is followed by a preface—introduced by "hear this word" (Amos 3:1)—concerning the new role of the prophet (Amos 3:3–6, 8) and from v. 12 the compilation of older oracles. The redactional techniques can be discerned in the first section, Amos 3:12–15. The original metaphor and participial saying—an original woe utterance—have been related to one another so that the one provides the reason for the other: the lion will consume the Israelites, skin

and hair, because some Samarians—the metaphor relates it to all Israelites—lounge on divans.

> As the shepherd rescues from the mouth of the lion two legs, or
> a piece of an ear, so shall the people of Israel be rescued, those
> who live in Samaria with the corner of a couch and part of a bed.
> (Amos 3:12)

The verse in Amos 3:15, which is an addition and once followed v. 12
directly, takes up the social-critical implication of the justification and attributes the catastrophe announced in the metaphor to an act of God. The
words of the prophet turn into a divine speech:

> I will tear down the winter house as well as the summerhouse; and
> the houses of ivory shall perish, and the great houses shall come
> to an end, says YHWH. (Amos 3:15; cf. v. 12: "Thus says YHWH")

The tradents and scribes of the Book of Amos reworked the material in
the same or a similar manner in Amos 4:1–3; 5:1–3, 7; 5:18–20. Although
the collection originated at about the same time as the literary traditions
in Isaiah and Hosea, there is a new set of accents. Through the woe utterances, attention is drawn in particular to social problems, the luxury of
the upper class, and the dispensation of justice. Attributed to the whole
population, these problems are reckoned as the cause of the catastrophe.
Isolated grievances are generalized and interpreted as an offense against
God. Later authors elaborated the social indictments (Amos 5:10–17)
and, probably under the influence of Isaiah and Hosea (but also the rest
of the Hebrew Bible), supplemented them with cultic and political polemic. Cultic polemic can be found in the addition Amos 3:13–14 that
was inserted between v. 12 and v. 15, and in many other places (Amos
4:4–5; 5:4–6; 5:21–27). The political polemic is found above all in the
outer frame of the older collection in Amos 3:9–11 and 6:1–14. A comprehensive domestic and foreign political reform program arises just as
little as it does from the social and cultic criticisms of Isaiah, Hosea, and
the other prophets. Nevertheless, as God's stipulations, the political, social, and cultic standards gain greater significance and are deemed suitable
for effecting world change. Theological reflections on the election of the
people as the reason for the disaster (Amos 3:1–2) as well as on the many
warnings and possibilities for repentance, which God had offered to his
people (Amos 4:6–12; cf. 5:14–15), reveal the historical-theological plan
that underlies them.

The framing sections of both books, which were added later, are also
concerned with the divine plan and purpose. Here the tradition gives in-

sight into the overturning of God's heart (Hos 11:8). In the older collection of the prophetic sayings the theological reworking turns, above all, around the break in relationship between God and his people. The books' framing sections, however, largely address the theological basis of the relationship with God, which implies his numerous indictments and punitive interventions.

In the Book of Hosea, it is the deficient knowledge of God that provokes the question: who is the YHWH that the people should have acknowledged but have forgotten? The answers given in Hos 2 and 9–13 (beginning in 9:10) call to mind numerous moments in the sacred history of Israel. The desert wanderings and the giving of the land, the exodus, and the patriarchs serve as examples of how YHWH since time immemorial has turned to his people Israel and made them his own. The regular apostasy of the people from YHWH is tantamount to a termination of the relationship with God. What Hos 1–3 make clear, using the children and the marriage of the prophet as examples, also applies to the people's current offense and its punishment by God. He terminates the broken relationship and revokes his election: "You are not my people, and I am not yours" (Hos 1:9). Once the relationship is destroyed, the reasons for this development might include current accusations as well as concrete political events that occurred a long time before (Hos 1:4; cf. in relation to the nations Amos 1:3, 6, 11, 13; 2:1)—such as the bloodshed of Jezreel (2 Kgs 9–10).

Thus, the historical retrospect provides the indictments and condemnations of the prophetic books with even greater theological weight. On the other hand, Israel's historical origins gain significance through the divine judgment that now threatens. Both justify the exclusive relationship between YHWH and Israel, which must be expressed through internal and external demarcation: against their own cult and against Baal and the other gods. It is not by accident that we find in the Book of Hosea the clearest echoes of the First Commandment and the Decalogue. Indeed, the prophetic recriminations in Hos 4:2 most likely served as a model for the latter. At the same time, the retrospect on the historical-theological foundations of the relationship with God opens up the possibility of a new beginning. Either YHWH himself changes his mind all of a sudden (Hos 2:16–25; 11:8–11), or the people (Hos 3:5; 14:2–9), or even only a selection of the righteous who walk in his ways return to YHWH (Hos 14:10).

The theological issues are even more directly expressed in the Book of Amos. Here, it is not Israel's sacred history that brings God's relationship with Israel back to mind (cf., however, Amos 2:9–11; 3:1–2; and 9:7) but only the candid declaration of its end: "The end has come for my people Israel" (Amos 8:2). The declaration is preceded by the cycle of visions in

Amos 7–9 in which the prophet converses with God and intercedes for "little Jacob." Twice he is successful and moves God to remorse: "it shall not happen" (Amos 7:1–6). However, in the third and fourth vision, God is implacable. Enough is enough; the end has come: "I will no longer pass them by" (Amos 7:7–8; 8:1–2). Quite differently from Amos 3:3–6:8, where the call to be a prophet of judgment derives from the evidence of facts, the visions fulfill the principle of Amos 3:7: YHWH does nothing "without revealing his secret to his servants, the prophets." The inexorable end of Israel is placed in an international context in Amos 1–2, while the fifth vision in Amos 9:1–4 and its appended doxology in vv. 5–6 (cf. Amos 5:8; 8:8) place it in a cosmic setting. Here again, the future salvation presupposes judgment and selection (Amos 9:7–15).

CHAPTER 6

"Behold, I Put My Words in Your Mouth"

The Formation of the Prophetic Tradition

In describing the *Fortschreibung* in the books of Isaiah, Hosea, and Amos, we have already encountered all the periods in which the prophetic tradition was shaped. Anticipating later periods was unavoidable in order to examine the books as a whole and not to be constantly jumping backward and forward between them. Now we will be concerned with the transition from one period to the next. We can best observe the transition in cases where a tradition originates at the change of epochs. This is the case for the Book of Jeremiah, which has its earliest origins during the shift from the Neo-Assyrian to the Neo-Babylonian period, a period of transition that involved the end of the kingdom of Judah. Ezekiel also has the fall of Jerusalem as its theme, although it originates from a much later time.

1. The End of the Kingdom of Judah

The end of the kingdom of Israel and the Neo-Assyrian domination of Syria and Palestine were not bad times for Judah. The small state in the south of Palestine had nothing to fear so long as it paid its tribute to the Assyrian king. The exertions that were necessary to produce tribute had a positive effect on the economy. So for a long time after 701 B.C.E. there was peace and economic prosperity, particularly during the reign of King Manasseh (669–642 B.C.E.) who appears in the Neo-Assyrian inscriptions as a loyal vassal (ANET, 291). At this time, the cult also profited, as YHWH was thanked for the peace and the abundant yields. After the collapse of the kingdom of Judah in 587 B.C.E., however, the theological tradition perceived instead a "Canaanization" of Judah after the Israelite model and invented "the Assyrian crisis of Israelite religion" (2 Kgs 21:1–18).

This interpretation was already worked out in the prophetic tradition of the seventh century, insofar as the view was held that the end of

Samaria had already determined the fate of Judah and Jerusalem. Since the expectation came true, we cannot say in detail whether such prophecies and their justifications emerged before or after 587 B.C.E. This is especially difficult when no reference to the kingdom of Israel is present or has only been added later.

This is the case in the Book of *Micah*. If we disregard the heading in Mic 1:1, which is obviously secondary, and the framework in 1:2–7 and 3:12, we find in Mic 1:8–16 (minus the theological interpretations in vv. 8–9, 16 and further glosses in vv. 10–15) a poem that is difficult to understand and full of wordplays. It describes solely the invasion and destruction of Judean towns in the Shephelah. Therefore, it could originate just as well from the events that occurred around 701 B.C.E. as from the period between 597 and 587 B.C.E. The same is perhaps true of one or another of the laments about social grievances in Mic 2–3 (e.g., 2:1–2). The combination, theological interpretation, and literary reworking of the older oracles within the framework of Mic 1–3 belong to the postexilic period. This is also true of the various *Fortschreibungen* in Mic 4–7 that presuppose the Zion theology in the Book of Isaiah. During the reign of Manasseh (first half of the seventh century), however, the prophetic tradition may have stalled. The expected end was for the time postponed beyond reach.

The palace revolution against Amon (641–640 B.C.E.), the son and successor of Manasseh, and the elevation of the eight-year-old Josiah to the throne of Judah (639–609 B.C.E.) introduced a decisive political change. The star of the Neo-Assyrian Empire was waning, and on the far horizon, the Medes and Babylonians were beginning to emerge. In 626/625 B.C.E., Babylon broke free from Assyrian hegemony and Nabopolassar (625–605 B.C.E.), the founder of the Neo-Babylonian or Chaldean kingdom, took the throne. In 616 B.C.E., the Mede Cyaxares defeated the Scythians, who were the unwilling allies of the Assyrians. In 612 B.C.E. Nineveh, the capital of the Neo-Assyrian Empire, fell. It was followed in 610 B.C.E. by the Assyrian rump state in north-Syrian Haran, though it received support once more in 609 B.C.E. from the Egyptian Pharaoh Necho II (610–595 B.C.E.), who, of course, was pursuing his own agenda. Finally, at the battle of Carchemish in 605 B.C.E., the Neo-Babylonian king Nebuchadnezzar II (605–562 B.C.E.) successfully concluded the conflict between the great powers for the dominance of Syria and Palestine to his advantage.

The Judean prophets greeted the end of the Neo-Assyrian Empire with corresponding propaganda. The core of the Book of *Nahum* has preserved an example of this. The two poems mocking Assyria in Nah

2:2–14 and 3:1–19 probably stem from around 612 B.C.E. and gloat over the conquest of the city of Nineveh by the Medo-Babylonian alliance. The events are ascribed to YHWH (Nah 2:14; 3:5). As in the Book of Isaiah they are regarded as retaliation for Assyria's offenses against Judah and other nations (Nah 2:3; 3:1, 4, 19; cf. Isa 10:5ff., etc.). The theological reflection in Nah 1 originates much later, partly formulated as an acrostic, a poetic form where each verse begins with the next letter of the alphabet. In this poem, the confessional statement about YHWH's patience from Exod 20:5–6; 34:6–7 is interpreted and turned against YHWH's enemies among the nations.

The same statement about YHWH's patience is present in the climax of the little Book of *Jonah* (4:2), which like Nah 1 stems from the postexilic period. It also contemplates the fate of Nineveh, though it allows the city to be spared. The name of the prophet is taken from 2 Kgs 14:25. The conflict a prophet experiences when God feels remorse and changes his mind is reflected in Jonah's own person. On the one hand, this is used to explain the conflicting posture of YHWH toward the nations, whereby the Assyrians can be deployed as a means of judgment and yet ultimately be punished for it. On the other hand, a new type of relationship between YHWH and the nations is established based on their piety.

However, let us return to the course of history. The defeat of the Neo-Assyrian kingdom at the end of the seventh century B.C.E. provided Judah with room to maneuver, which the leading circles around King Josiah would probably have exploited. We learn about it only indirectly through Josiah's tragic death, when in 609 B.C.E. he approached (and perhaps opposed) Necho II at Megiddo and paid for his youthful recklessness with his premature death (2 Kgs 23:29). In the slipstream of the Medo-Babylonian alliance, he had attempted to free Judah from Assyrian domination and that threatened by Egypt, as well as expanding his own dominion over the territory of the former northern kingdom. His political daring was highly esteemed. After the catastrophe of 587 B.C.E., the theological tradition chose him as a champion for YHWH and as a fighter for the Law of Moses. They attributed to him a radical reform of the cult in accordance with Deuteronomy (2 Kgs 22–23) and thus made him an example of release from their own (destroyed) past.

Because of Josiah's unwise political behavior, Judah ultimately found itself sucked into the conflict between Egypt and Babylon for dominance in Syria and Palestine. Josiah's successor on the throne of David was Jehoahaz, one of his sons. It appears that he wanted to continue the policies of his father, and in the year of his coronation he was arrested by

Necho II in the Syrian city of Riblah and then displaced to Egypt, where he died (2 Kgs 23:33–34). Jeremiah gives us a moving lament over Jehoahaz, whom he calls Shallum: "Do not weep for him who is dead (i.e., king Josiah), nor bemoan him. Weep rather for him who goes away, for he shall no more return, nor see his native land" (Jer 22:10). His successor was Eliakim, renamed as Jehoiakim (608–598 B.C.E.), who was also a son of Josiah and king by grace of Egypt. After the battle of Carchemish (605 B.C.E.), which overnight made him a vassal of Nebuchadnezzar, his days were numbered. Jehoiakim was not to be trusted (cf. 2 Kgs 24:1). It was not he, however, who was relieved of his royal rights and duties, but his son and successor Jehoiachin. After the first capture of Jerusalem in 597 B.C.E. Jehoiachin was deported to Babylon, where he was treated generously and in 562 B.C.E. elevated to be fed from the royal table of Amel-Marduk (2 Kgs 24:8–17; 25:27–30).

Jehoiachin was replaced as king of Judah by Mattaniah, the third son of Josiah, who was renamed Zedekiah (597–587 B.C.E.). When he too allowed himself to be tempted to break away from the Babylonian king and enter into negotiations with Egypt, the end of the kingdom of Judah had come. After a siege of a year and a half, Jerusalem fell in 587 B.C.E. The king was imprisoned and had to watch his children being killed before his eyes at Riblah. Afterward, in order to ensure that the shocking image was impressed on him, he was blinded and sent off to Babylon. The walls of Jerusalem and the temple were torn down and burned, while part of the population was deported (2 Kgs 25). Many fled to Egypt after the murder of Gedaliah, the Judean governor whom Nebuchadnezzar had installed in Mizpah (2 Kgs 25:22–26).

Just as Israel needed the prophets at the end of the eighth century, this was also the case for Judah as it met its end. Since the political situation was often difficult to discern and the camps divided, they took sides in different ways. Many, perhaps the majority, would vote with the reigning monarch. Following Josiah and Jehoahaz they initially made a tactical alliance with Babylon against Egypt (and Assyria), but subsequently they followed the politics of Jehoiakim and Zedekiah and sided with Egypt against Babylon. We hear about negotiations with Egypt from Lachish Ostracon No. 3 (see above, chap. 2.1, pp. 13–14). Anti-Babylonian propaganda was the business of the prophets of salvation, such as the prophet Hananiah in Jer 28, who were concerned about Judah's political sovereignty. In the Book of Jeremiah, however, they are dismissed as "lying (i.e., false) prophets."

The other side advised against backing Egypt and trying to rebel against Babylon. The prophet *Jeremiah, son of Hilkiah*, from a priestly family in Anathoth in the land of Benjamin appears to have belonged to this party. In Lachish Ostracon No. 6 (ANET, 322; COS II, 80–81; WAW, 215–17) a group of such people is said to "make the hands droop." This reminds us of the accusation of defeatism made against Jeremiah (Jer 38:4). In the Book of Jeremiah, his position is justified by YHWH's decision to surrender Judah and Jerusalem into the hand of the Babylonians as punishment for their sins. This, however, is a later theological interpretation of the historical facts. In reality, the preaching of Jeremiah and all those who shared his opinion (cf. Jer 26:20–24) was also politically motivated. They had not followed the change of opinion under Jehoiakim and Zedekiah but maintained the policies of Josiah and his son Jehoahaz. They saw— probably not incorrectly—that Judah's salvation and future probably lay as a Babylonian vassal state, as a buffer state against Egypt. In this respect, they also behaved loyally to the Judean king. However, their views clashed unavoidably with the politics of the reigning king and his officials. With good reason, both political parties imagined YHWH to be on their side.

The extent to which not only the prophets of the brand of Hananiah, but also Jeremiah and those like him, thought along the lines of the classic court and cult prophets is apparent from the original oracles that have been preserved from them. Whoever did not believe in a victory over the Babylonians envisaged a massive defeat coming upon Judah and Jerusalem. The omens for the day of YHWH, which arose from observations of the days and months, were correspondingly bad:

> The great day of YHWH is near, near and hastening fast;
> the sound of the day of YHWH is bitter,
> the warrior cries aloud there.
> That day will be a day of wrath,
> a day of distress and anguish,
> a day of ruin and devastation,
> a day of darkness and gloom,
> a day of clouds and thick darkness,
> a day of trumpet blast and battle cry against the fortified cities and
> against the lofty battlements. (Zeph 1:14–16)

The poem is presumably the only genuine oracle in the book of the prophet Zephaniah, who is given an unusually long genealogy (Zeph 1:1). Zephaniah is said to have appeared during the reign of Josiah, but the oracle is more suitable for the situation around 597–587 B.C.E. It pictures the wrath of YHWH, which has to be appeased (see above, chap. 5.1, on Amos 5:18, p. 40). Everything else is an explanation of the day of YHWH, which, according to the scribal prophecy of Zeph 1–3, has become the day of the great judgment on Judah and Jerusalem, the neighboring nations, and the entire earth. Only the pious in Israel and the nations will survive (see Isa 2:12; 13:6, 9; 22:5; 34:8; Jer 46:10; Ezek 13:5; 30:3; Joel 1:15; 2:1, 11; 3:4; 4:14; Obad 15; Zech 14:1).

A series of laments are handed down from *Jeremiah* that describe the coming disaster with enormous inner empathy on the part of the prophet:

> A lion has gone up from its thicket, a destroyer of nations has set out; he has gone out from his place. (Jer 4:7)

> A hot wind comes from me out of the bare heights in the desert toward my poor people, not to winnow or cleanse. (Jer 4:11)

> Look! He comes up like clouds, his chariots like the whirlwind; his horses are swifter than eagles—woe to us, for we are ruined! (Jer 4:13)

> My anguish, my anguish! I writhe in pain! Oh, the walls of my heart! My heart is beating wildly; I cannot keep silent; for I hear the sound of the trumpet, the alarm of war. Disaster overtakes disaster, the whole land is laid waste. Suddenly my tents are destroyed, my curtains in a moment. How long must I see the standard, and hear the sound of the trumpet? (Jer 4:19–21)

In the laments, the prophet speaks, not YHWH. He is appalled at what he has come to see and hear. Precisely what this is he only hints at, but this much is clear: it is not YHWH who punishes Judah and Jerusalem for their sins but a gargantuan war machine that is marching against them. In other texts, the enemy is precisely located. It comes "from the north":

> Flee for safety, O children of Benjamin, from the midst of Jerusalem! Blow the trumpet in Tekoa, and raise a signal on Bethhaccherem; for evil looms out of the north, and great destruction. (Jer 6:1)

> See, a people is coming from the land of the north; a great nation is stirring from the farthest parts of the earth. They grasp the bow and the javelin, they are cruel and have no mercy, their sound is like the roaring sea; they ride on horses, equipped like a warrior for battle. (Jer 6:22–23)

2. The Book of Jeremiah

The laments of Jeremiah are arranged in the collection Jer 4–6 under the heading in Jer 1:1. The collection begins as follows:

> Declare in Judah, and proclaim in Jerusalem, and say: *Blow the trumpet* through the land; shout aloud and say, "Gather together, and let us go into the fortified cities!" Raise a standard toward Zion, *flee for safety*, do not delay, *for I am bringing evil from the north, and a great destruction*. (Jer 4:5–6)

This opening is taken from the older laments in 6:1 and 6:22, which were placed at the end of the collection:

> *Flee for safety*, O children of Benjamin, from the midst of Jerusalem! *Blow the trumpet* in Tekoa, and raise a signal on Beth-haccherem; *for evil looms out of the north, and great destruction*. (Jer 6:1)

> *See, a people is coming from the land of the north*, a great nation is stirring from the farthest parts of the earth. They grasp the bow and the javelin, they are cruel and have no mercy, their sound is like the roaring sea; they ride on horses, equipped like a warrior for battle. (Jer 6:22–23)

Both the opening verses in Jer 4:5–6 and the older laments at the end in 6:1, 22 form a literary frame around the collection in Jer 4–6. Thus, Jer 4:5–6 cites Jer 6:1, 22. However, Jer 4 says something different from the original in Jer 6. In the original laments, it is the people from the north themselves who advance, while in the citation of the original in Jer 4, it is YHWH, speaking in the first person, who leads the enemy against Jerusalem. The prophetic speech has become a divine speech. The difference marks the step from the original lament of the historical prophet to the prophecy of judgment. In this way, the tradition explains the destruction of Jerusalem and the end of the kingdom of Judah as the will of YHWH. This is the origin of the Book of Jeremiah.

The interpretation of Jeremiah as a prophet of judgment is accompanied by additions to the lament, such as accusations and elaborations on the judgment. They are directed to a female who is addressed abruptly with the second-person singular feminine. It concerns "daughter Zion," the personified Jerusalem:

> A lion has gone up from its thicket, a destroyer of nations has set out; he has gone out from his place *to make your land a waste; your cities will be ruins without inhabitant*. (Jer 4:7)

> See, a people is coming from the land of the north; a great nation is stirring from the farthest parts of the earth. They grasp the bow and the javelin, they are cruel and have no mercy, their sound is

like the roaring sea; they ride on horses, equipped like a warrior
for battle, *against you, O daughter Zion!* (Jer 6:22–23)

The remonstrations that justify the judgment are likewise addressed to the
personified Jerusalem or to the people of God in Judah and Jerusalem—
partially also portrayed as a woman. The people of God in Judah and Jerusalem is obviously compared or equated with Israel, the former northern
kingdom. The accusations are rather general, and almost all amount to the
same thing: the rupture in the relationship between God and his people.
This is no different in the preceding chapters, Jer 2–3, and in the following
chapters up until Jer 23. In these chapters, again, we occasionally find an
old oracle of Jeremiah or of another prophet that has served as the basis
for further interpretation and *Fortschreibung.*

So far, the interpretation in the Book of Jeremiah moves along the
usual lines of the prophetic tradition and above all bears a certain relationship to Hosea. This cannot be explained as the prophetic tradition
belonging to the general theological education of priests and prophets.
On the contrary, the prophetic books suggest that the priests and prophets
in preexilic Judah knew absolutely nothing about the prophetic tradition
that has come down to us. Rather, only with the destruction of Jerusalem
and the end of the kingdom of Judah was the older tradition confirmed
and granted the importance that it deserved. This is reflected after 587
B.C.E. both in the *Fortschreibung* of the older books as well as in the draft-
ing of new writings such as the basic layer of the Book of Jeremiah, which
could build upon the foundations of its predecessors when reworking and
supplementing the underlying oracles. It appears that the authors of the
prophetic books knew of each other and cultivated an exchange of texts.

The further development of the prophetic tradition in the Book of
Jeremiah goes its own way. The distinctive element is the person of the
prophet, who gained increasing significance as a mediator and as an em-
bodiment of the word of God. On the one hand, this finds its expression
in a series of sign-acts that are fashioned as first-person accounts of the
prophet. They are inserted between the words about the enemy from the
north in Jer 2–10 (up to 10:22) and the sayings about the kings (priests
and prophets) in Jer 13 and Jer 22–23 (see Jer 13; 16; 18; 19). The sign-
acts presuppose the interpretation of the laments as words of judgment.
Unlike the laments, they see the coming disaster as Yhwh's work right
from the beginning. Unlike the interpretation of the laments, they offer
no reason. Rather, they simply demonstrate the retributive judgment of
God. Their distinctiveness consists of the connection between sign and
word. Both are the word of God to the prophet manifested in his person.

Thus, the sign-acts reflect the effect of the word of God and the role of the prophet as its representative in history. As the vision of Jeremiah's call in Jer 1 formulates programmatically: "Now I have put my words in your mouth" (v. 9) and "I am watching over my word to perform it" (v. 12).

In addition to the sign-acts, the person of the prophet also appears in the foreground in the narratives about his life and suffering (Jer 20; 26–29; 36–45). Surprisingly, the real name of "the enemy from the north" never occurs in the texts discussed so far. This strongly suggests that the texts are still close to the events of 597 and 587 B.C.E. As more time elapsed and the events became distant, they had to be named more precisely and reconstructed. This is one of the reasons why historicizing glosses were applied in texts such as Isa 7–8 (7:4b; 8:6b, 7b) or why the tradition in Isaiah (Isa 7; 36–39) as also in Jeremiah increasingly shifted to narration. Here, the portrayal of Isaiah is explicitly that of a prophet of the Assyrian epoch, and Jeremiah's is that of a prophet of the Babylonian (or Chaldean) epoch.

The narratives about Jeremiah are animated by the memory of the preexilic prophet, who moved in the political direction of Josiah and was opposed to the politics of making a treaty with Egypt, as was conducted by Jehoiakim and Zedekiah and supported by other prophets. Jeremiah apparently also advised Zedekiah in a similar manner (Jer 37). Both parties could invoke Yhwh in good conscience. Yet, after history had proven Jeremiah to be right and the others to be "false prophets," the tradition reformulated the political dilemma into a theological alternative: a decision for or against Yhwh. The narratives are composed on this basis. Some put the controversy with "false" prophets or the other opponents of Jeremiah's prophecy right at the center (Jer 20; 27–28; 36), while others focus on Jeremiah's life until he was displaced to Egypt (Jer 37–44). Babylon and Nebuchadnezzar not only play a role as the tool of judgment but also receive a far-reaching task that will last up to seventy years, according to Jer 25:11–12 and 29:10. As the appointed world leader and servant of Yhwh (Jer 27:5–8), Nebuchadnezzar will care for the survival and welfare of those who willingly submit to him, whether in Judah (Jer 32; 37–44) or in exile (Jer 29). For whoever submits to Babylon submits to Yhwh. Cautiously, this points to a perspective for the period after the disaster had occurred. Among exegetes, the formula "salvation in judgment" has become popular for this concept. The juxtaposition of the good and the bad figs in the vision of Jer 24 restricts this perspective to the Babylonian exiles. This restriction serves as a program for the following narratives (Jer 26–45) as well as the oracles against the nations (Jer 46–51), which are anticipated in Jer 25 and culminate in the great poem against Babylon (Jer 50–51).

Submission to YHWH, however, requires more than submission to Babylon. This is explained in a series of speeches that are delivered in prose and adopt a tone that is familiar from Deuteronomy and the deuteronomistic redaction of the Former Prophets (Jer 7; 11; 16; 18; 19, etc.). The speeches resemble sermons. In many cases, they draw upon a sign-act or its interpretation (e.g., Jer 16:10ff.) or other prophetic words that serve as a sort of sermon text. They presuppose the announcement of divine justice in the sign-acts and narratives but introduce new standards. First, they identify the neglect of God's word that Jeremiah has brought into the world with disobedience of God and defection to other gods. In sum, they regard it as a transgression of the First Commandment. The word of God in the mouth of the prophet thus becomes law. Historical retrospects trace the disobedience back to the ancestors in Exodus. Second, the speeches challenge the addressee to make a decision for or against YHWH and his prophets. In the historical fiction of the prophetic book, this conception offers to the preexilic generation a chance to repent. This opportunity, which was squandered long ago, remains open to all future generations, including the reader.

What future generations might expect can be gleaned from the book's prophecies of salvation—some conditional, some unconditional—which are collected above all in Jer 30–33. They promise the abolition and recompense of all that YHWH did to his people as punishment for their disobedience. The promise includes the annihilation of Babylonian rule in the context of a general judgment against the nations (Jer 25; 46–51) and the return of the Babylonian prisoners (Jer 24:5–6; 27:22; 29:10) and of the worldwide Diaspora (Jer 16:15; 23:3, 8; 29:14; 32:37). Furthermore, it comprises the reestablishing and unification of the two kingdoms under a new David in a rebuilt Zion-Jerusalem (Jer 23:5–6; 30–33). Also included, above all, is the restoration of the broken divine-human relationship. Since human capabilities are not sufficient, YHWH will conclude a new covenant with Israel and Judah, placing the law in their hearts. For the first time, what YHWH had intended since the exodus from Egypt will become reality: "they shall be my people and I will be their God" (Jer 31:31–33; cf. 24:7; 30:22; 32:38–39 as well as Ezek 11:19–20; 36:26–27).

The laments, sign-acts, and narratives of the Book of Jeremiah place the person of the prophet in the foreground in a particular way. To the extent that the prophet stands for the word of God and embodies the judgment of God, the prophet comes increasingly into conflict. Not only with the people and the false prophets but also with God himself. The tradition reflects this theological problem in a very special group of texts called the "confessions of Jeremiah" (Jer 11:18–12:6; 15:10–21; 17:14–18; 18:18–23; 20:7–18). These texts express the self-understanding of the prophet before his God in the language of individual laments, just like the ones found in the Psalter. The "I" of the prophet stands both for the prophet and for every righteous individual among the people. In his person, the righteous suffers the judgment of the sinful people. In the confessions, the prophet of the Book of Jeremiah—and with him every righteous person—does not suffer from judgment, which, on the contrary, is highly desired. Instead, they suffer under God himself who appears to punish the righteous and spare the sinner. It is not the historical Jeremiah who speaks in the confessions but rather the scribes who write under his name and count themselves among the righteous. It is the same here as elsewhere in the tradition of saints: the more you know about the person and the inner life of the prophets, the farther away you are from the historical origins.

3. The Book of Ezekiel

The Book of Ezekiel appears to be even more distant from the events it describes. It is dated throughout to the time after the first deportation in 597 B.C.E. and predicts the final capture and destruction of Jerusalem in 587 B.C.E. The priest Ezekiel, son of Buzi, is considered to be the author of the first-person account, acting as a prophet among the exiles in Tel-Abib by the river Chebar (Ezek 1:3–3:15) between 593 and 571 B.C.E. (Ezek 1:1; 29:17). The book maintains this historical fiction throughout, even when Israel in the land is the main subject and addressee of the priestly prophet. The wording and theology of the speeches point to the fifth and fourth centuries B.C.E.

The origins of the book are in large part obscure. The analysis is made even more difficult by the uniform style, which combines prophetic speech with priestly and deuteronomic-deuteronomistic phraseology and has a preference for lengthy speeches. It is clear that the speeches cannot be attributed to a single author, but in many instances we are lacking the criteria needed to interrelate the numerous waves of *Fortschreibungen* and to identify the literary core of the tradition, let alone the original oracles of the prophet-priest. The framework of the composition is formed by two visions: the departure of the "glory of Yhwh" (see Isa 6:3; 40:5; cf. Exod 24:16–17; 29:43; 40:34–38) from the temple and its return to Jerusalem in Ezek 8–11 and 40–48. Both visions take as their starting point the call scene in Ezek 1–3. In contrast, the sending of the prophet to the house of Israel (Ezek 2:3–7; 3:4–9) was added later. The many sign-acts and judgment speeches addressed to all Israel in Ezek 1–24, the prophecies of judgment and salvation in Ezek 33–39, as well as the oracles against the nations in Ezek 25–32 are all dependent on this sending of the prophet. The Book of Ezekiel evidently argues for the primacy of the (returned) Babylonian exiles above those who had remained in the land. Among the exiles was the "glory of Yhwh" (see Ezek 11:22–25). Only at a later stage of tradition did the book address all Israel and Israelites scattered across the world.

On the whole, the book leaves the impression that one has already read or heard everything elsewhere. This is because the book in large measure depends upon literary models that it cites and explains. This is obvious in the call vision of Ezek 1–3, where Ezekiel eats a scroll. The motif interprets Jer 15:16 ("your words were found, and I ate them") and makes the prophet appear to be the personified word of God. The appointment of the prophet as "watchman over Israel," who is responsible with his own life (Ezek 3:16–19; 33:1ff.), points in the same direction, as do the many sign-acts, to which many long speeches are attached (Ezek 4–5; 12; 24:15ff.; 37). Even more than in Jeremiah, the person and the biography of the prophet have become a "sign for Israel" (Ezek 12:6), so much so that some scholars have diagnosed Ezekiel as having pathological traits.

The long threats (e.g., Ezek 6–7; 13–14) are reminiscent in kind and phraseology to Jeremiah and his prose speeches. Others such as the parables (Ezek 15; 16; 17; 19; 21; 24; 34; 37; 38–39), visions (Ezek 1–3; 8–11; 40–48), and historical reviews (Ezek 16; 20; 23) echo Isaiah, Amos, and Hosea. The book repeatedly circles around the same theme: the destruction of Jerusalem and the collapse of the Judean monarchy. Both the reasons for the foreseen judgment and the predictions of salvation strike something of a monotonous tone and contribute little new in comparison to their precursors and literary models. Israel will receive punishment for murder, adultery, incest, perjury, and many other offenses that since time immemorial have infringed the sacred ordinances and breached the law, especially the First Commandment. Nevertheless, under certain conditions—for example, under the condition of individual retribution (Ezek 18; cf. Jer 31:29–30)—Israel has reason to hope that Yhwh may reinstate the divine-human relationship. As a result, the scattered people would be regathered and brought home, the land restored, the northern and southern kingdoms reunited, the nations punished, and, finally, the city of Jerusalem and its temple, the dwelling place of "the glory of Yhwh," rebuilt.

Ezekiel's presentation draws upon a prophetic tradition that is diverse but that had already taken on certain characteristic themes. The *topoi* are interpreted from a priestly-cultic perspective, focusing on themes such as clean and unclean or holy and profane and centered around the divine-human relationship. Nevertheless, we still encounter surprising new moves. Particularly noteworthy are the insider perspective on the heavenly world and the celestial plan for the New Jerusalem. We may compare the visions in Ezek 1–3, 8–11, and 40–48 to Isa 6. The book is a kind of Midrash; in other words, it is an interpretation of written prophecy in the form of prophecy, and as such it is a repository for later Jewish apocalypticism and mysticism.

Ezekiel is "not only a prophet but a theologian as well" (Gerhard von Rad). Actually, he is more of a theologian than a prophet. The doom he predicts lies already in the past. However, it gains current relevance in the Book of Ezekiel, which reflects the disaster in light of the earlier prophetic tradition, looking for the theological meaning of both the event and the tradition and their remaining validity. This theological interest is nowhere clearer than in the formula "so that you may know that I am Yhwh," which frequently concludes the speeches. The announcement of judgment like the promise of salvation serves solely the knowledge of Yhwh. Judgment and salvation, focused on the absence and presence of the "glory of Yhwh," do not occur (only) to place Israel under judgment or announce salvation. They primarily bring the divinity of God to light. The destruction of Jerusalem is the paradigm for "the end"—Ezekiel cites the prophet Amos (8:2)—that is to come. The assembling of Israel out of the nations—Ezekiel cites Isa 52:5–6—will demonstrate the holiness of God's name.

> Therefore say to the house of Israel, Thus says the Lord Yhwh: It is not for your sake, O house of Israel, that I am about to act, but for the sake of my holy name, which you have profaned among the nations to which you came. I will sanctify my great name, which has been profaned among the nations, and which you have profaned among them; and the nations shall know that I am Yhwh, says the Lord Yhwh, when through you I display my holiness before their eyes. (Ezek 36:22–23)

Disaster and salvation increase exponentially in the Book of Ezekiel. This has its basis in the theocentric view of both: the holier Yhwh's name, the greater the guilt and the harder the judgment; the greater the salvation, the holier his name.

This idea is put into effect in three extensive historical reviews: the history of God with Jerusalem (Ezek 16), the personified capitals of both kingdoms (Ezek 23) and the people of God as a whole (Ezek 20). In each case the theology of history better known from Jewish apocalyptic literature is already emerging (see chap. 8 below). Jerusalem and Samaria are reproached for the fact that since birth (Ezek 16) or since their youth (Ezek 23) they have been characterized by obscenity, faithlessness, and whoredom—in other words, godlessness. The cities are portrayed as women, and their propensity to godlessness is traced back to their Canaanite origins; it is, so to speak, hereditary. In this context, the election or marriage with YHWH appears in a new light. It has happened not only without reason but even against all inducement and is due only to the sovereignty of YHWH. Consequently, the judgment against the cities of Jerusalem and Samaria is even harder.

The same is true for the history of the people, whose crimes go back to their election in Egypt. That YHWH has repeatedly spared the people is the result not of grace, remorse, or compassion, and it is certainly not merited. Rather, it is only for the sake of YHWH's holy name—"so that it shall not be profaned in the sight of the nations" (Ezek 20:8f., 13f., 21f.)—that he comes to their rescue. In a similar way, the judgment of God (vv. 23ff.) and the salvific new beginning (vv. 33ff.) demonstrate the inviolability, integrity, and uniqueness of YHWH. The entire history of Israel thus becomes a witness to the holy name of God:

> And you shall know that I am YHWH, when I deal with you for my name's sake, not according to your evil ways, or corrupt deeds, O house of Israel, says the Lord YHWH. (Ezek 20:44)

CHAPTER 7

"Comfort, Comfort My People"

The Endings of the Prophetic Tradition

Not only the Book of Ezekiel but also several parts of the other prophetic books investigated in the previous chapters belong to the late phase of the prophetic tradition from Persian and Hellenistic times. This is especially true of the oracles of salvation, which all belong to a later stage. They presuppose the end of the kingdoms of Israel and Judah and reactivate on this basis the old, preexilic prophecy of salvation. Under changed circumstances, this form of prophecy takes on a new shape. Yet, it does not exclude the possibility that announcements of doom remain valid, be it as a recollection of the past (and continuing) doom or as the announcement of an imminent end followed by salvation. The reawakening of the prophecy of salvation can be observed best during the transition from the Babylonian to the Persian period, which is reflected in the second part of the Book of Isaiah (from Isa 40) but also in the books of Haggai, Zechariah, and Malachi.

1. The Second Temple of Jerusalem

The first year of the Persian king Cyrus II (559–539 B.C.E.) in Babylon (539 B.C.E.) marks the beginning of a new era for the biblical tradition. It is the year when the seventy years announced for Babylon by Jeremiah, during which time the land was laid waste and served its sentence (Lev 26:34), came to an end. At Cyrus's behest, the deported could return from Babylon to the land of their fathers and the temple in Jerusalem could be rebuilt at its former location (2 Chr 36:20–23; Ezra 1; 6:3–5).

The biblical picture does not correspond to the historical realities. It originates from a time when the temple, restored during the reign of Darius I (522–486 B.C.E.), was already standing. Further, this biblical picture is reconstructed from various passages of scripture. The account comes from those who claimed to have returned from Babylonian captivity and wanted to be in charge of the Second Temple community. For them, the capture of Babylon under Cyrus II and the beginning of Persian rule over Syria and Palestine marked the end of the period of judgment and the beginning of salvation. In the eyes of this group, Cyrus and his successors the Achaemenids were the legitimate heirs of the Davidic dynasty appointed by YHWH himself. As such, the Persian kings are responsible in the tradition for the rebuilding of the temple (Ezra 1–6; 7:27), the introduction of the law (Ezra 7–10; Neh 8), as well as for the external and internal reconstruction of Jerusalem (Neh 1–13). It is hardly a coincidence that it is told that Persian rulers dispatch envoys and officials from the circle of the Babylonian exiles, the so-called Golah: Sheshbazzar, Zerubbabel, Jeshua, Ezra, and Nehemiah.

In reality, however, the date 539 B.C.E. did not mark a change for the Jews in Babylon and Jerusalem. They may have projected their hopes onto Cyrus, who had conquered Media and Lydia and was obviously going to target Babylon next. Yet the conquest of the city did not entail the liberation from the Babylonian yoke for which they had hoped. To the contrary, Cyrus did not destroy Babylon but caused it to surrender without a fight. He restored the Babylonian cults and assumed the title "King of Babylon." Babylon remained the capital of the West under Persian rule. Cyrus's accession to power in Babylon was primarily a disappointment to the Jews. As a result, the prophetic tradition continued to be written as if one were still living under the Babylonian yoke.

A change for the better only occurred with the reconstruction of the Jerusalem temple under Darius I. He ascended the Achaemenid throne after Cambyses II (530–522 B.C.E.) had defeated Egypt and led the Persian Empire to the height of its power. Under the rule of Darius, the idea of a Persian multiethnic state developed. Every conquered people was allowed to live according to their own customs and laws as long as they accepted the Achaemenid king—authorized by the highest god and creator of the world order Ahuramazda—as the ruler and did not plan any revolts. According to the dating system in the Book of Haggai and in Ezra 5–6, the building of the Second Temple was carried out during the years 520–515 B.C.E. As this building project depended on the permission of the Persian authorities, Judah and Jerusalem enjoyed the same experience that Babylon had twenty years previously: the granting of cultic and soon afterward ethnic autonomy. Judah became a Persian province and Jerusalem got a protective wall.

Two prophetic oracles of the prophet *Haggai* have come down to us from the time of the building of the temple. They express YHWH's support for the project advanced by the Persian king:

> Is it a time for you yourselves to live in your paneled houses, while this house lies in ruins? Go up to the hills and bring wood and build the house, so that I may take pleasure in it and be honored, says YHWH. (Hag 1:4, 8)

> Who is left among you that saw this house in its former glory? How does it look to you now? Is it not in your sight as nothing? The latter splendor of this house shall be greater than the former, says YHWH of hosts. (Hag 2:3, 9a).

The rhetorical questions show that the building project did not cause enthusiasm everywhere. There were other worries, and many were simply discouraged by the amount of destruction. Maybe some harbored doubts about whether an enterprise sanctioned by the Persian authorities was in the interests of YHWH who, after all, had punished Jerusalem with the destruction of the temple. The appeals of the prophets that encourage the construction of the temple counter such doubts and continue the preexilic tradition of cultic prophecy. They emphasize the "glory of YHWH" that dwells in the temple (Isa 6:3) and reflects his external appearance. The destruction of the temple is not YHWH's will. Rather, he wants to delight in the house and to fill it with "glory."

The two oracles of the prophet Haggai seem to have found their way into the archives. As is common in the ancient Near East, each oracle includes a date: "In the second year of Darius the king, in the sixth month, on the first day of the month" and "In the seventh month, on the twenty-first day of the month the word of YHWH came by Haggai the prophet . . ." (Hag 1:1 + 1:4, 8; 1:15b/2:1 + 2:3, 9a). Dating the oracles according to the reign of the Persian king suggests that the contemporary political circumstances are in line with the will of YHWH. In the biblical tradition, these dates served as a point of departure to connect the words regarding the temple spoken by Haggai with the visions of Zechariah in Zech 1–8 and thus form some sort of prophetic chronicle similar to Ezra 1–6 (cf. Hag 1:1, 15a; 1:15b/2:1; 2:10, 20; Zech 1:1, 7; 7:1).

The visions of the prophet *Zechariah, son of Iddo* only indirectly relate to the building of the temple but are roughly contemporary compositions. They consist of individual visionary scenes that were gradually developed. The oldest pair deals with the rebuilding of the city Jerusalem (Zech 2:5–9 and 4:1–6a, 10b–14). A further pair places the rebuilding within the framework of a pacified world (1:8–11 and 6:1–8), a heavenly likeness of the Persian Empire with Jerusalem as its center. Historical figures (Zech 3; 4:6–10) as well as the perception of external and internal dangers (2:1–4; 5:1–4, 5–11) maintain the symmetry of the visionary cycle, but they were added later.

In the additions, one encounters the prophetic tradition. The tradition is responsible for the various comments and *Fortschreibungen* in Zech 1–8 (esp. chap. 1–2; 6:9–15; 7–8) that relate the visions explicitly to the building of the temple under Zerubbabel and Joshua and thus connect Zechariah with Haggai. In this composition, the temple marks the watershed between curse and blessing (Hag 1:6, 9–11: 2:15–19; Zech 8:9–13) or, in other words, between judgment and salvation (cf. Deut 28 and Lev 26). The introduction of this alternative was the basis for the addition of exhortations, penitential sermons, and other requirements to achieve the blessing that were gradually supplemented to the books of Haggai and Zechariah as well as the Book of *Malachi*, a further literary continuation of the composition consisting of Haggai and Zechariah 1–8. The temple alone was not enough. Without internal repentance and without pure sacrifices, the "glory of YHWH" will not appear and the curse bearing down on the people will not turn into a blessing.

It is impossible for the prophetic tradition of the Hebrew Bible to think about salvation without judgment preceding it. This is the reason why the temple oracles of Haggai and the visions of Zechariah were connected in a single composition and reworked in the way described above. As soon as salvation stalled, there was increased reflection on the guilt of the people and impending judgment. This process reached its climax during the transition from Persian rule to the Hellenistic period toward the end of the fourth century B.C.E. For this period we do not have any prophecy in the classic sense, nor do we find propaganda for or against Ptolemaic or Seleucid rulers, and there are no prophetic books explicitly addressing this period. The prophetic tradition moves toward its end. It summarizes its point of view in various late *Fortschreibungen* that portray YHWH as sitting in judgment over all the nations of the whole earth. By using various criteria, the pious in Israel and among the nations are excluded from this judgment. This development is apparent in the literary continuation of Zech 1–8 in Zech 9–14 and in several later pieces of prophetic literature. The books of *Joel*, *Obadiah*, and *Habakkuk* belong here, for they were mostly, if not entirely, written in the Hellenistic Period. In the following section, I will trace this development in the Book of Isaiah, whose second part (Isa 40–66) partly belongs in the Persian period and partly in the Hellenistic period.

2. Deutero-Isaiah

The Book of Isaiah is clearly divided into two parts, Isa 1–39 and Isa 40–66. Both parts differ in regard to language and reflect different historical circumstances. While the first part of the book contains material from the eighth to the second century B.C.E., the second part completely presupposes the end of the kingdom of Judah during the sixth century and the exilic-postexilic period following it. This is the reason why we speak of a "First" and a "Second" Isaiah. Following Bernhard Duhm, scholars often distinguish within "Second Isaiah" further between a "Second" and a "Third" Isaiah, usually called Deutero-Isaiah (Isa 40–55) and Trito-Isaiah (Isa 56–66). This differentiation can be justified, because Deutero-Isaiah, unlike the late parts in first Isaiah (Proto-Isaiah) and unlike Trito-Isaiah, was originally handed down separately or under the name of another prophet before it was extended into Trito-Isaiah. Both Deutero- and Trito-Isaiah were then added to Proto-Isaiah, and every part was dovetailed together.

With Deutero-Isaiah, something new begins in the prophetic tradition. The basic layer (*Grundschrift*) that can be found in Isa 40–48 is pure prophecy of salvation. It is not, as is usually the case, simply the reversal of the prophecy of doom. We can ask whether this basic layer can be traced back to an old-school cultic prophet who ministered among the exiles in Babylon as if nothing happened. When looking at the text, however, it is impossible to distinguish older oracles from the later literary tradition. In contrast to the oracles concerning the temple in Haggai or the visions of Zechariah, the Deutero-Isaianic speeches do not continue preexilic cultic prophecy. Rather, they presuppose the concept of God developed in the prophetic tradition. The prophecy of salvation in Deutero-Isaiah is not shaped as a counterpart to the prophecy of doom, although such prophecy forms the background of every single word. This can be seen in the way that the genres, types, and theological thought patterns from the national religion of the preexilic period are taken up and aligned with the new historical circumstances.

Every child in the ancient Near East could tell you that God is the creator and sustainer of the earth. Some form of this knowledge was part of the creed of the preexilic national religion in Israel or Judah. Deutero-Isaiah recalls this knowledge:

> Who has measured the waters in the hollow of his hand and marked off the heavens with a span, enclosed the dust of the earth in a measure, and weighed the mountains in scales and the hills in a balance? (Isa 40:12)

> Have you not known? Have you not heard? Has it not been told you from the beginning? Have you not understood from the foundations of the earth? It is he who sits above the circle of the

earth, and its inhabitants are like grasshoppers; who stretches out the heavens like a curtain, and spreads them like a tent to live in. (Isa 40:21–22)

Lift up your eyes on high and see: Who created these? He who brings out their host and numbers them, calling them all by name; because he is great in strength, mighty in power, not one is missing. (Isa 40:26)

The rhetorical questions are part of the style of a hymnic presentation of the creator god. In Deutero-Isaiah, they gain a new tune. Here they react to the doubts about God's ability and desire to help his weak people and to protect them against hostile nations and their gods. Israel's desperate lament, "My way is hidden from Yhwh, and my right is disregarded by my God" (Isa 40:27), forms the background here. In the form of a disputation, Yhwh aims to rebut such an accusation by reminding Israel that he is the creator and sustainer of the earth whose actions in nature and history have been apparent since the foundation of the earth. This argumentation grants an entirely new and independent significance to belief in creation.

The direct reassurance of weal is achieved by using the genre of an oracle of salvation. It is the same type used by the ancient Near Eastern prophets, who announced to the king the assistance of the gods and victory over his enemies. Both aspects resonate in the variants of the genre in Deutero-Isaiah:

But you, Israel, my servant, Jacob, whom I have chosen . . . do not fear, for I am with you, do not be afraid, for I am your God; I will strengthen you, I will help you, I will uphold you with my victorious right hand. Yes, all who are incensed against you shall be ashamed and disgraced; those who strive against you shall be as nothing and shall perish. You shall seek those who contend with you, but you shall not find them; those who war against you shall be as nothing at all. . . . For I, Yhwh your God, hold your right hand; it is I who say to you, "Do not fear, I will help you." (Isa 41:8–13)

The most significant change to the original use is the addressee. The people of Israel, who are granted the honorific title "servant of God" and are called after the patriarch Jacob, now replace the king. In other parts of Deutero-Isaiah, Cyrus (44:28; 45:1ff.), the anonymous servant (42:1–4; 49:1–6), or Zion-Jerusalem (54:4–6) can be addressed similarly. It was Yhwh who created them all and called them from the womb just like the Davidic king who no longer exists. The content of the promise of salvation also changes. Besides the delivery from their enemies (41:8–13), the royal people of God are promised to be kept from various general dangers (43:1–4) and are granted restitution by the spirit of God (44:1–5). Both can be understood metaphorically. However, they can equally be regarded as a concrete promise of the return of the exiles (cf. 43:5–7) or the natural provision and increase of the people during their return (cf. 41:17–20; 42:14–16; 43:14–21). Here, it is not creation that forms the basis of faith but rather the divine election of the king that is not revoked after the demise of kingship but simply reoriented. Now, the people benefit where the king once did.

The most radical transformation of the conventional belief concerns YHWH himself and his position among the gods. As far as Deutero-Isaiah is concerned, YHWH is not merely the highest deity, nor even the one God who tolerates no other gods beside him. Rather, he is the only God beside whom there is no other. This is the origin of monotheism in the strict sense. The singularity of YHWH is demonstrated by a probing of the evidence that is reminiscent of a court case. The nations and their gods are accused. Israel is called as a witness, and Cyrus, the conqueror of the nations, is produced as evidence. YHWH is both prosecutor and judge. The case centers on the question of who is responsible for the past and the future. The one who is able to predict and implement them is the only God:

> Set forth your case, says YHWH; bring your proofs, says the King of Jacob. Let them bring them, and tell us what is to happen. Tell us the former things, what they are, so that we may consider them, and that we may know their outcome; or declare to us the things to come. Tell us what is to come hereafter, that we may know that you are gods; do good, or do harm, that we may be afraid and terrified. You, indeed, are nothing and your work is nothing at all; whoever chooses you is an abomination. (Isa 41:21–24)

YHWH, however, has called someone to subdue the nations and he has appeared (41:25 cf. 41:1–4; 46:9–11). As a consequence, YHWH is God and no one else: "I am YHWH, the first, and with the last; I am he" (41:4; cf. 44:6; 48:12). The line of argument may not be watertight, but it was certainly compelling. Later scribes openly ridiculed the common ancient Near Eastern practice of producing and honoring idols (40:19–20; 41:6–7; 44:9–20; 45:20; 46:1–2, 6–7).

Deutero-Isaiah's monotheism did not emerge out of the blue. Nevertheless, it marks a turning point in the religious history of ancient Israel. Older concepts of God still shine through. For example, the statement about Yhwh's incomparability (40:18, 25; 44:7) derives from polytheism. It is attested in the ancient Near East several times for other gods. The royal title in 41:21 (cf. 43:15; 44:6) is reminiscent of the titles "lord over all the earth" and "king of all the gods," which were assigned to Yhwh in the preexilic cult (Ps 47:3; 95:3; 96:4; 97:5, 9) but who has now become the king of Israel. Within the older basic layer of Isa 40–48, the old (Israelite-Judean) myth of the enthronement of Yhwh (cf. Ps 29; 93) serves as a picture for the reentry of Yhwh in Jerusalem before the eyes of all nations (Isa 40:1–5; 52:7–10). In ancient times, Yhwh was regarded as the highest god among many. Already prior to Deutero-Isaiah, he was declared the one and only God of Israel (Deut 6:4–5; Exod 20:2–6/Deut 5:5–9). Only Deutero-Isaiah offers decisive "proof" that he is the only God and that there is none beside him. The reasoning, however, presupposes the conclusion. Based on the prophetic tradition, with its notion of a transcendent God who stands above Israel and the nations, this conclusion imposed itself almost automatically upon the authors of Deutero-Isaiah. Within the religious-historical framework of the Persian period, all gods were allocated a place under the canopy of Ahuramazda, the highest Persian god. The authors of Deutero-Isaiah sought to resist these leveling tendencies not only by having their God in place of the Persian highest god but also by making him take the place of all other gods.

In the basic layer of Deutero-Isaiah (Isa 40:1–5; 40:12–48:21; 52:7–10), the scene is dominated by Jacob-Israel, the royal servant, and by Yhwh, the creator and sustainer, ruler over Israel and the nations, and the only God. Both are on their way home from Babylon to Jerusalem—a second exodus (cf. Isa 43:14–21; 48:20–21), materialized in the return of the glory of the Lord (40:1–5) and his enthronement in Zion–Jerusalem (52:7–10). The judgment of Israel and Jerusalem is over, their sins are forgiven, and salvation is near: "Comfort, comfort my people, says your God. Speak tenderly to Jerusalem" (Isa 40:1–2). We do not know exactly what triggered this confidence and exultation about the things to come. It may have been the hopes connected to the Persian conquest of Babylon. It may have been the rebuilding of the temple and other benefits granted under Persian rule or even the manifold revolts in Babylon that the Persians squashed. Possibly all of these gave Deutero-Isaiah reason to declare the divine judgment over and to use elements of preexilic cultic prophecy to proclaim the dawn of salvation.

Nevertheless, the onset of salvation was slow in coming. The rubble of Jerusalem was not yet cleared, the Jews deported all over the world stayed where they were—whether because they were unable to return or because they simply saw no reason to come back to Palestine. As usual, the tradition responded with the reinterpretation of the older material. Gradually, those pieces in Isa 49–55 and 60–62 were added that revolve around Zion-Jerusalem. The city inherits the royal title from Jacob-Israel and is transformed into a person. She is addressed as the wife of the God and king YHWH. Her remaining inhabitants and the Israelites dispersed among the nations are referred to as her and YHWH's children. The rebuilding of the destroyed city is promised, as is the return of the children, who shall be offered as tribute to Queen Zion by the nations. The startled questions in Isa 49:21 ("who bore these for me," "by whom, then, were these reared," "and where have these been") reveal that the hopes are already directed to the second generation. Isaiah 60, then, focuses more on the expected precious items than on the returnees. YHWH's victory over the nations, too, is long in coming. Isa 51:9–10 calls upon "the arm of YHWH" to finally step in against the nations as he had done at the beginning of the world when he fought against Chaos and was victorious (cf. Ps 93) and as had occurred during the exodus from Egypt (cf. Exod 15). However, with time the scribes realize that it is not YHWH's fault that salvation is slow in coming. Rather, Israel and the children of Zion are responsible for the delay. Their mother was sold into slavery because of their sins and remains there (Isa 50:1–2; cf. 51:12–13).

Another figure assumes the role of king in Deutero-Isaiah in addition to the people Jacob-Israel and the city Zion-Jerusalem. This character has no name and is simply called "the servant of YHWH." The texts relating to him are called "Servant Songs." The servant has royal and prophetic traits. As the king elected and appointed by YHWH but also as YHWH's prophet the servant is sent to the nations. He will establish the order of law among the people and instruct them in it (Isa 42:1–4). For the first time in the prophetic tradition, the nations (i.e., all humankind) will participate in the salvation of YHWH (cf. Isa 45:22). First, however, the servant is sent to fulfill a mission for the people of Jacob-Israel, so he cannot be identical with this people: he is to raise up the tribes of Jacob and restore the survivors of Israel (Isa 49:1–6). Finally, he shares the fate of most of the prophets: he will be despised, treated with hostility, and eventually killed. His personal fate, however, is part of his mission. The suffering and death of the servant of the Lord is said to take place on behalf of the many (Isa 50:4–9; 52:13–53:12).

Nobody knows who this servant was. Usually, scholarship identifies him with the prophet "Deutero-Isaiah." True, such identification is anchored in the tradition, but even here opinions differ. Some passages identify him with the prophet himself (cf. Isa 43:10; 44:26; 50:10–11; 59:21 referring to Isa 42:1 and Jer 1:9), while others argue for Cyrus as the good shepherd and Messiah who liberates the captives and rebuilds the temple in Jerusalem (Isa 42:5–7; 44:28; 45:1–7, 12–13). A third group of texts suggests that he is identical with a part of Israel that helps to provide salvation for the other part (Isa 42:18–25; 49:3, 7–13; cf. "the servants" in Isa 63–66) or that the servant is Zion-Jerusalem (Isa 54:11–17 referring to 50:4–9; cf. 60–62). There are no limits to the interpretation, since the relevant texts probably neither deal with a concrete person nor are they written by a single author. They are animated by the topics and motifs of the book and project them onto a single person so that the reader can identify himself with this person and, as a result, with the message of the book. In this respect the identification of the servant with Deutero-Isaiah is certainly correct, only that Deutero-Isaiah is not a real person but rather a book, and the servant, in turn, is the incarnation of word of God in the book of Deutero-Isaiah.

3. Trito-Isaiah

The "Third" Isaiah or Trito-Isaiah is neither a prophet nor a prophetic book. It is simply the designation for the textual complex Isa 56–66, which was added successively to Deutero-Isaiah and the Book of Isaiah as a whole. The literary kernel can be found in Isa 60–62. In Isa 60, we read an exegesis of the motif of the pilgrimage of the nations to Zion originally found in Isa 49, and from here everything else follows. This updating (or *Fortschreibung*) continues the editing of Deutero-Isaiah in light of the Zion-theology and paints the glorification of Zion in ever-changing colors. The literary kernel presupposes the Second Temple and was probably written in the Persian period. As we saw in the visions of Zechariah, Jerusalem represents the center of a multiethnic state. The "light of the nations" (Isa 49:6) emanates from Zion.

One topic that receives little attention in Isa 60–62 is the return of the children of Zion. A possible reason for this may be that other problems were at the fore when the chapters were written, or perhaps it was felt that the topic was treated exhaustively in Isa 40–55. Even more striking is the fact that Isa 62 concludes with a call to the returnees (Isa 62:10–12) that is not only reminiscent of the beginning of Deutero-Isaiah (40:1–11) but also of Proto-Isaiah. It seems to describe the last part of the route mentioned in Isa 11:11–16; 27:15 and Isa 35. The verses in question are a late supplement and were added by a redactor who connected Proto-Isaiah and Deutero-Isaiah. Isa 62:10–11 once formed the conclusion of the Book of Isaiah.

This edition envisages a universal judgment as announced in Isa 24–27 and Isa 34. The historical background of such an expectation, which can also be found in other prophetic books (cf. Jer 25:27ff.; Ezek 38–39; Joel 4; Obad 15ff.), is the disintegration of the empire of Alexander the Great into the Diadochi and especially into the Seleucid and Ptolemaic kingdoms, which were constantly at war with each other. These wars also gave new impetus to the theme of the return. Before the whole earth can be judged, the Jews from all over the world have to be assembled in either Jerusalem or the reunited kingdoms of Israel and Judah. This is the only way they can survive the judgment. In Zech 9–10, this historical context is palpable: according to a scribal gloss (Zech 9:13) the sons of Zion are mobilized against the sons of "Javan" (Greece). It is not Alexander the Great (cf. Josephus, *Ant.* XI.329–339) but the Judean king, righteous, and poor who will enter Zion (Zech 9:9). The expectation of a new David fits this picture, too. He is the "good shepherd" who will replace the "evil shepherds"—that is, Hellenistic foreign rule (Zech 10:3; 11:3). He will rule over the united kingdoms of Israel and Judah and their returnees (cf. Isa 11:10–16; Jer 23:1–8; Ezek 34:1ff., 23ff.; 37:15–28; Mic 5:1ff.).

The second wave of *Fortschreibung* in Trito-Isaiah also writes against the "evil shepherds." It is represented in the texts in Isa 56–59 (beginning at 56:6), which are inserted between Isa 1–55 and Isa 60–62. Here, however, as in the allegory of Zech 11 (shaped after the model of Ezek 34), it is not the foreign rulers who are addressed but rather the leaders of the Jewish people who were appointed for good or ill by Yʜᴡʜ. As so often in the history of the prophetic tradition, there are problems within the Jewish community that serve as a reason for the delay in the advent of salvation—that is, the advent of light from Isa 60: "We hope for light and behold there is darkness; for a gleam and we must walk in gloom" (Isa 59:9). This time, the concern is with cultic practices and social upheaval brought in the wake of the Hellenistic era. They provoke old and new prophetic polemic and result in admonitions that replace the official cult and ritual fasting with a radical ethic of poverty and call for the observance of the Sabbath. The text is animated by quotations from the Book of Isaiah that are interpreted in a peculiar way. In scholarship, this kind of hermeneutics is called "spiritualization," but it might be more appropriate to call it "ethicization." The homecoming of Isa 62:10–12 must be preceded by repentance to "remove" all obstacles to salvation "from my people's way" (Isa 57:14). The liberation from the nations has to be preceded by the manumission of and provision for the poor so that the light of Isa 60–62 can shine forth and the glory of Yʜᴡʜ can appear (Isa 58:6–12).

Again, a certain affinity to the late additions in the Book of Zechariah is obvious. After an attack of the nations against Jerusalem, which is spared (Zech 12), the cult will be cleansed from idols and especially from the prophets and the unclean spirit (Zech 13). In view are the classic ecstatics that the Hebrew Bible calls "false prophets." They also appeared in Hellenistic times, but in the Book of Isaiah they are denied the prophetic spirit. However, even in the prophetic tradition of the Hebrew Bible the prophetic spirit gradually disappears. The law takes its place, and more and more supplants the historical and the literary prophets.

Before the prophetic spirit ceased and the *Fortschreibung* in the Book of Isaiah ground to a halt, Isa 63–66 were added. Again, the delay of the glorification of Zion announced in Isa 60–62 triggers this extension. YHWH, dripping with blood, comes from Edom where he has sat in judgment over the nations (Isa 63:1–6 following Isa 34). Yet, salvation does not occur. Such is the opinion of the authors of the grand penitential and petitionary prayer in Isa 63:7–64:11, who call themselves "servants" of YHWH and who do not call Abraham or Israel, but rather YHWH, their "father" (Isa 63:16–17). For them, Zion-Jerusalem and the temple still lay in ruins (Isa 64:9–10), as if nothing had happened. Neither Zerubbabel nor Nehemiah matters to them. All that counts is the guilt before God that weighs on the people and has not been forgiven. For this group, the judgment of 587 B.C.E. continues into their own (Hellenistic) times.

Their hopes are not for the temple, which these scribes despise (cf. 65:1–7, 11–12; 66:1–4, 17), but for something greater: they expect a new heaven and a new earth (Isa 65:17) that will surpass the former creation of Gen 1, which was revoked in Isa 24–27. As part of this new creation, all the things that the Book of Isaiah has previously announced or promised (Isa 65:18ff.; 66:7ff.) will be realized in Jerusalem. Not only the new heaven and the new earth (cf. Isa 1:2) but also a whole plethora of literary and linguistic references in Isa 65–66 build a bridge from the end to the book's beginning in Isa 1.

Not everybody, however, will participate in the promises. There is a deep rift in Israel that separates the righteous and the chosen "servants of YHWH" from the sinners (Isa 65:9–16; 66:5). The sharp distinction between the righteous and the wicked, also known in Habakkuk and outside the prophetic literature in late Psalms (Ps 1) and in Wisdom literature, is characteristic of the *Fortschreibung* in Isa 65–66. It is an expression of group formation in Judaism of the Hellenistic period and a result of the social and religious exclusion triggered by the economic and cultural boom of Hellenism, which would culminate in the crisis of the Maccabean period (see below, chap. 8). In Trito-Isaiah, the separation will be car-

ried out in judgment against Israel and the nations. Since neither genealogy nor ethnic origin count, but only loyalty to YHWH, we find the pious
among the nations being admitted into salvation and the eschatological
cult on Zion alongside the "servants of YHWH" (Isa 66:15–24; cf. 56:1–8
and Zech 14).

4. The Extinction of Prophecy

The prophetic tradition had its origin in the crisis and breakdown of
the usual cultic relationship between YHWH and his worshipers. In the entire tradition of the Hebrew Bible, this rupture triggered reflection on this
relationship and on the question of how it would be possible to restore it.
One fruit of this reflection was the idea of the "covenant" YHWH makes
with Israel by grace alone: "I will be your God and you will be my people."
How the covenant is spelled out in detail differs. Most often, covenant
specifies a commitment to the law that follows from the election of Israel.
In Isa 59:21, we read of an unusual definition of the covenant.

> And as for me, this is my covenant with them, says YHWH: my
> spirit that is upon you, and my words that I have put in your
> mouth, shall not depart out of your mouth, or out of the mouths
> of your children, or out of the mouths of your children's children,
> says YHWH, from now on and forever.

In view are those in Zion-Jerusalem and those among the people of Jacob-
Israel who turn away from sin and are saved (Isa 59:20). The covenant
is made with them. The addressee, however, is an individual person who
can only be identified with the prophet of the book, Isaiah. He is identified with the servant of YHWH from Isa 41:1 (cf. 61:1) who—like Isaiah
(8:16)—has offspring (52:10). In addition, he is placed alongside Jeremiah and Ezekiel, who also had YHWH's words placed into their mouth—
orally in Jer 1:9, physically in Ezek 2:8–3:3. Deut 18:18 prescribes this
for every prophet who will be like Moses. According to Isa 59:21, Isaiah
is the prophet par excellence because the words of God are in his mouth.
These words are handed down to his children and his children's children,
among whom one must include the scribes and authors of the book. It is
thus not the law (cf. Deut 6:6–9) but rather the Book of Isaiah that serves
as the deed of covenant between YHWH and his people Israel—from now
until eternity.

This is a grand claim, which—when we take the cross-references and
combination of quotations seriously—is not only asserted for the Book of
Isaiah but also for the complete prophetic corpus. In the textual tradition,

Isaiah stands out as first in the series of prophetic books. It contains everything that is developed in the following books. Dated like Hosea, Amos,
and Micah (Isa 1:1 par. Hos 1:1; Amos 1:1; Mic 1:1) to the eighth century B.C.E., his "prophecy" spans the Assyrian (Isa 1–12; 28–31; 36–38),
Babylonian (Isa 13–27; 33–35; 39), and Persian periods right up to the
end of the world (Isa 40–66). The book offers a view of the eschatological
destiny of Israel (Judah and Jerusalem) written from the perspective of the
Hellenistic period—that is, the perspective of the most recent editors of
the book. With this comprehensive view of world events and the role of
God in them, Isaiah stands for the whole of the prophetic tradition. Compilation, literary adaptations, and cross-references ensure that the global
perspective that the Book of Isaiah articulates characterizes the whole collection. What Israel needs in order to live and to die before God, it finds
not (only) in the Torah of Moses, but (also) in the Book of Isaiah and the
complete prophetic corpus.

In the development of theological thought, the law follows the
prophets and presupposes them. With time, however, this relationship was
reversed. The canonical division of the "Prophets," which included the
historical books from Joshua to Kings, has a different perspective from the
prophetic corpus. In the framework of the canonical "Prophets," the law
is granted precedence over the prophets.

> Only be strong and very courageous, being careful to act in ac-
> cordance with all the law that my servant Moses commanded you;
> do not turn from it to the right hand or to the left, so that you
> may be successful wherever you go. This book of the law shall not
> depart out of your mouth; you shall meditate on it day and night,
> so that you may be careful to act in accordance with all that is
> written in it. For then you shall make your way prosperous, and
> then you shall be successful. (Josh 1:7–8).

The prophets become mere exegetes of the law and authors of sacred
history (Chronicles) as well as famous and pious men of a former age
(Sir 44–49) whom Israel should take as an example. Tradition, therefore,
allows the prophetic spirit to burn brightly from the time of Moses until
Artaxerxes, the Persian king whom Ezra and Nehemiah served. After that
period, the prophetic succession is broken (Josephus) and will remain so
until the end comes and a prophet will rise again (cf. 1 Macc 4:46; 9:27
and 14:41). Until then, the motto of the tradition is:

> Remember the teaching of my servant Moses, the statutes and or-
> dinances that I commanded him at Horeb for all Israel. Lo, I will

send you the prophet Elijah before the great and terrible day of
YHWH comes. He will turn the hearts of parents to their children
and the hearts of children to their parents, so that I will not come
and strike the land with a curse. (Mal 3:22–24 NRSV Mal 4:4–6).

The notion of the disappearance of prophecy coincides with the end of
literary production in the prophetic books during the Hellenistic period.
The tradition itself draws the line in the Persian period. The latest dates
refer to the building of the temple under Darius and the two prophets
Haggai and Zechariah (cf. Ezra 5:1; 6:14). After them, only Malachi as
well as Ezra and Nehemiah are seen as replete with the prophetic or Mosaic spirit. Everyone else is a "false prophet." This demarcation, however,
does not reflect a feeling of inferiority with respect to the older tradition
but instead a certain consciousness of living at the end of time. After the
change from the Persian period to the Hellenistic period, the authors of
the prophetic books expected the end of the world. The closure of prophecy and the compilation of the tradition in the prophetic corpus helped
to provide self-clarification and orientation for the pious as they faced the
eschatological age.

In contrast, the canon with the Torah of Moses as its center comprehended a longer period. The emerging theory of a canon that we can grasp
in Chronicles, Ben Sira, as well as with Josephus and the Rabbis, elevates
the demarcation "from Moses to Artaxerxes" to a dogma. According to
this theory, the cessation of prophecy is a sign that the time of divine
revelation has come to an end. From this point on it is clear, and for Judaism an obligation, how a life pleasing to God should be lived in the future,
no matter how long it is until the end comes. The prophetic tradition, too,
realized that the end might drag on. This became the dominant theme in
Jewish apocalypticism.

CHAPTER 8

"The End Is yet to Come"

The Book of Daniel and Jewish Apocalypticism

The spirit blows where it wills. As soon as it ceased in the prophetic tradition, it flared up again elsewhere: in Jewish apocalypticism. Among scholars, there is much speculation about the origins of apocalypticism as well as over the exact meaning of the term. This speculation is pointless, because the apocalyptic writings have not one but in fact many roots. Nor do they all say the same thing. It is not so much certain literary genres and content that connects the apocalyptic writings but rather the manner in which these writings introduce a broad array of traditions into the service of eschatology. As far as their historical origin is concerned, they also have in common that their eschatology—unlike their precursors—was kindled by the religious crisis during the reign of the Seleucid king Antiochus IV Epiphanes (175–164 B.C.E.). There are abundant examples, but I will limit myself to the Book of Daniel as the only apocalyptic writing that is part of the Hebrew Bible. At Qumran, Daniel is counted among the "prophets," as is also the case in the Septuagint and in modern (Christian) translations of the Bible. In the Hebrew Bible, Daniel belongs to the "Writings," the third part of the canon.

1. Aramaic Daniel

The Book of Daniel is bilingual. The first part—the narratives in Dan 2–6 and the vision reported in the first person singular in Dan 7—is written in Aramaic. It is preceded by a Hebrew introduction in Dan 1:1–2:4a that is most likely a translation from Aramaic. The Aramaic part in Dan 1–7 is followed by the Hebrew visions in Dan 8–12. Like Dan 7, the visions are written in the style of a first-person account. The linguistic and stylistic evidence points roughly to the origin of the Book of Daniel: it starts with the collection of the Aramaic narratives in Dan 1–6. This collection was supplemented by an Aramaic vision in Dan 7 and then by the Hebrew visions in Dan 8–12. The addition of the Hebrew material also prompted the translation of Dan 1:1–2:4a into Hebrew.

Originally, the narratives in Dan 1–6 had nothing to do with either apocalypticism or eschatology. The heroes of the narratives, Daniel and his three friends (who only appear in Dan 1–3) are members of the Jewish exiles, the Golah, brought to Babylon by Nebuchadnezzar (Dan 1). There, they excel because of exceptional mantic abilities (Dan 1–2; 4–5). They distinguish themselves because of their unwavering commitment to their God (Dan 3 and 6). Finally, thanks to the help of their God, they carve out a career at the court of Nebuchadnezzar (Dan 1–4), his son Belshazzar (Dan 5), and at the court of the "Mede" Darius up until the first year of the Persian king Cyrus (Dan 6; cf. 1:21).

The narratives date back to the Persian period. In part, they rely on older material about inner-Babylonian conflicts between the last Neo-Babylonian king Nabonidus and his son Belshazzar. In the Book of Daniel, Nabonidus becomes Nebuchadnezzar. The collection belongs to the same milieu as the Chronistic writings. It represents the position of the Babylonian exiles: God turns the heart of the Babylonian and Median kings toward the exiles. Unlike the books of Ezra and Nehemiah, this not only happens during the Persian period but already during the seventy years of the exile. Consequently, the pagan rulers become followers of the Jewish God, as is known from Deutero-Isaiah (Isa 45:3–4), as well as Ezra and Nehemiah in the case of Cyrus and his successors. As long as the kings realize that God has appointed them as successor to the Davidic dynasty, for the benefit of all people and especially for the benefit of the Jewish Golah, world empire and kingdom of God exist in perfect harmony. The hymnic parts—put into the mouth of Daniel or the pagan rulers—express the spirit of the narratives in poetic terms (Dan 2:19–23; 2:47; 3:28–29; 3:31–33/4:31–34; 5:18ff.; 6:26–28). The collection of narratives concludes in Dan 6:29, as it began in 1:21, with an anticipation of the central date of salvation for the Babylonian Golah taken from 2 Chr 36:22–23/ Ezra 1: "So this Daniel prospered during the reign of Darius (the Mede) and during the reign of Cyrus the Persian."

The narratives in Dan 1–6 know of two exceptions that confirm the rule: in Dan 4, the hubris of Nebuchadnezzar, who converts, and in Dan 5, the sacrilege of Belshazzar, who does not convert and is therefore superseded by Darius the Mede. In Dan 7, the exception suddenly becomes the rule. It is not by chance that the reader is taken back to the time of Belshazzar—more precisely, to the first year of his rule (Dan 7:1). Toward

the end of Babylonian rule the fall of all empires is announced: four animals, representing the four empires, emerge from the sea and strike terror
on earth; the fourth animal is the worst of all. The divine court convenes,
chaired by the "Ancient of Days," the highest God, and dooms the four
empires to perdition. After that, "one like a human being" comes with the
clouds of heaven. To him and to the "holy ones of the Most High," kingship and everlasting dominion are given.

Much energy has been spent finding analogies from the ancient Near
East for the peculiar series of animals and for the "son of man" in Dan
7—with moderate success. This is hardly surprising, since the antagonism
between bestial and human rule originates in Dan 4 and most of the for-
mulations in Dan 7 stem from Dan 1–6. The "son of man" is not yet an
independent figure in Dan 7 but a symbol for the "holy ones of the Most
High," which are most likely angels in the original text. The "son of man"
is only transformed into a person during the reception of Dan 7 in the
similes of 1 Enoch (OTP I, 5–89), in 4 Ezra (OTP I, 517–559), and in
the New Testament.

Dan 7, however, is not the original continuation of Dan 1–6. Rather,
the chapter represents an addition that casts the narrative collection in a
different light. This new perspective can be explained by the role of the
fourth animal. After the first three animals, which symbolize the empires
already present in Dan 1–6—namely Babylon, the Medes, and Persia—the
fourth animal represents the Greek Empire, from which the ten horns, the
Ptolemaic and Seleucid kings, proceed. The disintegration of the Persian
Empire after the death of Alexander and the brutality of the wars of the
Diadochi led to a change of mind. This change is visible in Dan 7 as well
as in the interpretation of the dream in Dan 2 (vv. 31–45). Originally, the
two images of Nebuchadnezzar's dream—the statue with the golden head
and the stone that becomes a mountain—referred to the change from the
Babylonian Empire to the empire of the Medes and Persians. Now the
statue is transformed into a symbol of the four empires and the stone is a
symbol of the kingdom of God, which shatters the empires of the world.
The supplements in Dan 2 are so close to Dan 7 that one is tempted to
assume the same author here. For this author, the theological stance of the
narrative collection of Dan 1–6 is shattered in the face of this new reality.
As a result, he abandons the empires and preserves the kingdom of God
eschatologically. From now on, the dream of the king in Dan 2 refers to
"what is to be at the end of days" (Dan 2:28).

It is more or less a matter of taste whether or not one wants to use the
term "apocalyptic" for Aramaic Daniel. In any case, Dan 7 and the corresponding supplements to Dan 2 constitute a move toward eschatology.

Eschatology is a prerequisite for Jewish apocalypticism but is not identical with it. It is, however, typical of apocalyptic thought that it uses various material and traditions to contemplate Israel's fate within the context of universal history. In 1 Enoch, astronomical material (1 Enoch 72–82) and an eschatologized exegesis of the story of the flood in Gen 6–9 serve as the basis for the interpretation of the history of Israel from its beginnings to the time of the religious crisis under Antiochus IV. Here, in the Book of Daniel, it is the didactic narratives about Daniel and his friends and the eschatologization of the collection in Dan 7. The fate of Israel is only introduced by the Hebrew visions in Dan 8–12.

2. The Hebrew Visions

The Hebrew visions in Dan 8–12 can also be characterized as *Fortschreibung* and hence as an interpretation of Aramaic Daniel. They operate consistently in the historical context of the narratives and let Daniel, from the perspective of the exile, foresee the history of the empires and the people of Israel until the Hellenistic period. The goal is the events during the reign of Antiochus IV, who in the years 169–167 B.C.E.—and not without the consent of the Jewish elite—implemented radical and rigid reforms in Jerusalem. After looting the temple and entering the holy of holies, he installed the cult of Zeus Olympius, the god of the Greeks, and he is said to have rendered the Jewish law inoperative by decree (1 Macc 1). As a result, the Maccabean resistance opposed Antiochus IV. Their rebellion led to the revocation of the reform and to the rededication of the temple in December 164 B.C.E. (1 Macc 4:36–59; 2 Macc 10:5–8).

Within the Book of Daniel, Antiochus IV appears as the epitome of the ungodly king. In Dan 8, as in the corresponding additions to Dan 7, he is the small horn speaking great things and waging war against the Most High and his holy ones (Dan 7:8, 20–21, 24–25; 8:9–12, 21–25). He is the last of the kings from the North, the "despicable man" of Dan 11:31–25 who set up the "appalling abomination" in Jerusalem (Dan 11:31; cf. 9:26f.; 12:11). However, the authors of the visions are not among the Maccabean warriors from whom the Hasmonean kingship would later emerge. For the authors of Daniel, the Maccabees are simply "a little help" (Dan 11:34). They count on their God who—following the historical fiction—let Daniel reveal to them in advance the tribulations that would come upon them during the period in which they live. Like Daniel and his friends, they should only adhere persistently to their declared belief in God and be patient. From the fictional perspective of Daniel as from the authors' perspective: "the end is yet to come" (Dan 11:27; cf. 8:17, 19; 9:27; 11:35, 40; 12:13).

However, even if all of the visions are all focused on the "end" they move toward it in very different ways. They are constantly seeking to determine the "end." The transition to the first attempt is prepared by the addition of Dan 7:18b: even after the interpretation of Dan 7, Daniel remains anxious and keeps the matter in his mind. Two years later, in the third year of Belshazzar, he receives a second vision. The difference is not very great, but it is significant. The vision of the four animals and the "son of man" in Dan 7 still uses the imagery and language of Dan 1–6. Additionally, it is close to the narratives in terms of its content, since it juxtaposes world empire and kingdom of God. By contrast, Dan 8, which uses the imagery of the ram and the goat and their horns, only focuses on the empires. The vision of Dan 8 attempts to determine the "end" by translating Dan 7 into Hebrew as well as by explicitly naming the Median, Persian, and Greek Empires, which were only revealed as ciphers in Dan 7. As was the case in Dan 7, everything relating to the small horn (Antiochus IV) represents a later addition inspired by Dan 11.

According to Dan 8:27b, Daniel, once again, does not understand this vision and cannot explain it—another bridge for the next attempt to determine "the end." The vision in Dan 10–11 is illuminating here. The vision focuses on Gabriel, the interpreting angel already mentioned in Dan 7 and Dan 8, and continues the description of the history of the four empires, summarized in Dan 11:2–4, until the period of suffering under Antiochus IV. The use of metaphors is completely abandoned and the vision turns its attention to the immediate details of the politics of the day, the wars and marriages between the king of the North (Seleucids) and the king of the South (Ptolemies), and the assault on the people of God. The guiding principle, however, is not historiography but a theological interest. The word of God conveyed by the interpreting angel takes the place of vision and explanation. In the word of God, every detail is recorded and attributed to divine determination as an indication of the expected end. This is supplemented by the fact that the information provided by the angel in the Book of Daniel is often taken from prophetic tradition and especially from Isaiah (cf. Dan 11:10, 40 with Isa 8:8; Dan 11:36 with Isa 10:23). In the historical constellation encountered in the Book of Isaiah, with Jerusalem standing between Assur and Egypt, the authors of the visions of Daniel were reminded of their own situation pinned between a king in the North and a king in the South. Such an understanding also supports the view that the Book of Isaiah was once read (and supplemented) along these lines.

The exegesis of a passage taken from the prophets is also the focus of Dan 9—a chapter secondarily inserted between Dan (7–)8 and Dan 10–12. Here, it is the seventy years of Jer 25:11–12; 29:10 that cause Daniel quite a headache, for the deadline has already expired. Following Dan 6, the episode is dated to the time of Darius the Mede (Dan 9:1)—that is, shortly before the first year of Cyrus (Dan 1:21; 6:29)—a date that is to turn the tide but that, according to the date in Dan 10:1, is already past.

The problem gives rise to an extensive penitential prayer (Dan 9:4–20) that recapitulates the history of Israel and repents of the sins of the ancestors. The prayer is probably a later addition but elucidates the theological basis of the visions. It is the same theological concept that we have already encountered in the penitential prayer of Isa 63–64. It is no coincidence that the authors of the visions identify themselves with the Daniel of the exilic period. For them, the wrath of YHWH, specifically the destruction of Jerusalem and the temple, continues until their present time under Antiochus IV. In their view, they too—like the generation of 587 B.C.E.—live under judgment and bear the consequences of the sins of their ancestors as well as their contemporaries. In the face of this, only God can help. This is why they do not take part in the Maccabean revolt and simply wait patiently for God and for the "end" predetermined by him.

The authors of Dan 9 are especially concerned with the question of when this "end" will come. To answer this question, the exegesis of the seventy years from Jer 25—a prime example of inner-biblical exegesis—offers a particular contribution. If taken literally, the deadline will soon expire. Since the wrath extends from the destruction of Jerusalem to the defilement of the temple under Antiochus IV the deadline is elongated: the seventy years are transformed into seventy weeks of seven years each, that is $7 \times 70 = 490$ years (Dan 9:24). In Dan 9:25–27, the 490 years fall into three phases, although the calculation does not quite tally. The first phase comprises of seven weeks (49 years) and possibly extends from the destruction of Jerusalem (587 B.C.E.) to the first year of Cyrus and the feeble reconstruction of the city (539 B.C.E.). This roughly fits the math. The last phase comprises just one week (7 years) and refers to the events under Antiochus IV between 169 and 164 B.C.E.. In between we have 62 weeks (434 years). Generations of scholars have had a tough time of it with the calculation without being able to solve the riddle. Perhaps the 62 weeks simply arise from the difference after the subtraction of 7 + 1 weeks, or perhaps the age of Darius the Mede, who was 62 years old when he began to rule (Dan 6:1), was the point of reference. Be that as it may, the Book of Daniel itself started the calculations. Here, the interest focused on the last phase and the bisection of the last week in Dan 9:27. Thus, in

Dan 7:25 and 12:5–7, the last half is again dissected into three phases of two, one, and half a time; in Dan 8:13–14 and 12:8–13, the individual days are counted.

The periodization of the history of Israel to calculate the end of times is not unique to the Book of Daniel. Chronology was always of central importance, especially in royal annals and in the cult to calculate the festivals. Astronomy served the same purpose as it attempted to harmonize the earthly calendar with the order of the luminaries (identified with gods or angels) controlled by God. There is an intrinsic link between the course of the heavenly bodies, the divine order of the cosmos, and the order on earth. This is especially true for the cult, where heaven and earth meet. Considering this, it is understandable why Antiochus IV's attack on the cult (cf. Dan 7:25) was seen as reaching for the stars (cf. Dan 8:10–11) and why there was such a debate about questions concerning the calendar in 1 Enoch and in the many writings from Qumran.

The Book of Jubilees (OTP II, 35–141) carries this out consistently for the period from creation to the exodus from Egypt (Gen 1–Exod 15). The rewriting of the biblical text is structured by a chronological framework of years of weeks (7 years) and Jubilees (7×7 years). History is thus classified according to the temporal structure of creation, the seven-day week with the Sabbath of God at the end of the first week (Gen 1:1–2:4). The historical outline of the Apocalypse of Weeks (1 Enoch 92–93 + 91:11–17) and the Animal Apocalypse (1 Enoch 83–90 + 91:1–10, 18–19) in the Book of Dreams and the Parenetic Book of 1 Enoch follow a different chronological scheme. In a *vaticinium ex eventu*, both recapitulate the history of Israel from Adam to the Maccabees as the prophecy and revelation of Enoch. The latter was taken up to heaven before the flood and therefore has knowledge of the heavenly secrets (Gen 5:21–24). As in Dan 9, the history of Israel in 1 Enoch is seen from the perspective of sin and continuing judgment and is divided into periods until the end.

This kind of exact calculation and recalculation in light of the history of the last days—still practiced in some circles today—may seem absurd and ridiculous to us. However, we have to take into account the circumstances under which it originated. Then and now, they emanated from a deep uncertainty about the signs of the times that is counteracted by exact calculation of the days until the end. Much more interesting than the calculations themselves are their causes and the self-critical view of one's own past, which—at least in ancient Judaism—arose out of the calculation of history. Both saved Jewish apocalypticism from overestimating human possibilities and from establishing a theocratic state. Like all the "pious" (Hasidim) of this period, apocalyptic thinkers were fundamentalists. Fundamentalism, however, does not necessarily need to have a violent streak. In most cases, other interests are at play, the enforcement of which requires violence and tends to exploit the "pious."

The Hebrew visions in Dan 8–12 say strikingly little about what will come after the "end." For the "pious" who yearned for the end, the termination of the current period of suffering seems to be the only goal. Only Dan 12 offers some hints of what will await them: a general resurrection, for some eternal life and for some eternal shame, and the prospect to shine like the stars of the sky (Dan 12:2–3; cf. Mal 3:20–21). The Book of Daniel shares with the late layers of the prophetic tradition the hope for an eschatological separation of the righteous from the wicked. This motif is broadly developed in other apocalyptic literature—for example, 1 Enoch—and implemented in ethical thought. For the visions of Daniel, this separation seems more important than the prospect of the kingdom of God (Dan 2 and 7) embedded in the book itself. In other words, the kingdom of God is where the shepherd places sheep to the right and goats to the left.

Antiochus IV died in 164 B.C.E., shortly after the cleansing and rededication of the temple. This was not the "end." The Jewish festival of Hanukkah commemorates this event until today.

CHAPTER 9

"Its Interpretation Is"

The Prophets in the Dead Sea Scrolls

Many, but not all, participated in celebrating the rededication of the Jerusalem temple. The Maccabees had most cause for joy. Following their triumph over Antiochus IV, they continued their fight for national and political independence, and after their victory over the weak Seleucids, they established the Hasmonean kingdom. In their celebrations, they were joined by the ruling priests at the Jerusalem temple, whom Flavius Josephus called Sadducees. Also among those rejoicing were many from the group of the "pious," the Hasidim, who espoused the Jewish law and occasionally allied themselves with the Maccabees. They were to grow into a powerful religious party, which sometimes exercised considerable influence, a group that Josephus called the Pharisees. The majority of the Hasidim, however, had similar opinions to those advocated in the Book of Daniel and stayed away from the celebrations of the first Hanukkah festival. This included the Qumran community, whom we encounter in the Dead Sea Scrolls. In their circles, the prophetic tradition of the Hebrew Bible took a prominent place, as has already been pointed out in various ways in the previous chapters.

1. The Qumran Community

About sixty years ago, eleven caves were stumbled upon at the northwestern end of the Dead Sea near the settlement at Khirbet Qumran. They contained fragments of Hebrew and Aramaic manuscripts and even a few Greek ones. Similar fragments were also found in the region around Qumran and Masada. It soon became apparent that it was the twentieth century's most spectacular find of Jewish manuscripts. The manuscripts originate from between 250 B.C.E. and 150 C.E., but in many cases reflect much older texts.

Scholars refer to the various texts by the place they were found and either a number or an abbreviation for the title: for instance, 1QIsa[a] for manuscript "a" of the Book of Isaiah from cave 1 at Qumran; 1Q8 = 1QIsa[b] for manuscript "b" of the Book of Isaiah from cave 1 at Qumran.

Three types of texts were found in the caves at Qumran and its vicinity. First, manuscripts of biblical books, which are the oldest we know; second, Hebrew and Aramaic originals of apocrypha and pseudepigrapha, which were either completely unknown or had previously been known only from ancient translations such as the Septuagint; third, texts that originated in the Qumran community itself.

Prominent examples from the third group are the rules for the organization and the common life of the community: the Community Rule, *Serekh ha-Yahad* (QS), and the Damascus Document (QD); a collection of prayers called the Thanksgiving Scroll or *Hodayot* (QH); the description of a holy, eschatological war called the War Scroll or *Serekh ha-Milhamah* (QM); and, last but not least, commentaries on the biblical prophets or *Pesharim* (Qp). The designation of these commentaries as *pesher* (pl. *pesharim*) derives from the formula that is frequently used in them: *pishro* "its interpretation" or "its meaning." These texts were also fully unknown previously. They provide insights into the life and thinking of the religious group that was responsible for the production and transmission of the manuscripts.

What kind of community was it? Until recently it seemed that we might be able to identify it with one of the religious parties of ancient Judaism from the Greco-Roman period, known to us from Flavius Josephus and the New Testament. Alongside Sadducees, Pharisees, Zealots, and the early Christians, Josephus and other sources speak of the Essenes. The sources attribute to this party a sort of biblical fundamentalism and a radical lifestyle. Based on numerous points of contact, scholarship concluded that the Qumran community and the Essenes must be the same group. This opinion is, however, no longer uncontested, such that we are best to keep with the self-description of the community from their own writings.

The group designated itself as *ha-yahad*, which means quite simply "the community." They had separated from other parts of Judaism and claimed to be the only true Israel. The separation may already have taken place toward the end of the third or the beginning of the second century B.C.E. The reasons for the separation were social and religious dislocations that resulted from the politics of the Hellenistic period. Indications of such dislocations are already to be found in the latest parts of the Hebrew Bible in the contrast between the righteous and the wicked. This contrast is pithily expressed in Psalm 1 of the Hebrew Bible: "Blessed is the man who does not walk in the counsel of the wicked, nor stand in the way of sinners, nor sit in the seat of the scoffers, but his desire is in the law of YHWH and in his law he meditates day and night" (Ps 1:1–2).

Over time, the community steadily grew. We have several editions of the rules for their common life (QS and QD), reflecting adaptation to new conditions and ever-increasing differentiation. Within the community, there appear to have been doctrinal disputes that led to a split. In the Damascus Document (QD) and other texts, this split is associated with a figure called the "Teacher of Righteousness," about whom opinions in the community differed. In addition, the community was increasingly embroiled in controversy with the Sadducees and Pharisees, who had established themselves in the Hasmonean kingdom at the temple in Jerusalem after the successful revolt of the Maccabees.

In the course of the intellectual dispute, the books of the prophets came to have a central significance. The community increasingly developed an eschatological self-understanding and imagined themselves to be living in the last times, "the end of days," when the predictions of the prophets would be fulfilled and God would judge the wicked and save the righteous. That the members of the community were numbered among the righteous goes without saying. In order to understand themselves and their situation, they immersed themselves in the Bible and its related literature and derived their own perspectives from them.

In this way, works were composed that employed cosmological speculation about the divine plan for the world or described the eschatological battle of good and evil spirits in heaven as well as on earth. The community began to determine its own place within biblical, sacred history and to extend their reflection on this history as it reached the expected "end of days." Apart from the biblical history in the Torah and Former Prophets, the Latter Prophets played a decisive role: here, the prophetic books including the Book of Daniel and the Psalms of David, which were also regarded as prophecy, come into play. The many copies of biblical prophetic books, citations from the prophets, prophetic apocrypha, as well as the interpretations of entire prophetic books in the *pesharim* attest to this.

The Qumran community did not experience the "end of days," upon which they had set all their hopes, either. Although they did not actively participate in the Jewish rebellions against the Roman occupiers in the years 66–74 and 132–134 C.E., they were victims of the Roman armies that overran the western shore of the Dead Sea and defeated the rebellions. In order to protect the manuscripts of their holy books from the impure hands of the Romans, the members of the community hid them in the caves of Qumran and the surrounding area. Apart from isolated discovery in antiquity, there they remained for about 2,000 years, unfortunately badly decaying, until their rediscovery in the middle of the twentieth century.

2. Prophets and Scribal Learning

In his work about the Jewish war of the first century c.e., the Jewish historian Flavius Josephus writes the following on the Essenes:

> There are some among them who profess to foretell the future, being versed from their early years in holy books, various forms of purification and apothegms of prophets; and seldom, if ever, do they err in their predictions.

This description is usually taken as a confirmation of the identification of the Essenes with the Qumran community. The testimony is, however, not quite so clear. Josephus has in mind an active ability to prophesy about contemporary events, and in his main work, the *Jewish Antiquities*, he adduces various examples of Essene predictions that were fulfilled. However, the Dead Sea Scrolls never speak in this manner. Quite the opposite: the Qumran community appears to have stuck to what is found in Neh 6 and Zech 13, regarding their contemporaries as "false" prophets. It is no coincidence that a list of the names of "false" prophets was found at Qumran. This enumeration of well-known prophets from the biblical tradition was possibly augmented with a contemporary prophet. Unfortunately, the text is too damaged to be able to say anything certain.

Accordingly, in the Dead Sea Scrolls the Hebrew word for prophetic utterances (the root *n-b-ʾ*) is used exclusively for biblical prophets and "false prophets." No member of the community was awarded the title "prophet" or "seer," nor were there people who pronounced in God's name a new word from God. When prophetic predictions were made about the future and the "end of days," these were always derived from the biblical prophets or related scriptures. The prophecies were placed in the mouth of biblical authorities like Enoch, the patriarchs, or the twelve sons (tribes) of Israel. Alternatively, they were formulated with reference to the predictions of the biblical prophets that were copied, cited, and interpreted. In every case, they were related to the Qumran group and their times.

This does not mean that the prophetic spirit did not also blow in Qumran. It only means that it did not blow directly but rather was mediated

through the books of the biblical prophets. It emerges from the *pesher* on
the Book of Habakkuk (1QpHab VI–VII) that the interpretation of the
prophets was understood as decoding the "mysteries of God." These were
hidden away in the transmitted texts of the prophetic books and were to
be elicited from them. The "mystery" lay in determining to which period
the prophecy was to be related and whom they concerned. Decoding the
"mystery" required a special form of interpretation. Precisely this is the
idea behind the word *pesher* 'interpretation', the technical term for commentary on the prophets. This term has a long prehistory. On the one
hand, it belongs to the realm of the professional interpreter of dreams and
mysteries (cf. Dan 2–5); on the other hand, it means the knowledge that
the ancient Near Eastern scribe has about omens and divination. Scribal
learning and (prophetic) inspiration do not exclude one another; rather,
they originally belong together.

In the Habakkuk *pesher*, a distinctive presupposition of the interpretation is that a contemporary divine revelation was granted to a priest
(1QpHab II) or to a certain "Teacher of Righteousness" (1QpHab VI–
VII). According to the Habakkuk *pesher*, God announced the mysteries
to him and gave him insight so that he could interpret the words of the
prophets. The *pesher* on the Book of Habakkuk and the *pesharim* on other
prophetic books do their interpretation based on this special revelation.
What this "teacher" was in historical terms—whether he was perhaps a
hermeneutical construct or a real figure only later reimagined—does not
emerge clearly from the texts. The idea of a special revelation providing
the hermeneutical key to the interpretation of the prophets reminds us of
the interpreting angel in Daniel 9, who conveys to Daniel the heavenly
revelation about the meaning of the 70 years prophesied in the Book of
Jeremiah.

With or without this hermeneutical means, the interpretation of the
prophets in Qumran was a professional and, at the same time, an inspired
undertaking of scribal learning. It continued what we have already seen in
the origins of the biblical prophetic books and their various types of gradual revision and supplementation (*Fortschreibung*). It is an activity that
uses different techniques of textual tradition and reception in order to un-
lock the relevance of the biblical writings for the community in the present
or the future, or, vice versa, to explain the community's own situation by
recourse to the biblical tradition. This scribal activity consisted of copying
and caring for biblical manuscripts as well as the citation of biblical texts,
their reformulation in *rewritten scripture* texts, and commentating on entire biblical books in the *pesharim*, where the decoding of the "mysteries

of God" occurred in the often mysterious and puzzling interconnection between biblical text and interpretation.

3. Copying and Citing

Before we turn to the *pesharim*, let us take a brief look at the other techniques of prophetic interpretation at Qumran that predated the genre of *pesharim* and paved the way for them. We begin with a textual variant that, alongside fidelity and faithfulness to the text, shows great freedom with respect to the letters: Isa 8:11.

> For Yʜᴡʜ spoke thus to me while his hand was strong upon me, and warned me not to walk (or: he dissuaded me from walking) in the way of this people, saying . . .

In the great Isaiah scroll from Qumran (1QIsaᵃ), however, we read,

> For Yʜᴡʜ spoke thus to me while his hand was strong upon me, and he dissuaded us from walking in the way of this people, saying . . .

The difference is marked in the Hebrew text by only two letters but is of enormous significance. The older (Masoretic) text presents a lexical problem, for its spelling allows two alternatives. Through the addition of a vowel-letter, the scribe of the Qumran manuscript solves the problem. He makes clear that he has in mind the verb "to avert," in the causative stem "to dissuade," and not the other possibility "to warn." Furthermore, the scribe alters the personal pronoun of the problematic verb ("and he dissuaded me/us"), in which he makes use of the visual similarity between the Hebrew for 'me' (*-eny*) and 'us' (*-enu*).

The reading in 1QIsaᵃ reflects a conscious alteration of the text in order to relate it to the contemporary context of the scribe's own situation. What Yʜᴡʜ has revealed to the prophet is a revelation to "us." The "us" is the Qumran community that follows in the prophetic footsteps and consequently walks in the right way, the opposite direction to the rest of the people. This emerges clearly in an exegetical work, the Florilegium 4Q174, in which a part of an interpretation of Ps 1 is explicitly quoting Isa 8:11:

> Midrash of *"Happy is [the] man who has not followed the counsel of the wicked."* (Ps 1:1). The interpretation of the passa[ge conc]erns those who turn aside from the way [. . .] which is written in the

Book of Isaiah the prophet concerning the latter days, *"And it was
as with a strong* [. . .] *this people."* (Isa 8:11)

The phrase is also found in one of the rule texts from Qumran, the Damascus Document, but without an explicit reference to Isaiah. This rule is
preserved in two manuscripts (CD A VIII 16 = B XIX 29):

So this is the judgment of the converts of Israel, who turned away
from the path of the people.

In this way, the biblical manuscripts from the Dead Sea afford us a unique
view into textual transmission during the Greco-Roman period. The hab-
its and customs of the ancient scribes testify to their absolute fidelity to the
text. Nevertheless, there was no single standard text, and alterations such
as the one we have described were quite possible. Indeed, the manuscripts
from the Dead Sea give the impression of considerable diversity. Thus,
for example, the great Isaiah scroll (1QIsa^a) represents its own text type
in comparison to the version preserved in the Masoretic Text. Fragments
have been preserved of the Book of Jeremiah, some of which follow the
Masoretic version (4QJer$^{a, c, c}$), while some attest to the short, divergent
text of the Greek translation of the Septuagint (4QJer$^{b, d}$). At the same
time, there are also harmonizing and standardizing revisions, to which
the Hebrew and Greek manuscripts of the Twelve Prophets from Wadi
Muraba'at (Mur 88) and Nahal Hever (8Hev 1) testify.

How to explain this diversity is a much-discussed problem. Some pos-
tulate an original text, or one as close as we can get to it, from which
the diversity developed. Others, however, argue for textual traditions that
originated independently of each other. Given the high percentage of
agreement among the texts, the first possibility seems to be more likely.
At any rate, it is clear that the diversity did not alter the authority of the
text and the esteem in which it was held. There was anything but a slavish
word-for-word fidelity. Even if readings differed, for the scribes and readers of the biblical books, the same text always contained the word of God
for all time, and consequently for them and their time.

A third way between the textual tradition and the composition of a
fresh work is perceptible in the category of *rewritten scripture*. In texts of
this category, biblical material was reformulated and related to new situations. This was also done to the prophets Jeremiah, Ezekiel, and other
biblical figures to whom prophetic qualities were attributed. In all the
texts, the narratives about the prophets in their biblical context now and
again give way to predictions about eschatological time. It is not always
easy to decide whether such works of the category of *rewritten scripture*

originated in the Qumran community itself or whether they stem from elsewhere and were appropriated by the community. In any case they fit perfectly the picture that has emerged of textual transmission, as well as the interpretation of the biblical prophets at Qumran.

Before the Qumran community started to write commentaries upon entire biblical books in the form of the *pesharim*, individual texts had been chosen and interpreted. The obvious interpretations to examine are the explicit citations, which increased in frequency in the writings of the community as time passed. So, for example, a citation of Isa 40:3 is inserted into a version of the Community Rule (1QS VIII,14) that is not (yet) present in another manuscript of the same work (4QS^d). The citation conveys that the journey of the community "into the desert" to study the Torah is a fulfillment of a prophetic prediction.

If we turn to the other, more recent set of instructions for the community, the Damascus Document, we find considerably more explicit biblical citations in comparison to 1QS or even 1QM. In the Damascus Document, we have an interpretation of a citation that combines Isa 7:17 and Isa 8:14 (CD VII 9–13). The texts are oriented to the future and concern future retribution against the wicked and the despisers of Torah. Their fate, according to the author of the Damascus Document, is already announced in the prophetic books:

> But those who reject the commandments and the rules (shall perish). When God judged the land bringing the just deserts of the wicked to them, that is when the oracle of the prophet Isaiah son of Amoz came true, which says, *"Days are coming upon you and upon your people and upon your father's house that have never come before, since the departure of Ephraim from Judah"* (Isa 7:17), that is, when the two houses of Israel separated, Ephraim departing from Judah.

The division of the kingdom under Solomon and Jeroboam I (when "the houses of Israel separated"; cf. Isa 8:14, quoted in CD VII 12) serves in the Damascus Document as also in the Book of Isaiah as a historical model and comparison for the future judgment. If this applies to the Judean monarchy during the time of king Ahaz in the eighth century B.C.E. according to the Book of Isaiah, then the same judgment is promised to the contemporary opponents of the Qumran community at the turn of the second to first century B.C.E.

The other manuscript of the Damascus Document (CD B XIX) has much the same, although it contains citations from Zechariah and Ezekiel in the same context rather than from Isaiah, Amos, and Numbers. The relationship between the two parallel manuscripts is extremely complex. The differences suggest a literary dependence on both sides. Whatever the case, the findings make clear that the Qumran community wrestled with the biblical tradition. Repeatedly they sought to reconstruct and interpret both their history and their present situation in light of biblical, and especially prophetic, citations. In doing so, they also hoped to gain a perspective on the future, the "end of days."

4. *Text and Commentary*

The "end of days" was also firmly in the sights of the *pesharim*, the commentaries on the biblical prophets. Alongside the transmission of the biblical text and the reformulation of biblical materials in *rewritten scripture* texts, the practice of citing biblical texts and interpreting them developed into the collection of excerpts and entire exegetical works. These revolved around certain themes, mostly of an eschatological nature. We can speak of thematic *midrashim* or thematic *pesharim*. Well-known representatives of this group of texts are the collection of excerpts, 4Q175 (Testimonia) and 4Q176 (Tanhumim), as well as the exegetical works 11Q13 (Melchizedek) and 4Q174 (Florilegium). The latter was joined together with 4Q177 (Catena A) to form a single work, the Midrash on Eschatology (4QMidrEschat). In addition, a list of other texts appear as "commentaries" to diverse biblical books, especially Genesis. All of these texts listed above can be found conveniently in the sixth volume of the bilingual version of Charlesworth (DSS.C 6B, 2002).

The thematic *midrashim* (or thematic *pesharim*) and "commentaries" are the precursors of the genre of continuous *pesharim*. In the *pesharim*, entire prophetic books or a select part was cited verse by verse and interpreted, with the commentary marked by the formula *pishro*, 'its interpretation is'. Consequently, the distinguishing characteristic of this genre in comparison to the thematic *midrashim* (or thematic *pesharim*) and other exegetical works is, above all, the formal arrangement. The biblical text was interpreted in its traditional arrangement and order, not as a selection of biblical citations or passages. In addition, the genuine *pesharim* are focused on the prophetic books and the Psalms.

According to the important new edition by Maurya P. Horgan (in DSS.C 6B, 2002), we can definitively identify 17 examples in total as continuous *pesharim*: 6 manuscripts on the Book of Isaiah; 2 each on Hosea, Micah, and Zephaniah; 1 each on Nahum and Habakkuk; and 3 manuscripts on the Psalms of David, which were counted among the prophets. In most cases only fragments have been preserved. Only the *pesher Habak-*

kuk (1QpHab) is mostly intact, and this is the case with *pesher Nahum* (4QpNah) in many sections as well. Both the *pesharim* on Habakkuk and on Nahum are some of the youngest manifestations of the genre and exemplify it in an especially mature form.

5. Biblical and Contemporary History

Regardless of which prophetic book is being interpreted or which text from the biblical book is under discussion, the interpretations of the *pesharim* often sound very similar. External enemies among the nations are spoken about; they are called the "Kittim" and are only very rarely mentioned by name. Much is also said about internal enemies who made life difficult for the Qumran community. The internal enemies also have aliases: Ephraim and Manasseh, the house of Absalom and the house of Peleg, "the seekers-after-smooth-things," "the wicked priest," "the man of lies," and "the preacher of lies." Finally, the *pesharim* often refer to the community as "the elect," "the doers of Torah," or simply "the community"—claiming the "Teacher of Righteousness" to be its master and viewing itself as the true Judah or true Israel.

Most of these designations in the interpretive sections of the *pesharim* stem directly from biblical expressions or can be derived from them. Nevertheless, the *pesharim* do not simply retell biblical stories but rather describe a vital confrontation between actual, contemporary individual groups. The *pesharim*, of course, side with only one group, the Qumran community, and polemicize against their external and internal opponents in Judah and Jerusalem in the sharpest manner. The aim of the confrontation is the great and imminent turn of events "at the end of days," which according to the *pesharim* is predicted in the prophetic writings. God will finally bring the enemies down and save his faithful ones, the members of the community, from all evil.

In light of this evidence, the following questions come to mind. How are the original biblical texts related to the biblical metaphors in the interpretive sections? And, how are both related to the contemporary history in which the urgent confrontation is taking place? Here is a more-or-less random example from the *pesher* on the Book of Nahum (4QNah II 1–2 and III 1–9):

> "*Woe city of blood.*" She is all [deception with pilla]ge, she is filled (Nah 3:1). Its interpretation: "*she*" is the *city* of Ephraim, the Seekers-after-Smooth-Things at the end of days, that the[y will] conduct themselves in *deception* and falsehoo[d].

. . .

> *"And I will cast upon you detested things, and I will [de]grade you
> and I will make you despicable [MT: a spectacle] and all who see
> you will flee from you."* (Nah 3:6–7) Its interpretation concerns
> the Seekers-after-Smooth-Things whose evil deeds will be *revealed*
> at the end of time to all Israel, and many will understand their
> iniquity and hate them and *despise them* because of their insolent
> guilt. And upon the revelation of the glory of Judah, the simple
> ones of Ephraim will *flee* from the midst of their congregation
> and will leave those who mislead them and will join themselves
> to [. . .] Israel.

> *"And they shall say [MT: it is said], Nineveh is despoiled; who will
> mourn for her? Where shall I seek comforters for you?"* (Nah 3:7) Its
> interpretation [concerns] the Seekers-after-Smooth-Things whose
> counsel will perish and their assembly will be broken up and they
> will not continue to mislead [the] congregation and the simple
> [ones] will not support their counsel any more.

> *"Are you better than Am[on situated among] the rivers?"* (Nah 3:8)
> Its interpretation: *"Amon"* is Manasseh, and *"the rivers"* are the
> nobles of Manasseh, the honored ones of the [. . .]

At first glance, the biblical text, which is cited verse by verse, and the interpretation of the *pesher*, which is introduced with the words "its interpretation is," have little in common. The original core of the biblical text of the
Book of Nahum stems from the late seventh century B.C.E. The prophetic
writing is found in all three chapters. This includes the section cited here,
Nah 3:1–8, a prediction against Nineveh, the capital of the Neo-Assyrian
Empire, which had fallen in 612 B.C.E. Through an ironic rhetorical question, its fate is compared with that of the Egyptian city No-Amon. More
familiar to us as Thebes, this city was captured and devastated in 664
B.C.E. by Assurbanipal, himself an Assyrian. The prophetic oracles against
the "bloody city" Nineveh express the relief and triumph of Judah and its
national God YHWH at the demise of its former oppressor.

The interpretation of the *pesher* has nothing to say about this. Rather,
in accordance with the hermeneutical rules of the "Teacher of Righteousness" mentioned in the Habakkuk *pesher*, the verses are interpreted in relation to the Qumran community and its time. Ephraim and Manasseh
are the opponents, whom the *pesher Nahum* identifies with the "bloody
city" Nineveh and the city No-Amon. They are "the seekers-after-smooth-
things" and mislead the "simple ones of Ephraim" as well as "the commu-

nity." The demise of Nineveh is the demise of the opponents of the community, which is expected at the imminent "end of days," when the "glory of Judah" will be revealed. At that time, the "simple ones of Ephraim" will convert and join the true Israel.

If we read the *pesher* once again and look more closely, we will nevertheless discover a certain connection between the biblical text and its interpretation. It consists of common catchwords, which are shown above in italics. These catchwords are introduced into the interpretation in two ways: either through a direct identification ("its interpretation: this is the city of Ephraim") or in the context of a sweeping comparison ("its interpretation relates to") that works with the wording of the biblical reference. Further connections occur that only a reader of the Hebrew text can perceive, such as assonance, paronomasia, homonyms, synonyms as well as catchwords to previous *pesher* sections on earlier biblical texts. Concealed behind all this is a subtle system of interpretive rules and techniques that reach back into the literary history of the biblical books and were used and refined in later rabbinic tradition and in the New Testament. In addition to ancient Near Eastern parallels to the genre of *pesher*, other inspirations could include the scribal education in the Greco-Roman period as well as Alexandrian philology and emerging commentary in Greek and Latin literature.

The techniques of interpretation allow us to recognize how the author of the *pesher* arrived at his interpretation. Nevertheless, they do not explain the relationship in content that exists between the biblical text and its interpretation. It is, however, not agreed whether such a relationship was even intended. In this respect Qumran scholarship appears to expect too little. It has become common only to examine the *pesher* sections, contextualize them historically and in this way to determine the intent of the *pesher*. The historical allusions in the *pesharim* and other documents from the Dead Sea are combined with other contemporary Jewish sources, most especially Josephus, in order to explicate the historical situation in the first century B.C.E. This in turn explains the interpretation of the prophetic books in the *pesharim*.

Fundamental to this approach is the fact that not only the preserved manuscripts of the *pesharim* but also the works themselves are not older than the first century B.C.E. and in fact contain not a few allusions to events in the late second and first centuries B.C.E. The manuscript of the *pesher* on Nahum, for example, originates from the time between 50–25 B.C.E. It also names some of its protagonists. In one place, the *pesher* speaks of "the kings of Javan from Antiochus until the appearance of the rulers of the Kittim." This delimits a period that we can determine with relative certainty to run from the time of Antiochus IV Epiphanes (175–164 B.C.E.) until the taking of Jerusalem by the Romans under the command of Pompey in 63 B.C.E. In the same context, a Seleucid king with the name Demetrius is mentioned, which can be understood to be Demetrius III Eucaerus (95–88 B.C.E.). During his reign, the Hasmonean king Alexander Jannaeus (103–76 B.C.E.) ruled in Jerusalem. In its interpretation of Nah 2:12, the *pesher* calls him "the lion of wrath." The leading circles of Judaism, presumably with the assistance of the Pharisees, rose up against him. The *pesher* refers to these with the ciphers "Ephraim" and "the seekers-of-smooth-things." Intermittently the insurgents allied themselves with Demetrius III and were consequently punished by Alexander Jannaeus in the cruelest ways. The *pesher* mentions the living being nailed to crosses, and this is confirmed by Josephus. The Sadducees, who were the leading party at the Jerusalem temple, appear to hide behind the cipher "Manasseh."

Thus, the *pesher* on Nahum can be situated historically rather precisely and be dated to the time after 63 B.C.E. Nevertheless, we have not sufficiently comprehended the central message of the *pesher* and its relationship to its biblical original. The purely historical explanation of the *pesher* overlooks the fact that the allusions to the historical circumstances that beset the Qumran community, as well as the hope that God will ultimately intervene, are expressed in ciphers. Moreover, these ciphers and images used in the interpretation of the prophetic book are largely derived from biblical texts. This corresponds with the fact that the formulation of the *pesher* sections often employs biblical phrases and even implicit citations from other biblical books.

Thus, the textual evidence suggests that the *pesharim* from Qumran with their contemporary references live entirely within the world of biblical Israel and aim to be related primarily to the biblical sacred history. This is nowhere as clear as with the use of the names Ephraim and Manasseh as designations for the opposing groups of Pharisees and Sadducees. The code was not invented by the *pesher* on Nahum for the first time. Rather, we have here a literary dependence on the *pesharim* and other exegetical works on Isaiah, Hosea, and Micah—in other words, those biblical books where an antagonism between Ephraim and Manasseh (both designate northern Israel, where hostile Samaria was located and the rival Samaritans lived) on the one hand and Judah (southern Israel with Jerusalem at its center) on the other plays a central role. In the older *pesharim*, the classical biblical antagonism between Ephraim and Judah appears to have served as a historical example of inner-Israelite or inner-Jewish conflicts or even as a means of anti-Samaritan polemic. The *pesher* Nahum goes one step further and transfers the historical antagonism into the conflict between the different religious parties in Judah.

Thus, the Judah, Ephraim, and Manasseh of the *pesharim* and other works are neither political-geographical designations nor simply ciphers for the religious parties in ancient Judaism. Instead, they invoke the biblical view of history where these names signify ideals and stand for actions, fates, and hopes that are connected to the future of biblical "Israel." The members of the Qumran community, who understood themselves as the representatives of biblical Israel, appear to have rediscovered the historical constellations of the sacred history in their own time, the circumstances of the second and first centuries B.C.E. They extended the biblical view of history accordingly or wrote themselves into this history. The conflict in which the community saw itself involved occurred in "Israel," where Judah and Ephraim (Manasseh) competed with one another. At the same time the conflict was in Judah, which represented (the true) Israel divided into the righteous and sinners—as too was Israel divided into seducer and seduced. Only "at the end of days," when the "glory of Judah" is revealed, will it again correspond to the biblical ideal of "all Israel."

6. *Prophetic Books and Pesher*

Those who live in the biblical history and locate their own time in it will regard the books of the biblical prophets as scripture that directly concerns them and their own time. As we have already seen, this is how the hermeneutical rules of the "Teacher of Righteousness" understood things in the *pesher* on the Book of Habakkuk. Thus, it would be strange if the interpretations in the *pesharim* had no substantial relationship to their biblical original whatsoever, apart from catchwords and other technical interpretive links. This question emerges especially in our example from the *pesher* on Nahum, where the external enemies of the seventh century B.C.E., Nineveh and No-Amon, are understood in relation to the Israelite powers, Ephraim and Manasseh, that correspond to the community's contemporary enemies within Israel and Judah in the first century B.C.E.

Up to now, scholarship has not given much consideration to this question. It is thought that in its allusions to contemporary historical conditions, the Qumran community read, more or less arbitrarily, the conditions it endured and whose end it earnestly desired into the text of the prophetic books and placed them into the interpretation, sometimes appropriately, sometimes not. This explanation, however, is in many respects unsatisfactory. It not only rests on a circular argument, in which the *pesharim* are used to reconstruct the history, which then serves to explain the *pesharim*, but also conceives the issue too narrowly. The historical allusions are not to be doubted, yet it must also be asked whether they are the origins or the results of exegetical activity in the *pesharim*. The alternative is to read the *pesharim* not primarily in relation to historical allusions but in relation to the biblical texts and their interpretive problems. However, if anything, this alternative is also mistaken, and it is likely that both influences—the text and contemporary events—are discernible. Hence, the *pesharim* should be understood as an intrinsic reflection on the received biblical text in the light of contemporary events and vice versa.

So that we can recognize the role that the biblical texts played for the *pesharim*, it is necessary to determine the literary history of the biblical books. Only when we understand the literary history of the biblical text will the history of its reception and interpretation—which is already part of the fabric of the biblical text itself—become apparent. For this literary history, the reader should refer to the previous chapters of this book (chaps. 4–8). The scholarly interpretation of the *pesharim* is therefore closely bound up with the scholarly investigation of the biblical prophetic books.

To return to our example, the *pesher* on the Book of Nahum, it is striking that the downfall of the city of Nineveh in the Book of Nahum is grounded in accusations that elsewhere in the Hebrew Bible are directed against Israel: Samaria or Jerusalem, Ephraim or Judah. Various explanations for this have been discussed. The most likely hypothesis is that the Book of Nahum was based upon older prophetic oracles against the hostile power Assyria and Nineveh. These were embellished with accusations against Israel from the repertoire of the classical written prophets through a process of redaction and *Fortschreibung*. The result is that the traditional text of the Book of Nahum is strongly influenced by this inner-Israelite polemic. When there are unclear syntactic structures or cryptic speech, the biblical text, in the Hebrew and even more so in the Greek versions, often raises the question of who is actually meant: the external enemy, Nineveh, or the Israelites? This is especially the case when the text is viewed in light of the entire biblical tradition. Had Daniel, in Dan 9, been poring over the Book of Nahum, he would presumably have understood as little or perhaps even less than in his reading of the Book of Jeremiah.

This appears to me to be the starting point for the interpretation of the *pesharim*, and we find the *pesharim* taken up with the same questions that concern modern scholarship. Who is the second-person singular feminine, the second-person singular masculine, the third-person singular masculine, or the third-person plural masculine in Nahum 1? Or, where is the "bloody city" in Nah 3:1, given that it is also spoken about in Isa 1 and Hab 2:12 and there identified with Jerusalem or an Israelite city? Or, where is the ruined Nineveh, when we are told in the Book of Jonah that Nineveh converted to the true God and escaped destruction? Or, where is the "No-Amon" that Nineveh took sides with and is associated with idol worship in Jer 46 and Ezek 30? These and other questions result from a close reading of the biblical text, especially if we consider the text not only in relation to the book (as we normally do) but interpret it verse-by-verse, cross-referencing it with biblical writings and other texts (as is common in Jewish exegesis).

It is these sorts of questions that stimulated the interpretation in the *pesharim* or at least may be expected to have done so. In the *pesher* on Nahum, they are answered by using the present and other writings to secure a meaning for the cited biblical verses. One of the youngest literary layers in the Book of Nahum may have been of assistance in orienting the author of the *pesher Nahum*: the hymn in Nah 1:2–8. In the biblical book, the text fulfills an important hermeneutical function. The text introduces the deity who executes judgment on Nineveh according to the predictions that will follow (Nah 2:14; 3:5–6). The feminine personal pronoun in v. 8, which constitutes the climax of the half-acrostic psalm, presumably points to this judgment, for otherwise it is left hanging. The God of judgment against Nineveh and this judgment gain a new character. He is the jealous, vengeful, and angry God who appears in the thunderstorm and before whom the earth trembles. He is a God who judges not only Nineveh but more generally distinguishes between his friends and enemies. In Nah 1:2b, 3a, we have an addition that echoes the wording of v. 8 and creates an *inclusio*. This verse has no other enemy in view but instead emphasizes (with reference to Isa 1:24; cf. Isa 59:18) the general opposition between the enemies of YHWH and those "who trust in him." With this new orientation to the book, Nineveh now stands on the same level as the enemies of YHWH among his own people. All the charges and pronouncements of judgment that the Book of Nahum directs against Nineveh can be taken over against them.

Based on Nah 1:2–8, it was possible for the author of the Nahum *pesher* to equate Nineveh and No-Amon with inner-Israelite opponents of his own time. He was able to resort to the influential typology or codification of the opponents as "Ephraim" and "Manasseh" that had already been developed in other exegetical works. This was despite the fact that, for *pesher Nahum*, unlike the interpretations of Isaiah, Hosea, or Micah, there was no direct clue in the biblical text of the Book of Nahum. Nevertheless, the relationship of the biblical original to the *pesher* is by no means arbitrary. Instead, the interpretation of the biblical text appears in any case to be directed or stimulated by exegetical problems arising from the received biblical text itself. These problems are solved by reference to contemporary history, which is the situation of the Qumran community, in accordance with the hermeneutical rule of the "Teacher of Righteousness" that determines to which time and to whom the predictions of the biblical prophets relate.

We observe here what can also be seen elsewhere—namely, that in many cases the interpretations of the *pesharim* form a seamless continuum with the problems and solutions that already played a role in the genesis of the biblical text. Not infrequently these issues within the biblical text are already negotiated with exegetical methods similar to those we find in the *pesharim* (catchwords, combination of various biblical texts, etc.). Thus, the interpretation of the *pesharim* continues the type of inner-biblical interpretation that can be observed in the literary and redactional history of biblical books—admittedly in a different genre, with text and commentary strictly divided from one another. Two things are achieved with this division that seem to be contradictory at first glance but in fact are compatible: first, an increase in the authority of the original biblical text to which the commentary relates, and second, the freedom of the commentator toward the biblical text, which he can now interpret in light of his own time and questions.

CHAPTER 10

"Not to Abolish But to Fulfill"

The Prophets in the New Testament

This is the beginning of the gospel of Jesus Christ, the son of God. As it is written in the prophet Isaiah: See, I am sending my messenger before you, who will prepare your way. It is a voice of one calling in the desert: prepare the way of the Lord, make his paths level. (Mark 1:1–2)

With this blended citation from Mal 3:1 and Isa 40:3, the oldest of the four gospels introduces the appearance of John the Baptist as preparer of the way and of Jesus of Nazareth as the announced Lord. Here and throughout the New Testament, the prophetic books of the Old Testament, cited according to the Greek translation of the Hebrew Bible, are regarded as the great promise that has taken human form in Jesus Christ and is verified in the future. With the exception of the Qumran community, there is scarcely any other Jewish group around the turn of the era that invoked the prophets as extensively to ground their own self-understanding as early Christianity. Jews and Christians had at the very least distanced themselves from one another and come into competition with one another. What is it that divided them?

The reason is not, at any rate, they way in which they received prophets. The many citations of the prophets and the appeal to "the law and the prophets" in the New Testament stand in continuity with Jewish interpretation of the prophetic books. As we have seen, interpretation of the prophetic books began in the books themselves and continued after the closing of the prophetic corpus in apocalyptic, the *pesharim* from Qumran, and many other writings from the Greco-Roman period. The New Testament authors share with all these the techniques and hermeneutical principles of textual interpretation. Selection, association, typology, and so on were in every case directed by a predetermined subject matter that was independent of the cited texts and formed the basis of interpretation.

However, this subject matter could not be brought to bear appropriately except through the words of scripture.

We have encountered two examples. In Dan 9 it is the revelation of the interpreting angel who explains the scriptures to Daniel. Conversely, the seventy years of Jeremiah, calculated according to the revelation of the angel, illuminate Daniel's situation and open a view to the future for the author and readers of the Book of Daniel. In the *pesher* on Habakkuk (1QpHab VII), there is the additional revelation to the "Teacher of Righteousness," who enables the interpreter of the prophetic writings in the Qumran community to extract the meaning of the text for his own time. Habakkuk had no inkling of this interpretation, but it was intended by God. The significance for a later time is inherent in the text, and it obviously cannot be uttered without it.

It is no different in the New Testament. "Do you understand what you are reading?" Philip asks the treasurer from Ethiopia who has visited Jerusalem and is reading the Book of Isaiah on his return journey (Acts 8:30). Philip explains the difficult passage Isa 53:7–8, which concerns the death of "the servant of God," by preaching to him about the gospel of Jesus Christ, whereupon the treasurer allows himself to be baptized. Anyone who reads a little further in Isa 53 is guided to relate it to the substitutional suffering of the servant of God upon the cross and Jesus' devotion "for you" (1 Cor 11:25) or "for (the) many" (Mark 14:24), as is found in the inauguration of the Last Supper. In addition, the promise of the servant of God in Isa 53:10–11 is seen as the promise of Easter.

It is not, therefore, the *type* of scriptural interpretation that divided Jews and Christians. Nor is the eschatological orientation of the interpretation a sufficient reason. This, too, can be documented many times in the Jewish writings from the Greco-Roman period and especially in the *pesharim* from Qumran. After the domestication of prophetic and apocalyptic expectations by the law in the Hebrew canon and in Jewish tradition, in the Christian tradition the prophets soon became teachers of the law as well (see above, chap. 1.3, pp. 5ff.).

The development is, in fact, comparable. The Christian tradition begins, as does the prophetic tradition, with the crisis and break of the divine-human relationship. The judgment of God that the prophets announce corresponds to the cross. On both occasions, faith in the preserving and saving power of God is shattered, and as long as God is not perceived in these events, there is doubt and disappointment. "My way is hidden from my God, and God has passed by my right" (Isa 40:27); "My God, my God, why have you forsaken me" (Matt 27:46); "but we had hoped that he would redeem Israel" (Luke 24:21). Yet, for faith—that is, from an emic perspective—the break is an act of God, and it is precisely the break that establishes the old divine relationship anew. In judgment, the promise announces itself, and in the cross, the resurrection. The break appeals for change and promises new life in light of the judging and saving God. It is upon this basis that the entire tradition of the Old and New Testaments has been formed, sometimes placing in the foreground the demand of God (the law) and at other times the promise (the gospel). Both are derived from the interpretation of defeat as divine judgment that Israel in its history and Jesus on the cross in his own body have experienced.

The analogy would be misunderstood if we were to place Jesus and the gospel directly in the succession of the prophets. The prophets are in the first place "the founders of the religion of the law, not the forerunners of the gospel" (Julius Wellhausen). After the two catastrophes that he was responsible for in Israel and Judah, YHWH has survived above all in the law, Jesus in the gospel. In addition, the gospel is built upon both "the law and the prophets." Thus, the relationship has to be understood in a different way. Perhaps in the following: just as in the history of Israel there was a shift—initiated by the prophets—from the preexilic religion of Israel and Judah to the theological tradition of the Hebrew Bible now reflected in "the law and the prophets," something similar happened in the history of Jesus Christ. Here, too, a radical shift took place. As the fundamental experience of the gospel and its hermeneutical norm, the cross and the resurrection of Jesus place in question and provide a new basis for the religion of ancient Judaism as it was practiced at the turn of the era. This is just the same as how the developing tradition of the Hebrew Bible placed in question and provided a new basis for the preexilic state religion of Israel and Judah from its own experience of judgment.

It appears that it was precisely at this point that the ways of Judaism and Christianity parted. The scales were tipped by neither the kind of prophetic interpretation nor its focus. The decisive factor was the fact that the key to the understanding of the prophets and the scriptures as a whole—namely, the cross and the resurrection of Jesus Christ—became the object of faith. Jesus was a Jew and not Christ. We might say that the "scandal of the cross" (1 Cor 1:23) made him into the Christ overnight and all who confessed him into Christians. It was not an unavoidable development, but neither was it an accident of religious history. It happened and immediately showed its effect, not least in the interpretation of the prophets.

Cross and resurrection were not simply a hermeneutical rule or a new piece of data to which the scriptures were to be related. They were not easily placed within the biblical sacred history. As especially Matthew's gospel shows, it was only possible to present them as the climax and fulfillment of Old Testament predictions with great exegetical investment. Rather, the cross and resurrection of Jesus turned on its head all the expectations concerning religious orders and hopes based on "the law and the prophets." Cross and resurrection came to be identified by the early Christian, New Testament tradition with the divine revelation in "the law and the prophets," but in reality they took their place. This meant, in fact, the annulment of the Jewish religion, which was based on the Hebrew Bible. This was achieved by preserving intact and endorsing Judaism's fundamental authority, scripture in the form of "the law and the prophets" (and of course the other writings of the canon), as far as they testified to Jesus Christ.

Jesus came not to annul the prophets but rather to fulfill them (Matt 5:17), says the New Testament. In the famous Beatitudes (Matt 5:1–12; Luke 6:20–23) the author of the gospel of Matthew allows Jesus to show what this means. Some of the Beatitudes cite the prophets. The poor, to whom the kingdom of God belongs, and the mourners, who will be comforted, remind us of Isa 61:1–2, , while the reference to the hungry, who will be satiated, is reminiscent of Isa 55:1–2. Jesus does not "fulfill" these predictions as we might expect. Poverty, grief, and hunger do not cease with him; if anything, the opposite is true. He himself takes the way of the poor, the hungry, and the mourning—unto the cross. Nevertheless, it is precisely in this way—and only in this way according to the Beatitudes— that he "fulfills" what the prophets had predicted. Hence, "fulfillment" does not mean simply the realization of all that the prophets had in view, even if the gospels sometimes suggest this in their post-Easter biographies of Jesus. Rather, it should be the "completion" of the divine promise, and this meant their final establishment in the gospel of Jesus Christ. "The blind receive their sight, the lame walk, the lepers are cleansed, the deaf hear and the dead are raised, and the poor have good news brought to them" (Matt 11:5; Luke 7:22)—all of this is what the prophets promise (Isa 35:5–6; 61:1 etc.); and all of this is what the gospel of the scandal of the cross promises: "blessed is anyone who takes no offense at me" (Matt 11:6; Luke 7:23).

In order to understand the process and assess it correctly, it must be made clear that the same hermeneutic that is applied in the New Testament and the Christian tradition to the Hebrew Bible is also appropriate for the New Testament itself. The Christian interpretation in the New Testament does not distinguish between Old and New Testaments or Jewish and Christian perceptions, even if it sometimes appears this way in Christian polemics against Jewish opponents. Rather, the boundary between "law" and "gospel" or "letter" and "spirit" applies to the entire Old Testament as well as to the New, depending on whether we follow our own dogmatic system or, in the sense of the biblical testimony, surrender to God the word, who has proven his freedom in the cross and resurrection and who alone brings freedom.

Christianity has often lacked this freedom. It is also part of freedom to acknowledge the truth that, alongside the Christian use of the Hebrew Bible, there is a legitimate Jewish use without Jesus Christ and the New Testament. It is God alone who can judge between them. Since the time of the cross and the resurrection, Christians wait for the return of their Lord Jesus Christ. When he comes, it is promised, he also will be subjected to God, so that finally God may be all in all (1 Cor 15:20–28).

CHAPTER 11

Research on the Prophets

Problems and Perspectives

It is not unusual to find the expression "paradigm shift" in recent overviews of research on the Hebrew Bible. This is also the case in an overview of research on the prophets of the Hebrew Bible by Martti Nissinen (2009), who primarily describes the English-speaking discussion in considerable detail. Uwe Becker (2004), who also considers German-speaking research, is slightly more careful and speaks of the "rediscovery of the prophetic books." More or less the same is meant in each case: the prophet as an individual has been left behind and attention is given instead to the prophetic literature in the Hebrew Bible. This trend within research can be observed beginning in the 1970s and has resulted in the rediscovery of old observations and the formation of new questions. Indicative of the current discussion is the flow of new edited collections as listed below.

In what follows, I wish to discuss the problems that have arisen from this recent trend in scholarship (see Schmid 1996; Barstad 1993; 2009). I will be concerned with older and newer European literature, mostly in German but increasingly also in English, that concentrates on the literary genesis of the prophetic books, even if this question is unfashionable now. As Hugh Williamson so incisively observes in his introduction to a collection of essays that do not appear to know recent research (Firth and Williamson 2009), reading such works is rewarding even if you do not agree with them. For, as a rule, these works lead to a closer and more precise reading of the biblical text than is the case in so many descriptions of the textual surface in "canonical" or "close" readings.

Research Reports

Barstad, Hans M. "No Prophets? Recent Developments in Biblical Prophetic Research and Ancient Near Eastern Prophecy." *Journal for the Study of the Old Testament* 57 (1993): 39–60.

_____ . "What Prophets Do: Reflections on the Past Reality in the Book of Jeremiah." Pp. 10–32 in *Prophecy in the Book of Jeremiah*. Beihefte zur

Zeitschrift für die Alttestamentliche Wissenschaft 388. Edited by H. M. Barstad and R. G. Kratz. Berlin: de Gruyter, 2009.

Becker, Uwe. "Die Wiederentdeckung des Prophetenbuches. Tendenzen und Aufgaben der gegenwärtigen Prophetenforschung." *Berliner Theologische Zeitschrift* (2004): 30–60.

Nissinen, Martti. "The Historical Dilemma of Biblical Prophetic Studies." Pp. 103–20 in *Prophecy in the Book of Jeremiah*. Beihefte zur *Zeitschrift für die Alttestamentliche* Wissenschaft 388. Edited by H. M. Barstad and R. G. Kratz. Berlin: de Gruyter, 2009.

Schmid, Konrad. "Klassische und nachklassische Deutungen der alttestamentlichen Prophetie." *Zeitschrift für neuere Theologiegeschichte* 3 (1996): 225–50.

Recent Collections of Essays

Ben Zvi, Ehud, ed. *Utopia and Dystopia in Prophetic Literature*. Publications of the Finnish Exegetical Society 92. Helsinki: Finnish Exegetical Society/ Göttingen: Vandenhoeck & Ruprecht, 2006.

Ben Zvi, Ehud, and Michael H. Floyd, eds. *Writings and Speech in Israelite and Ancient Near Eastern Prophecy*. Society of Biblical Literature Symposium Series 10. Atlanta: Society of Biblical Literature, 2000.

Firth, David G., and Hugh G. M. Williamson, eds. *Interpreting Isaiah: Issues and Approaches*. Nottingham: Apollos/Downers Grove: IVP Academic, 2009.

Fischer, Irmtraud, Konrad Schmid, and Hugh G. M. Williamson, eds. *Prophetie in Israel: Beiträge des Symposiums "Das Alte Testament und die Kultur der Moderne" anlässlich des 100. Geburtstags Gerhard von Rads [1901–1971] Heidelberg, 18.–21. Oktober 2001*. Altes Testament und Moderne 11. Münster: LIT, 2003.

Floyd, Michael H., and Robert D. Haak, eds. *Prophets, Prophecy, and Prophetic Texts in Second Temple Judaism*. Library of Hebrew Bible/Old Testament Studies 427. New York/London: T. & T. Clark, 2006.

Gordon, Robert, and Hans Barstad, eds. *"Thus Speaks Ishtar of Arbela": Prophecy in Israel, Assyria, and Egypt in the Neo-Assyrian Period*. Winona Lake, IN: Eisenbrauns, 2013.

Grabbe, Lester L., and Alice O. Bellis, eds. *The Priests in the Prophets: The Portrayal of Priests, Prophets, and Other Religious Specialists in the Latter Prophets*. Journal for the Study of the Old Testament Supplement 408. New York/ London: T. & T. Clark, 2004.

Grabbe, Lester L., and Robert D. Haak, eds. *'Every City Shall Be Forsaken': Urbanism and Prophecy in Ancient Israel and the Near East*. Journal for the Study of the Old Testament Supplement 330. Sheffield: Sheffield Academic, 2001.

Kaltner, John, and Louis Stulman, eds. *Inspired Speech: Prophecy in the Ancient Near East: Essays in Honor of Herbert B. Huffmon*. Journal for the Study of the Old Testament Supplement 378. New York/London: T. & T. Clark, 2004.

Kelle, Brad E., and Megan B. Moore, eds. *Israel's Prophets and Israel's Past: Essays on the Relationship of Prophetic Texts and Israelite History in Honor of John H. Hayes*. Library of Hebrew Bible/Old Testament Studies 446. New York/London: T. & T. Clark, 2006.

Köckert, Matthias, and Martti Nissinen, eds. *Propheten in Mari, Assyrien und Israel*. Forschungen zur Religion und Literatur des Alten und Neuen Testaments 201. Göttingen: Vandenhoeck & Ruprecht, 2003.

Kratz, Reinhard Gregor. *Prophetenstudien: Kleine Schriften II*. Forschungen zum Alten Testament 74. Tübingen: Mohr Siebeck, 2011.

Nissinen, Martti, ed. *Prophecy in Its Ancient Near Eastern Context: Mesopotamian, Biblical, and Arabian Perspectives*. Society of Biblical Literature Symposium Series 13. Atlanta: Society of Biblical Literature, 2000.

Thelle, Rannfrid, Terje Stordalen, and Mervyn R. J. Richardson, eds. *New Perspectives on Old Testament Prophecy and History: Essays in Honour of Hans M. Barstad*. Supplements to Vetus Testamentum 168. Leiden: Brill, 2015.

Weippert, Manfred. *Götterwort in Menschenmund: Studien zur Prophetie in Assyrien, Israel und Juda*. Forschungen zur Religion und Literatur des Alten und Neuen Testaments 252. Göttingen: Vandenhoeck & Ruprecht, 2014.

1. The Person of the Prophet

If we are to understand the recent trend in the history of scholarship to concentrate on the prophetic literature, we must first keep in sight the point from which it departed. This point of departure is the fixation on the person of the prophet in both the ecclesial and the scholarly understanding of the prophets of the Hebrew Bible. This approach was dominant into the twenty-first century and in some cases continues even today. This fixation has a long prehistory and finds its beginnings in the biblical tradition itself. Poetic self-reflection, prophetic miracles or sign-acts, and narratives about the prophets draw attention to the person of the prophet as mediator of God's word. Here, the prophet is usually portrayed as a lone voice in the wilderness, disowned by the world, despairing of God and his mission. At the same time, the headings of the prophetic books ensure a historicization that places individual prophets at certain phases in the history of Israel and Judah.

The subsequent Jewish and Christian patterns of interpretation that we have already discussed in chapter 1 of this book have loosened this fixation on the person of the prophet a bit and integrated the prophets into their own theological systems: the lone voice in the wilderness became the writer of sacred history, the teacher of the law, the revealer of divine secrets or the preacher of Christ. Yet, also within these patterns, the prophets maintained their individuality. It is true that the words of the prophets—according to their books and even more so in the eschatological interpretations of the *pesharim* from Qumran or the New Testament—pointed in many ways beyond their own time. Nevertheless, for a long time, Jewish and Christian tradition had, with few exceptions, no reason to doubt the correctness of the historical information, the authenticity of the words and deeds of the prophets, or the authorship of the books that traditionally went under their names.

Even after the Enlightenment had taken its course and doubts had arisen that could no longer be suppressed, the interest in the figure of the prophet remained, but it was shifted to the original words of the prophet. In scholarship, historical and religious interests went hand in hand. The identification of the "real" words of the prophet, the *ipsissima verba*, appeared to open the door to encountering the prophet in a scholarly manner and to prove his authenticity. This coalesced with the romantic and pietistic idea that traces of the true, unadulterated testimony to God could be found behind the material of the biblical tradition and the traditions of synagogue and church.

The historical and religious dimensions of this line of interpretation climaxed in the characterization of the historical prophets as individual geniuses, adopting the biblical portrayal and reviving the notion of the lone voice in the wilderness. The prophets were seen as the epitome of individual piety, commissioned and instructed by God in mysterious ways. But they were also rigorously tested, misunderstood, and despised by their own people, faithfully fulfilling their role, acknowledging no other authority than God alone and their own conscience. As such, the prophets were heralds of a new—in truth, ancient—original and true religion and morality that had nothing of what the later biblical tradition would attribute to them. "Men of the eternally new" was what Bernhard Duhm named them (Duhm 1922: 7–8), which is to say, nothing other than the dictum of Julius Wellhausen that the prophets "proclaimed nothing new, only ancient truth" (Wellhausen 1885: 398f.; 6th ed. 1905: 398; 1914: 107).

The nineteenth-century image of the prophets lived on in the history of religions school (*Religionsgeschichtliche Schule*) and was confirmed form-critically through the discovery of the prophetic genres and theologically through dialectical theology. At the same time, increasing weight was placed on the orality of the prophetic oracles in contrast to a literary legacy, which was downgraded to a lower level. In this perspective, orality was and still is regarded as the guarantee of divine immediacy of both the mysterious experience of the biblical prophets and their original message in the forms of prophetic speech. In this way, it is not only the prophet and his contemporary audience that had unmediated access to the word of God but also we and every future reader or hearer of the Bible.

Comprehensive Overviews

Barton, John. *Oracles of God: Perceptions of Ancient Prophecy in Israel after the Exile*. London: Darton, Longman and Todd, 1986. 2nd ed. Oxford: Oxford University Press, 2007.

Blenkinsopp, Joseph. *A History of Prophecy in Israel*. Philadelphia: Westminster Press, 1983. 2nd ed. Louisville: Westminster John Knox, 1996.

Duhm, Bernhard. *Die Theologie der Propheten als Grundlage für die innere Entwicklungsgeschichte der israelitischen Religion*. Bonn: Marcus, 1875.

_____ . *Israels Propheten*. Tübingen: J.C.B. Mohr (Paul Siebeck), 1916. 2nd ed. Tübingen: J.C.B. Mohr (Paul Siebeck), 1922.

Ewald, Heinrich. *Commentary on the Prophets of the Old Testament*. 5 vols. Trans. J. F. Smith. London: Williams & Norgate, 1875–1881. (Trans. of *Die Propheten des Alten Bundes*. 2 vols. Stuttgart: Krabbe. 2nd ed. 3 vols. Göttingen: Vandenhoeck & Ruprecht, 1867–68.)

Gunkel, Hermann. *Die Propheten: Die geheimen Erfahrungen der Propheten; die Politik der Propheten; die Religion der Propheten; Schriftstellerei und Formsprache der Propheten*. Göttingen: Vandenhoeck & Ruprecht, 1917.

Hölscher, Gustav. *Die Profeten: Untersuchungen zur Religionsgeschichte Israels*. Leipzig: Hinrichs, 1914.

Koch, Klaus. *The Prophets, vol. 1: The Assyrian Period*. Trans. Margaret Kohl. London: SCM Press, 1982. (Trans. of *Assyrische Zeit. Vol. 1 of Die Profeten*. Stuttgart: Kohlhammer, 1978. 3rd ed. Stuttgart: Kohlhammer, 1995.)

_____ . *The Prophets, vol. 2: The Babylonian and Persian Periods*. Trans. Margaret Kohl. London: SCM Press, 1983. (Trans. of *Babylonisch-persische Zeit. Vol. 2 of Die Profeten*. Stuttgart: Kohlhammer, 1980. 2nd ed. Stuttgart: Kohlhammer, 1988.)

Lindblom, Johannes. *Prophecy in Ancient Israel*. Oxford: Blackwell, 1962. 9th ed. Philadelphia: Fortress Press, 1980.

Mowinckel, Sigmund. *Psalmenstudien, vol. 3: Kultprophetie und prophetische Psalmen*. Kristiania: Dybwad, 1923.

_____ . *Prophecy and Tradition: The Prophetic Books in the Light of the Study of the Growth and History of the Tradition*. Oslo: Dybwad, 1946.

Rad, Gerhard von. *The Message of the Prophets*. Trans. D. G. M. Stalker. London: SCM Press, 1968. (Trans. of *Die Botschaft der Propheten*. Munich: Siebenstern-Taschenbuch-Verlag, 1967. 4th ed. Edited by Eduard Haller. Gütersloh: Mohn, 1981.)

_____ . *Old Testament Theology, vol. 2: The Theology of Israel's Prophetic Traditions*. Trans. D. M. G. Stalker. Edinburgh: Oliver and Boyd, 1965. (Trans. of *Die Theologie der prophetischen Überlieferungen*. Vol. 2 of *Theologie des Alten Testaments*. München: Kaiser, 1960. 4th ed. Munich: Kaiser, 1965.)

Wellhausen, Julius. *Prolegomena to the History of Ancient Israel.* Trans J. S. Black and A. Menzies. Edinburgh: A. & C. Black, 1885. (Latest German version: *Prolegomena zur Geschichte Israels.* 6th ed. Berlin: G. Reimer, 1905.)

_____ . *Israelitische und jüdische Geschichte.* 7th ed. Berlin: Reimer, 1914 (repr. 10th ed. Berlin: de Gruyter, 2004).

Zimmerli, Walther. *The Law and the Prophets: A Study of the Meaning of the Old Testament.* Trans. R. E. Clements. Oxford: Blackwell, 1965. (Trans. of *Das Gesetz und die Propheten: Zum Verständnis des Alten Testaments.* Göttingen: Vandenhoeck & Ruprecht, 1963.)

2. The Books of the Prophets

The about-face in scholarship on the prophetic literature was at first not conceived as an alternative but instead as an augmentation to the conventional "classical" image of the prophet. From its beginning, the trend moved in two directions, one analytical and the other descriptive. The first looked for the subsequent literary history (Hertzberg 1962) of the original prophetic words and their collection. Tracing the history from the *ipsissima verba* onward, it would be possible to reconstruct the path from prophetic word to the book. Literary-historical and redaction-historical work, which have been developed especially in European scholarship, are devoted to this end (Kratz 2011: 32–48, 310–43).

The second approach aims particularly at the traditional text of the Masoretic canon, and for this reason its method is called the "canonical approach" or the like. The prehistory of the original oracles, their collection, redaction, and actualization (*Fortschreibung*) are not denied but effectively ignored or only taken into consideration if they can made useful in some way. In place of literary-historical reconstruction, this approach offers a more-or-less precise description of the linguistic and thematic architecture of the biblical text. The approach is indebted to theological concerns and increasingly to the interests of cultural and literary studies. It can now be found not only in English-speaking research, where it is very common, but also in other scholarly traditions (Clements 1966; see Rendtorff 1983 and 2005).

Both approaches, the analytical and the canonical, presuppose the "classical" picture of the historical prophet and his original message as it has been received from the nineteenth century. Nevertheless, they have, in fact, increasingly resulted in the evaporation of the person of the prophet. For historical or theological reasons, older scholarship did not show any interest in the literary phenomena of the prophetic books. By tracing these literary phenomena, the newer approaches have struck upon evidence that already played an important role in the pre-critical phase of interpreting the prophets. This evidence includes textual signals of literary composition or intertextual connections within a book, or even beyond it. While this evidence ensured the identity of prophet and prophetic book in the pre-critical period, they now often raise the question of what remains of the historical prophet and his original words. For even the supposedly original material is transmitted within the books of the prophets and has become an object of literary-critical investigation (Collins 1993).

For literary-historical and redaction-historical analysis, this means that it has to be applied also to passages usually considered to be the original oracles of the historical prophet. Consequently, it turns out that in no case do we encounter the original words of the prophets. Rather, so far as we can tell, from the very beginning—and this means from the first recording or inclusion in the context of a prophetic book—the prophetic oracles have been subject to redactional scribal reworking and alteration (Schottroff 1970; Steck 1982: 149–203; 1996/2000; 2001; Jeremias 1996a; 1996b; 1999; Davies 1996; Kratz 2011; de Jong 2011). This is no different in the Hebrew Bible from elsewhere in the ancient Near East (van der Toorn 2000; Nissinen 2000 as well as 2005; 2008a; 2009a). It is only that the process led to something "new" in the biblical tradition (Kratz 2011: 49–70, 310–43).

Some scholars today still try to avoid the consequences described above and insist on the historicity or authenticity of the prophetic oracles at least for a certain kernel of the prophetic book. They refer either to the oral tradition behind scripture or to the witness of scripture itself. The significance of orality in the transmission process has most recently been discussed by Carr (2005) and van der Toorn (2007). This undoubtedly very important aspect of the preserved material, however, can scarcely provide a control and consequently contributes very little to solving our problems. In addition, the stubborn recourse to the biblical text and its narrative implications does not help: it neither leads to the original prophet nor does it prove the historicity or authenticity of his words (see Jeremias 2013; Kratz 2013).

The prophets also disappear from view in the "canonical approach." The method has very little to do with history unless we underhandedly identify the literary composition of the book as a whole with the historical prophet or his theological concept and date it to the time the book itself suggests. However, recent studies have increasingly avoided this circular conclusion and viewed the traditional text in the historical context of the (presumed) time of the completion of the prophetic book. Thus, here too the question of the historical prophet has been abandoned (see Nissinen 2009a: 106–9). Steck (1996; English version 2000) already championed the claim of a historical reading of the "final" text and advocated the time of the oldest manuscript evidence—that is, the second century B.C.E.—as the historical context for such a reading. Nevertheless, as a rule, most scholars opt for the Persian and early Hellenistic periods, often without any justification, as a possible date for "the final shape" of the prophetic books.

The Dead Sea Scrolls have offered an additional approach to the prophet's "book." Here, manuscripts of more-or-less complete books have been found in Hebrew and, for the Twelve Prophets, also in Greek. In addition, the exegetical literature (Charlesworth 2002), especially the *pesharim* (Horgan 1979; 2002), grant a new perspective into the handling of the "final form" of the text—in other words, the reception and interpretation of the prophetic books in Palestinian Judaism of the Greco-Roman period.

Most recently, research has been occupied with the question of whether there was prophecy at Qumran and how prophets and scribes related to one another (Barstad 1994; Bowley 1999; Brooke 2000; 2006; 2008; 2009a; 2009b; Lange 2003; Nissinen 2008b, 2009b). In chapters 4 and 9 of this book an attempt was made to answer this question, for it concerns not only interpretation at Qumran but also the biblical books themselves in their literary genesis, understood as a process of inner-biblical interpretation. Future research will increasingly have to deal with the relationship of inner- and external biblical interpretation. My initial probes into this area have produced a number of surprising results (Kratz 2011: 99–145, 243–271, 359–79). The origin of the prophetic books and their reception at Qumran seem to be much closer than one usually thinks. Another field of future research is the historical and cultural background of the genre of the *pesharim* as commentaries (see Lange and Pleše 2011; Brooke et al. 2012; Kratz 2014).

Prophet and Prophetic Book

Carr, David M. *Writing on the Tablet of the Heart: Origins of Scripture and Literature.* Oxford: Oxford University Press, 2005.

Clements, Ronald E. *Old Testament Prophecy: From Oracles to Canon.* Louisville: Westminster John Knox, 1996.

Collins, Terence. *The Mantle of Elijah: The Redaction Criticism of the Prophetical Books.* The Biblical Seminar 20. Sheffield: JSOT Press, 1993.

Davies, Philip R., ed. *The Prophets.* The Biblical Seminar 42. Sheffield: Sheffield Academic Press, 1996.

Hertzberg, Hans W. "Die Nachgeschichte alttestamentlicher Texte innerhalb des Alten Testaments." Pp. 69–80 in *Beiträge zur Traditionsgeschichte und Theologie des Alten Testaments*. Göttingen: Vandenhoeck & Ruprecht, 1962.

Jeremias, Jörg. *Hosea und Amos: Studien zu den Anfängen des Dodekapropheton*. Forschungen zum Alten Testament 13. Tübingen: J.C.B. Mohr (Paul Siebeck) 1996. (= 1996a)

_____. "Die Anfänge der Schriftprophetie." *Zeitschrift für Theologie und Kirche* 93 (1996): 481–99. (= 1996b)

_____. "Prophetenwort und Prophetenbuch: Zur Rekonstruktion mündlicher Verkündigung der Propheten." *Jahrbuch für biblische Theologie* 14 (1999): 19–35.

_____. "Das Rätsel der Schriftprophetie" *Zeitschrift für die Alttestamentliche Wissenschaft* 125 (2013): 93–117.

Jong, Matthijs de. "Biblical Prophecy—A Scribal Enterprise: The Old Testament Prophecy of Unconditional Judgment considered as a Literary Phenomenon." *Vetus Testamentum* 61 (2011): 39–70.

Kratz, Reinhard G. *Prophetenstudien: Kleine Schriften II*. Forschungen zum Alten Testament 74. Tübingen: Mohr Siebeck, 2011.

_____. "Das Rätsel der Schriftprophetie: Eine Replik." *Zeitschrift für die Alttestamentliche Wissenschaft* 125 (2013): 635–39.

Nissinen, Martti. "Spoken, Written, Quoted, and Invented: Orality and Writtenness in Ancient Near Eastern Prophecy." Pp. 235–71 in *Writings and Speech in Israelite and Ancient Near Eastern Prophecy*. Edited by Michael H. Floyd and Ehud Ben Zvi. Society of Biblical Literature Symposium Series 10. Atlanta: Society of Biblical Literature, 2000.

_____. "How Prophecy became Literature." *Scandinavian Journal of the Old Testament* 19 (2005): 153–72.

_____. "Das Problem der Prophetenschüler." Pp. 337–53 in *Houses Full of All Good Things: Essays in Memory of Timo Vejola*. Edited by Martti Nissinen and Juha Pakkala. Publications of the Finnish Exegetical Society 95. Göttingen: Vandenhoeck & Ruprecht, 2008. (= 2008a)

_____. "The Historical Dilemma of Biblical Prophetic Studies." Pp. 103–20 in *Prophecy in the Book of Jeremiah*. Edited by Hans M. Barstad and Reinhard G. Kratz. Beihefte zur *Zeitschrift für die Alttestamentliche* Wissenschaft 388. Berlin: de Gruyter, 2009. (= 2009a)

Rendtorff, Rolf. *The Old Testament: An Introduction*. Trans. John Bowden. Philadelphia: Fortress, 1983. (Latest German edition: *Das Alte Testament: Eine Einführung*. 6th ed. Neukirchen-Vluyn: Neukirchener Verlag, 2001.)

_____. *The Canonical Hebrew Bible: A Theology of the Old Testament*. Trans. David W. Orton. Tools for Biblical Study 7. Leiden: Deo, 2005. (Trans. from *Kanonische Grundlegung*. Vol. 1 of *Theologie des Alten Testaments: Ein kanonischer Entwurf*. Neukirchen-Vluyn: Neukirchener Verlag 1999.)

Schottroff, Willy. "Jeremia 2,1–3: Erwägungen zur Methode der Prophetenexegese." *Zeitschrift für Theologie und Kirche* 67 (1970): 263–94.

Steck, Odil Hannes. *Wahrnehmungen Gottes im Alten Testament: Gesammelte Studien.* Theologische Bücherei 70. Munich: Kaiser, 1982.

_____ . *Gott in der Zeit entdecken: Die Prophetenbücher des Alten Testaments als Vorbild für Theologie und Kirche.* Biblisch-Theologische Studien 42. Neukirchen: Neukirchener Verlag, 2001.

_____ . *The Prophetic Books and Their Theological Witness.* Translated by James D. Nogalski. St. Louis: Chalice, 2000. (Trans. from *Die Prophetenbücher und ihr theologisches Zeugnis: Wege der Nachfrage und Fährten zur Antwort.* Tübingen: J.C.B. Mohr [Paul Siebeck], 1996.)

Toorn, Karel van der. "From the Oral to the Written: The Case of Old Babylonian Prophecy." Pp. 219–34 in *Writings and Speech in Israelite and Ancient Near Eastern Prophecy.* Edited by Michael H. Floyd and Ehud Ben Zvi. Society of Biblical Literature Symposium Series 10, Atlanta: Society of Biblical Literature, 2000.

_____ . *Scribal Culture and the Making of the Hebrew Bible.* Cambridge/London: Harvard University Press, 2007.

Prophecy at Qumran

Barstad, Hans M. "Prophecy at Qumran?" Pp. 104–20 in *In the Last Days: On Jewish and Christian Apocalyptic and Its Period.* Edited by Knud Jeppesen et al. Aarhus: Aarhus University Press, 1994.

Bowley, James E. "Prophets and Prophecy at Qumran." Pp. 354–78 in *The Dead Sea Scrolls after Fifty Years: A Comprehensive Assessment II.* Edited by Peter W. Flint and James C. VanderKam. Leiden: Brill, 1999.

Brooke, George J. "Prophecy." Pp. 694–700 in vol. 2 of *Encyclopedia of the Dead Sea Scrolls.* Edited by Lawrence H. Schiffman. 2 vols. Oxford: Oxford University Press, 2000.

_____ . "Prophecy and Prophets in the Dead Sea Scrolls: Looking Backwards and Forwards." Pp. 151–65 in *Prophets, Prophecy, and Prophetic Texts in Second Temple Judaism.* Edited by Michael H. Floyd and Robert D. Haak. Library of Hebrew Bible/Old Testament Studies 427. London: T. & T. Clark, 2006.

_____ . "The Place of Prophecy in Coming out of Exile: The Case of the Dead Sea Scrolls." Pp. 535–50 in *Scripture in Transition: Essays on Septuagint, Hebrew Bible, and Dead Sea Scrolls in Honour of Raija Sollamo.* Edited by Anssi Voitila and Jutta Jokiranta. Leiden: Brill, 2008.

_____ . "Prophets and Prophecy in the Qumran Scrolls and the New Testament." Pp. 31–48 in *Text, Thought, and Practice in Qumran and Early Christianity: Proceedings of the Ninth International Symposium of the Orion Center for the Study of the Dead Sea Scrolls and Associated Literature, Jointly Sponsored by the Hebrew University Center for the Study of Christianity, 11–13 January 2004.* Edited by Ruth A. Clements and Daniel R. Schwartz. Studies on the Text of the Desert of Judah 84. Leiden: Brill, 2009. (= 2009a)

_____ . "Was the Teacher of Righteousness Considered To Be a Prophet?" Pp. 43–60 in *Prophecy After the Prophets? The Contribution of the Dead Sea Scrolls to the Understanding of Biblical and Extra-Biblical Prophecy.* Edited by Kristin de Troyer and Armin Lange. Contributions to Biblical Exegesis and Theology 52. Leuven: Peeters, 2009. (= 2009b)

_____ . et al., ed. "The Rise of Commentary: Commentary Texts in Ancient Near Eastern, Greek, Roman and Jewish Cultures." *Dead Sea Discoveries* 19 (2012): 249–484.

Charlesworth, J., ed. *Pesharim, Other Commentaries, and Related Documents.* Vol. 6B of *The Dead Sea Scrolls: Hebrew, Aramaic, and Greek Texts with English Translation.* Tübingen: Mohr Siebeck/Louisville: Westminster John Knox, 2002.

Horgan, Maurya P. *Pesharim: Qumran Interpretations of Biblical Books.* The Catholic Biblical Quarterly Monograph Series 8. Washington, DC: Catholic Biblical Association of America, 1979.

_____ . "Pesharim." Pp. 1–201 in *The Dead Sea Scrolls. Hebrew, Aramaic, and Greek Texts with English Translation.* Vol. 6B. Edited by James Charlesworth. Tübingen: Mohr Siebeck/Louisville: Westminster John Knox, 2002.

Kratz, Reinhard G. *Prophetenstudien: Kleine Schriften II.* Forschungen zum Alten Testament 74. Tübingen: Mohr Siebeck, 2011.

_____ . "Text and Commentary: The *pesharim* of Qumran in the Context of Hellenistic Scholarship," Pp. 212–29 in *The Bible and Hellenism: Greek Influence on Jewish and Early Christian Literature.* Edited by Thomas L. Thompson and Philippe Wajdenbaum. Copenhagen International Seminar. Durham: Acumen, 2014. (German original: "Text und Kommentar: Die Pescharim von Qumran im Kontext der hellenistischen Schultradition." Pp. 51–80 in *Von Rom nach Bagdad: Bildung und Religion von der römischen Kaiserzeit bis zum klassischen Islam.* Edited by Peter Gemeinhardt and Sebastian Günther. Tübingen: Mohr Siebeck, 2013.

Lange, Armin. "Interpretation als Offenbarung: Zum Verhältnis von Schriftauslegung und Offenbarung." Pp. 17–33 in *Wisdom and Apocalypticism in the Dead Sea Scrolls and in the Biblical Tradition.* Edited by Florentino Garzía Martínez. Bibliotheca Ephemeridum Theologicarum Lovaniensium 168. Leuven: Leuven University Press, 2003.

_____ . and Zlatko Pleše. "The Qumran Pesharim and the Derveni Papyrus: Transpositional Hermeneutics in Ancient Jewish and Ancient Greek Commentaries." Pp. 895–922 in *The Dead Sea Scrolls in Context: Integrating the Dead Sea Scrolls in the Study of Ancient Texts, languages, and Cultures,* 2 vols. Edited by Armin Lange, Emanuel Tov, and M. Weigold. Leiden: Brill, 2011.

Nissinen, Martti. "Transmitting Divine Mysteries: The Prophetic Role of Wisdom Teachers in the Dead Sea Scrolls." Pp. 513–33 in *Scripture in Transition: Essays on Septuagint, Hebrew Bible, and Dead Sea Scrolls in Honour of Raija Sollamo.* Edited by Anssi Voitila and Jutta Jokiranta. Leiden: Brill, 2008. (= 2008b)

_____ . "Pesharim as Divination: Qumran Exegesis, Omen Interpretation and Literary Prophecy." Pp. 43–60 in *Prophecy After the Prophets? The Contribution of the Dead Sea Scrolls to the Understanding of Biblical and Extra-Biblical Prophecy.* Edited by Kristin de Troyer and Armin Lange. Contributions to Biblical Exegesis and Theology 52. Leuven: Peeters, 2009. (= 2009b)

Troyer, Kristin de, and Armin Lange, ed. *Prophecy After the Prophets? The Contribution of the Dead Sea Scrolls for the Understanding of Biblical and Extra-Biblical Prophecy.* Contributions to Biblical Exegesis and Theology 52. Leuven: Peeters, 2009.

3. Ancient Near Eastern and Greek Analogies

The question of the historical prophets has received new direction from a completely different angle. In the 1980s, ancient Near Eastern texts from Mari and Nineveh were made available to a wider public and enjoyed a greater impact than before upon the research on biblical prophecy (Nissinen passim; Köckert and Nissinen 2003; Stökl 2012; Weippert 2014; Gordon 2014). More recently, Greek parallels have increasingly been drawn upon as well (Hagedorn 2007; Huffmon 2007; Lange 2006, 2007).

The parallels show quite plainly what can be envisaged under the phenomenon "prophecy" in the ancient world and in the ancient Near East in particular. They provide insights into the origins, the different titles, and the work of prophets and prophetesses. They also provide information about the mysterious contact of the prophet with the deity, the circumstances of oracle reception, the forms of speech, and the content of their messages. They also allow us to recognize the alteration that takes place to the prophetic word during their (oral and literary) transmission, archiving, and collection. In comparison, the prophets of the Hebrew Bible appear in many respects to be a special exception. Certainly they share elements of the phenomenology with their ancient Near Eastern and Greek analogies. Yet, they are markedly distinct in the tradition of prophetic narratives and entire prophetic books as well as in the content of their messages.

Occasionally, scholars bring chronological, cultural, and generic differences into play against comparing biblical and ancient Near Eastern prophecy and its results, and no doubt such differences do exist. The possibility of comparison is questioned, either in order to interpret the biblical prophets entirely by themselves, taking them as a historical fact, or in order to dissolve the distinctive features on the basis of phenomenological analogies, declaring that biblical prophecy is entirely compatible with what we know of Near Eastern prophecy and can thus be judged as historical (Scherer 2005; Blum 2008).

Nevertheless, this objection overlooks the fact that the phenomenon of ancient Near Eastern prophecy is also documented in chronologically and geographically proximate locations (Balaam from Deir ʿAlla; Zakkur from Hamath) as well as sporadically for Judah itself (Lachish 3 and 16). Despite the distinctive cultural characteristics and viewed as a whole, all the documentation conveys a relatively consistent picture for the Mesopotamian and northwest Semitic area. This makes it quite suitable for comparison, the more so since the biblical evidence fits very well phenomenologically. We must not make the mistake of inferring the historicity of the information contained in the biblical sources from the phenomenology or, vice versa, filling the gaps of the phenomenological analogies with biblical material (Barstad 1993 and 2009). Rather, in the biblical sources themselves, we must distinguish between the phenomenology and the individual form. The phenomenology leads to the historical conditions in Israel and Judah, and the individual form within the biblical tradition leads to what is particular and new in the prophecy of the Hebrew Bible (Nissinen 2008: 346–47; 2009: 114–17; Kratz 2011: 49–70, 71–98). Up to now, we have only been able to consider this new perspective as a purely literary phenomenon. Where it has its historical place in ancient Israel, Judah, or Yehud is another question (Nissinen 2008).

As we have seen, the quest for the person of the historical prophets in biblical tradition is relativized in two directions: first, through the rediscovery of the literary nature of the biblical prophetic tradition, whether this resulted from literary-critical and redaction-critical analysis or through a canonical or holistic reading; and second, through a religio-historical comparison that has made apparent both the phenomenological similarities and cultural peculiarities, as well as the deep gap between historical (ancient Near Eastern, Israelite-Judahite) and literary (biblical) prophecy (Kratz 2011; similarly Nissinen 2004; 2008: 346–47; 2009: 108). Both the rediscovery of the literary nature of the prophetic tradition and the religio-historical analogies make the contours of the historical prophets behind the biblical tradition increasingly blurry.

Ancient Near Eastern Analogies

Barstad, Hans M. "Lachish Ostracon III and Ancient Israelite Prophecy." *Eretz-Israel* 24 (1993): 8*–12*.

_____ . "What Prophets Do: Reflections on the Past Reality in the Book of Jeremiah." Pp. 10–32 in *Prophecy in the Book of Jeremiah*. Beihefte zur *Zeitschrift für die Alttestamentliche* Wissenschaft 388. Edited by H. M. Barstad and R. G. Kratz. Berlin: de Gruyter, 2009.

Blum, Erhard. "Israels Prophetie im altorientalischen Kontext: Anmerkungen zu neueren religionsgeschichtlichen Thesen." Pp. 81–115 in *From Ebla to Stellenbosch—Syro-Palestinian Religions and the Hebrew Bible*. Edited by Izak Cornelius and Louis Jonker. Abhandlungen des Deutschen Palästina-Vereins 37. Wiesbaden: Harrassowitz 2008.

Gordon, Robert, and Hans Barstad, eds. *"Thus Speaks Ishtar of Arbela:" Prophecy in Israel, Assyria, and Egypt in the Neo-Assyrian Period*. Winona Lake, IN: Eisenbrauns, 2013.

Köckert, Matthias, and Martti Nissinen, eds. *Propheten in Mari, Assyrien und Israel*. Forschungen zur Religion und Literatur des Alten und Neuen Testaments 201. Göttingen: Vandenhoeck & Ruprecht, 2003.

Kratz, Reinhard G. *Prophetenstudien: Kleine Schriften II*. Forschungen zum Alten Testament 74. Tübingen: Mohr Siebeck, 2011.

Nissinen, Martti. "Die Relevanz der neuassyrischen Prophetie für die alttestamentliche Forschung." Pp. 217–58 in *Mesopotamica—Ugaritica—Biblica: Festschrift für Kurt Bergerhof zur Vollendung seines 70. Lebensjahres am 7. Mai 1992*. Edited by Manfried Dietrich and Oswald Loretz. Alter Orient und Altes Testament 232. Kevelaer: Butzon & Bercker / Neukirchen-Vluyn: Neukirchener Verlag, 1993.

_____. "Falsche Prophetie in neuassyrischer und deuteronomistischer Darstellung." Pp. 172–195 in *Das Deuteronomium und seine Querbeziehungen*. Edited by Timo Veijola. Schriften der Finnischen Exegetischen Gesellschaft 62. Göttingen: Vandenhoeck & Ruprecht/Helsinki: Finnische Exegetische Gesellschaft, 1996.

_____. *References to Prophecy in Neo-Assyrian Sources*. State Archives of Assyria Studies 7. Helsinki: Neo-Assyrian Text Corpus Project, 1998.

_____. "Spoken, Written, Quoted, and Invented: Orality and Writtenness in Ancient Near Eastern Prophecy." Pp. 235–71 in *Writings and Speech in Israelite and Ancient Near Eastern Prophecy*. Edited by Michael H. Floyd and Ehud Ben Zvi. Society of Biblical Literature Symposium Series 10, Atlanta: Society of Biblical Literature, 2000.

_____. "What Is Prophecy? An Ancient Near Eastern Perspective." Pp. 17–37 in *Inspired Speech: Prophecy in the Ancient Near East; essays in Honor of Herbert B. Huffmon*. Edited by John Kaltner and Louis Stulman. Journal for the Study of the Old Testament Supplement 378. New York/London: T. & T. Clark, 2004.

_____. "The Dubious Image of Prophecy." Pp. 26–41 in *Prophets, Prophecy, and Prophetic Texts in Second Temple Judaism*. Edited by Michael H. Floyd and Robert D. Haak. Library of Hebrew Bible/Old Testament Studies 427. London: T. & T. Clark, 2006.

_____. "Das Problem der Prophetenschüler." Pp. 337–53 in *Houses Full of All Good Things: Essays in Memory of Timo Veijola. Edited by Martti Nissinen and Juha Pakkala*. Publications of the Finnish Exegetical Society 95. Göttingen: Vandenhoeck & Ruprecht, 2008.

_____. "The Historical Dilemma of Biblical Prophetic Studies." Pp. 103–20 in *Prophecy in the Book of Jeremiah*. Edited by Hans M. Barstad and

Reinhard G. Kratz. Beiheifte zur Zeitschrift für die Alttestamentliche Wissenschaft 388. Berlin: de Gruyter, 2009.

_____ . "Biblical Prophecy from a Near Eastern Perspective: The Cases of Kingship and Divine Possession." Pp. 441–68 in *Congress Volume Ljubljana 2007.* Edited by André Lemaire. Supplements to Vetus Testamentum 133. Leiden: Brill, 2010.

Nissinen, Martti, ed. *Prophecy in Its Ancient Near Eastern Context: Mesopotamian, Biblical, and Arabian Perspectives.* Society of Biblical Literature Symposium Series 13. Atlanta: Society of Biblical Literature, 2000.

Nissinen, Martti, with contributions by Choon L. Seow and Robert K. Ritner. *Prophets and Prophecy in the Ancient Near East.* Edited by Peter Machinist. Writings from the Ancient World 12. Atlanta: Society of Biblical Literature, 2003.

Scherer, Andreas. "Vom Sinn prophetischer Gerichtsverkündigung bei Amos und Hosea." *Biblica* 86 (2005): 1–19.

Stökl, Jonathan. *Prophecy in the Ancient Near East: A Philological and Sociological Comparison.* Culture and History of the Ancient Near East 56. Leiden: Brill, 2012.

Weippert, Manfred. "Prophetie im Alten Orient." Columns 196–200 in vol. 3 of *Neues Bibel Lexikon.* Edited by Manfred Görg. 3 vols. Düsseldorf/ Zürich: Benziger, 2001.

Weippert, Manfred. *Götterwort in Menschenmund: Studien zur Prophetie in Assyrien, Israel und Juda.* Forschungen zur Religion und Literatur des Alten und Neuen Testaments 252. Göttingen: Vandenhoeck & Ruprecht, 2014.

Greek Analogies

Hagedorn, Anselm C. "Looking at Foreigners in Biblical and Greek Prophecy." *Vetus Testamentum* 57 (2007): 432–48.

Huffmon, Herbert B. "The Oracular Process: Delphi and the Near East." *Vetus Testamentum* 57 (2007): 449–60.

Lange, Armin. "Literary Prophecy and Oracle Collection: A Comparison between Judah and Greece in Persian Times." Pp. 248–75 in *Prophets, Prophecy, and Prophetic Texts in Second Temple Judaism.* Edited by Michael H. Floyd and Robert D. Haak. Library of Hebrew Bible/Old Testament Studies 427. London: T. & T. Clark, 2006.

_____ . "Greek Seers and Israelite-Jewish Prophets." *Vetus Testamentum* 57 (2007): 461–82.

4. Isaiah, Jeremiah, Ezekiel

It is not unusual to find the literary-historical analysis of the prophetic books dismissed on the grounds that this analysis does not lead to definitive results and, consequently, is not the appropriate means for explaining the tradition. This objection is understandable but obviously a rather naïve opinion of the character of historical scholarship, which only very rarely arrives at definitive results. Indeed, the alternative often recommended—namely, to limit attention to the available (Masoretic) "final form"—leads, as far as I can see, to results that are no more definitive. On the contrary, they lead to very diverse, often strongly divergent, results, and that is without considering the different versions of the canonical text (in Qumran, the Septuagint, and the other versions). Incidentally, it is often overlooked that the results of literary-historical analysis are in no way as disparate as many proponents of the canonical final form or those who simply are not so well informed claim. In what follows, therefore, I offer some bibliographical references to the state of research, divided into the "Major" and "Minor" prophets. The choice of literature is naturally subjective and anything but comprehensive. I consider and recommend in the first place studies dealing with the literary genesis of the prophetic books that are likely to deepen the portrayal given in this book.

The *Book of Isaiah* has a comprehensive review of research from Höffken (2004). Also instructive is the introduction by Williamson in the collection of essays edited by him (Firth and Williamson 2009). Here it has been agreed since Duhm (4th ed. 1922; repr. 1968) that a distinction must be made between a first Isaiah (chaps. 1–39) and a second and third Isaiah (chaps. 40–55 and 56–66). Only the first of these (First Isaiah or Proto-Isaiah) has its roots in the preexilic or, more precisely, the Assyrian period. The second and third (Deutero-Isaiah and Trito-Isaiah) stem from the late Babylonian, Persian, and Hellenistic times.

There is, however, especially with Deutero-Isaiah, a debate about whether the parts originated independently of one another and were only later subsequently combined (Steck 1985; Kratz 1991) or whether Deutero-Isaiah was always a continuation of First Isaiah (Williamson 1994). This discussion also leads to Trito-Isaiah and its relationship to Deutero-Isaiah and First Isaiah. Some continue to envisage a single prophet (Elliger 1928 and 1933; Koenen 1990) or author (Stromberg 2011), others a scribal school (Lau 1994), while others find diverse phases and layers of redaction and actualization or *Fortschreibung* (Steck 1991).

In this discussion, the question concerns not least how the different literary connections that exist between the individual parts of the book, as well as between Isaiah and the other prophetic books, are to be explained. Whether the inter- and intratextual links have a genetic relevance is here as elsewhere highly controversial (Willey 1997; Sommer 1998; Nurmela 2006; also Sweeney 2005). It is a question of fundamental importance. Therefore, it requires a more detailed discussion. To me, the literary scope of the textual links would appear to be a possible criterion for making a decision. Thus, quotations in the same literary context (i.e., intratextual connections), so far as they are meaningful and not merely a literary convention or a fixed expression, are quite relevant for the genesis of the book.

This is especially true of the self-referentiality of Deutero- and Trito-Isaiah, no matter whether one judges them to be one or two separate literary corpora. Given the close and direct literary connection and the compositional context within the Book of Isaiah, an artificial division of Deutero-Isaiah and Trito-Isaiah into two separate texts is meaningless. In both cases, each new literary layer contributes something to the whole. Apart from some individual additions that have only a limited horizon, at every level the respective "final form" and composition of the entire book must be viewed and interpreted in light of the literary expansions.

It is more difficult to assess the textual connections that exist between Deutero- and Trito-Isaiah, on the one hand, and First Isaiah on the other. It is certainly the case that these connections resonate within the same literary context of the Book of Isaiah and thus, in principle, have a priority over connections to Jeremiah, Ezekiel, or other biblical writings. On the other hand, the connections in First Isaiah are not always as easy to identify as those within and between Deutero- and Trito-Isaiah. In addition, they emerge in both cases in relatively late layers and do not appear to have been influential from the beginning. The criterion of literary scope must, therefore, be correlated with the relative chronology of the literary layers.

The question is most acute in relation to the base text (*Grundschrift*) of Deutero-Isaiah in Isa 40–48 and its first expansion in Isa 49–55 (see below). Here, we need to examine how far the intertextual connections permit an independent origin of Deutero-Isaiah or suggest an attachment to First Isaiah or even Jeremiah (Kratz 2011: 198–232). Since the connections to First Isaiah emerge in later literary layers of Deutero-Isaiah and, even more so, in Trito-Isaiah, it is certain that we are dealing with genetically relevant intratextual allusions within the Book of Isaiah. This assumption, in turn, is confirmed by the late "Deutero-Isaianic" material in First Isaiah (e.g., Isa 35). Where and when exactly the genetically relevant intratextual connections with First Isaiah begin to emerge is a matter that future research will have to uncover.

We will now turn to the individual sections of the Book of Isaiah. Since Duhm's commentary in 1882, a certain consensus has been reached that for First Isaiah the core of the literary tradition is to be found in Isa 6–8 and 28–31. There is also widespread agreement about the literary layers of the book, especially with regard to the later sections, but even with regard to the crucial chapters for the book's origins: Isa 5–10 and 28–31. The shift from an old prophet of salvation for Judah (Isa 7:4, 7–9; 8:1–4) to the biblical book's prophet of doom can be perceived in the Isaiah memoir, Isa 6–8 (Steck 1982: 149–203; Becker 1997; Kratz 2011: 49–70; differently, Williamson 2013). Scholars have, however, not yet agreed on how the individual literary layers are to be dated and whether the oldest core comes from the historical prophet and his pupils (Barth 1977; Barthel 1997; Kreuch 2011; Müller 2012) or from an anonymous scribal tradition (Vermeylen 1977, 1978; Becker 1997; de Jong 2007, 2011; see also Kratz 2011: 49–70, 160–97; in English, Kratz 2006, 2010, 2012). A distinct problem, still unsolved, is the presentation of Isaiah as a prophet of salvation in the narratives about the siege and deliverance of Jerusalem in 701 B.C.E. in Isaiah 36–39 par. 2 Kgs 18–20 and how this portrayal fits with the prophet of doom in First Isaiah (see Kratz 2015). For further details, see Becker 1999 and Höffken 2004; for further discussion, Schmid 2014.

For Deutero-Isaiah there is an emerging consensus that a distinction can be made between a core discernible in Isa 40–48 (Jacob-Israel), a comprehensive literary expansion (*Fortschreibung*) in Isa 49–55 (Zion), and additions in Isa 40–48 (Kiesow 1979; Kratz 1991; Steck 1992; van Oorschot 1993; Zapf 2001). Naturally, there are also other voices who hold, as earlier scholars did, to the unity of the prophet or the theological concept of Deutero-Isaiah (Hermisson 1998: 132–57; Albani 2000; Ehring 2007), or to the literary unity of the book of Deutero-Isaiah (Watts 1985, 1987; Berges 1998; Baltzer 2001). These voices are also some distance from a consensus. For further details, see Hermisson 1986 and 2000 as well as Höffken 2004.

It has already been shown several times that Trito-Isaiah developed from Isa 60–62 and is a scribal interpretation of Deutero-Isaiah and in parts an interpretation of the entire Book of Isaiah. Yet, even here no agreement can be reached on the question of whether we are dealing with the oracles of a prophet (Koenen 1990) or with learned scribal prophecy outside (Lau 1994) or within (Steck 1991; also Stromberg 2011) the literary context of the Book of Isaiah. Moreover, Trito-Isaiah has repeatedly generated interest as a source for postexilic religious and social history (Hanson 1975, 2nd ed. 1979; Achtemeier 1982; Schramm 1995; Ruszkowski 2000). To what extent the text gives information about the actual circumstances cannot be said with any certainty. It depends upon the circles in which the tradition originated and for whom it was intended. The common conclusion about the historical circumstances based on the content of the tradition is rather limited. For more details, see Höffken 2004 and Kratz 2011: 233–42.

Research on the *Book of Jeremiah* has been most thoroughly elaborated by Schmid (1996). The most important pioneers in redaction-critical
analysis were Mowinckel (1914) and Thiel (1973; 1981). Several scholars
have suggested that the origins of the literary development of the book are
to be found in Jeremiah's laments about the "enemy from the north" in
Jer 4–6 (Pohlmann 1978; 1989; Levin 1985; Biddle 1990; Schmid 1996).
Further differentiation comes quite naturally: indictments were developed
from the laments, which identified God as the originator of the judgment
and sought for the reasons in the social, cultic, and other offenses of the
people. Moreover, inspired perhaps by the very "personal" character of
the first-person laments, the figure of the prophet as mediator of the divine word moves into the center of attention. Various passages testify to
this development: the numerous sign-acts performed by the prophet that
depict God's judgment and are followed by long theological admonitions,
the narratives of his sufferings, and the so-called confessions of Jeremiah
(see Bezzel 2007). The scholarly discussion is not so much about the differentiation of the material but rather the question of how it is to be dated,
what goes back to the prophet, and where the rest comes from. Of particular interest is the origin of the predictions of salvation in the Book of
Jeremiah (Levin 1985; Schmid 1996).

Research on the *Book of Ezekiel* has been described in detail by Pohlmann (2006; 2008). The work of Hölscher (1924) and Zimmerli (1979)
was seminal. Ezekiel's striking dependence on previous prophetic tradition
has often been noticed (Wedel 1995) and was most recently investigated in
the work of Klein (2008) as an example of "inner-biblical interpretation."
Klein especially explains the origin of the prophecies of salvation. Moreover, she has found a new starting point for the difficult question about
the origins of the book. Klein assumes the original beginning of the book
was in Ezek 1:2–3a; 3:10–11, 15, 22–24 and its original end was in Ezek
43:2–5 (Klein 2008: 388–406). This is different from the position ven-
tured by Pohlmann (1992; 1996; 2001) and Rudnig (2000; 2001; for the
discussion and further literature, see Hiebel 2015). Klein's analysis means
that the oldest version of the book already addressed the Babylonian exiles
and presupposed the Book of Jeremiah, including the promises of salvation in Deutero-Isaiah and Jeremiah that are related to the Golah. From
its inception, Ezekiel balanced doom and salvation on the scales: doom for
the city and the land, salvation for the exiles. From this combination, there
emerged—in parallel to the developments in the books of Jeremiah and
Isaiah (Deutero- and Trito-Isaiah)—the long speeches against all Israel,
the promise of salvation for Israel and for the worldwide Diaspora. Last,
but not least, the vision of the new Jerusalem was developed with a cor-

respondence between the departure and arrival of the glory of YHWH in Ezek 8–11 and 40–48, a development that determined the architecture and theological color of the existing book (see Krüger 1989; Schöpflin 2002; Hiebel 2015).

Isaiah

Achtemeier, Elizabeth. *The Community and Message of Isaiah 56–66*. Minneapolis: Augsburg, 1982.

Albani, Matthias. *Der eine Gott und die himmlischen Heerscharen: Zur Begründung des Monotheismus bei Deuterojesaja im Horizont der Astralisierung des Gottesverständnisses im Alten Orient*. Arbeiten zur Bibel und ihrer Geschichte 1. Leipzig: Evangelische Verlagsanstalt, 2000.

Baltzer, Klaus. *Deutero-Isaiah: A Commentary on Isaiah 40–55*. Hermeneia. Trans. Margaret Kohl. Minneapolis: Fortress, 2001. (Trans. of "Deutero-Jesaja." Vol. 10/2 of *Kommentar zum Alten Testament*. Gütersloh: Gütersloher Verlagshaus, 1999.)

Barth, Hermann. *Die Jesaja-Worte in der Josiazeit: Israel und Assur als Thema einer produktiven Neuinterpretation der Jesajaüberlieferung*. Wissenschaftliche Monographien zum Alten und Neuen Testament 48. Neukirchen-Vluyn: Neukirchener Verlag, 1977.

Barthel, Jörg. *Prophetenwort und Geschichte*. Forschungen zum Alten Testament 19. Tübingen: Mohr Siebeck, 1997.

Becker, Uwe. *Jesaja—von der Botschaft zum Buch*. Forschungen zur Religion und Literatur des Alten und Neuen Testaments 178. Göttingen: Vandenhoeck & Ruprecht, 1997.

_____. "Jesajaforschung (Jes 1–39)." *Theologische Rundschau* 64 (1999): 1–37, 117–52.

Berges, Ulrich. *Das Buch Jesaja: Komposition und Endgestalt*. Freiburg (Breisgau): Herder, 1998.

Duhm, Bernhard. *Das Buch Jesaja übersetzt und erklärt*. Handbuch zum Alten Testament III/1. Göttingen: Vandenhoeck & Ruprecht, 1822. 4th ed. = Göttingen: Vandenhoeck & Ruprecht, 1922; 5th ed. = 1968.

Ehring, Christina. *Die Rückkehr JHWHs: Traditions- und religionsgeschichtliche Untersuchungen zu Jesaja 40,1–11, Jesaja 52,7–10 und verwandten Texten*. Wissenschaftliche Monographien zum Alten und Neuen Testament 116. Neukirchen-Vluyn: Neukirchener Verlag, 2007.

Elliger, Karl. *Die Einheit Tritojesaja (Jesaja 56–66)*. Beiträge zur Wissenschaft vom Alten und Neuen Testament 45. Stuttgart: Kohlhammer, 1928.

_____. *Deuterojesaja in seinem Verhältnis zu Tritojesaja*. Beiträge zur Wissenschaft vom Alten und Neuen Testament 63. Stuttgart: Kohlhammer, 1933.

Firth, David G., and Hugh G. M. Williamson, eds. *Interpreting Isaiah: Issues and Approaches*. Nottingham: Apollos/Downers Grove, Ill.: IVP Academic, 2009.

Hanson, Paul D. *The Dawn of Apocalyptic: The Historical and Sociological Roots of Jewish Apocalyptic Eschatology.* Philadelphia: Fortress, 1975. 2nd ed. Philadelphia: Fortress, 1979.

Hermisson, Hans-Jürgen. "Deuterojesaja-Probleme: Ein kritischer Literaturbericht." *Verkündigung und Forschung* 31 (1986): 53–84.

_____. "Einheit und Komplexität Deuterojesajas: Probleme der Redaktionsgeschichte von 40–55." Pp. 132–57 in *Studien zu Prophetie und Weisheit: gesammelte Aufsätze.* Edited by Jörg Barthel. Forschungen zum Alten Testament 23. Tübingen: Mohr Siebeck, 1998.

_____. "Neue Literatur zu Deuterojesaja." *Theologische Rundschau* 65 (2000): 237–84, 379–430.

Höffken, Peter. *Jesaja: Der Stand der theologischen Diskussion.* Darmstadt: Wissenschaftliche Buchgesellschaft, 2004.

Jong, Matthijs J. de. *Isaiah among the Ancient Near Eastern Prophets: A Comparative Study of the Isaiah Tradition and the Neo-Assyrian Prophecies.* Supplements to Vetus Testamentum 117. Leiden: Brill, 2007.

_____. "Biblical Prophecy—A Scribal Enterprise: The Old Testament Prophecy of Unconditional Judgment considered as a Literary Phenomenon." *Vetus Testamentum* 61 (2011): 39–70.

Kiesow, Klaus. *Exodustexte im Jesajabuch: Literarkritische und motivgeschichtliche Analysen.* Orbis Biblicus et Orientalis 24. Freiburg, Switzerland: Éditions Universitaires/Göttingen: Vandenhoeck & Ruprecht, 1979.

Koenen, Klaus. *Ethik und Eschatologie im Tritojesajabuch: Eine literarkritische und redaktionsgeschichtliche Studie.* Wissenschaftliche Monographien zum Alten und Neuen Testament 62. Neukirchen-Vluyn: Neukirchener Verlag, 1990.

Kratz, Reinhard G. *Kyros im Deuterojesaja-Buch: Redaktionsgeschichtliche Untersuchungen zu Entstehung und Theologie von Jes 40–55.* Forschungen zum Alten Testament 1. Tübingen: J.C.B. Mohr (Paul Siebeck), 1991.

_____. "Israel in the Book of Isaiah." *Journal for the Study of the Old Testament* 31 (2006): 103–28.

_____. "Rewriting Isaiah: The Case of Isaiah 28–31." Pp. 245–66 in *Prophecy and the Prophets in Ancient Israel.* Edited by John Day. Library of Hebrew Bible/Old Testament Studies 531. London: T. & T. Clark, 2010.

_____. *Prophetenstudien: Kleine Schriften II.* Forschungen zum Alten Testament 74. Tübingen: Mohr Siebeck, 2011.

_____. "The Two Houses of Israel." Pp. 167–79 in *Let Us Go Up to Zion: Essays in Honour of H. G. M. Williamson on the Occasion of His Sixty-Fifth Birthday.* Edited by Iain Provan and Mark S. Boda. Supplements to Vetus Testamentum 153. Leiden: Brill, 2012.

_____. "Isaiah and the Siege of Jerusalem," Pp. 143–60 in *New Perspectives on Old Testament Prophecy and History: Essays in Honour of Hans M. Barstad.* Edited by Rannfrid Thelle, Terje Stordalen, and Mervyn R. J. Richardson. Supplements to Vetus Testamentum 168. Leiden: Brill, 2015.

Kreuch, Jan. *Unheil und Heil bei Jesaja: Studien zur Entstehung des Assur-Zyklus Jesaja 28–31.* Wissenschaftliche Monographien zum Alten und Neuen Testament 130. Neukirchen: Neukirchener Verlag, 2011.

Lau, Wolfgang. *Schriftgelehrte Prophetie in Jes 56–66: Eine Untersuchung zu den literarischen Bezügen in den letzten elf Kapiteln des Jesajabuches*. Beihefte zur Zeitschrift für Alttestamentliche Wissenschaft 225. Berlin: de Gruyter, 1994.

Müller, Reinhard. *Ausgebliebene Einsicht: Jesajas "Verstockungsauftrag" (Jes 6, 9–11) und die judäische Politik am Ende des 8. Jahrhunderts*. Biblisch-Theologische Studien 124. Neukirchen: Neukirchener Verlag, 2012.

Nurmela, Risto. *The Mouth of the Lord Has Spoken: Inner-Biblical Allusions in Second and Third Isaiah*. Studies in Judaism. Lanham, MD/Oxford: University Press of America, 2006.

Oorschot, Jürgen van. *Von Babel zum Zion: Eine literarkritische und redaktionsgeschichtliche Untersuchung*. Beihefte zur Zeitschrift für die Alttestamentliche Wissenschaft 206. Berlin: de Gruyter, 1993.

Ruszkowski, Leszek. *Volk und Gemeinde im Wandel: Eine Untersuchung zu Jesaja 56–66*. Forschungen zur Religion und Literatur des Alten und Neuen Testaments 191. Göttingen, Vandenhoeck & Ruprecht, 2000.

Schmid, Konrad. "Die Anfänge des Jesajabuchs." Pp. 426–53 in *Congress Volume Munich 2013*. Edited by Christl M. Meier. Supplements to Vetus Testamentum 163. Leiden: Brill, 2014.

Schramm, Brooks. *The Opponents of Third Isaiah: Reconstructing the Cultic History of the Restoration*. Journal for the Study of the Old Testament Supplement 193. Sheffield: Sheffield Academic Press, 1995.

Sommer, Benjamin D. *A Prophet Reads Scripture: Allusion in Isaiah 40–66*. Stanford, CA: Stanford University Press, 1998.

Steck, Odil Hannes. *Bereitete Heimkehr: Jesaja 35 als redaktionelle Brücke zwischen dem Ersten und dem Zweiten Jesaja*. Stuttgarter Bibelstudien 121. Stuttgart: Katholisches Bibelwerk, 1985.

——————. *Studien zu Tritojesaja*. Beihefte zur Zeitschrift für die Alttestamentliche Wissenschaft 203. Berlin: de Gruyter, 1991.

——————. *Gottesknecht und Zion: Gesammelte Aufsätze zu Deuterojesaja*. Forschungen zum Alten Testament 4. Tübingen: Mohr, 1992.

Stromberg, Jacob. *Isaiah after Exile: The Author of Third Isaiah as Reader and Redactor of the Book*. Oxford Theological Monographs. Oxford: Oxford University Press, 2011.

Sweeney, Marvin. A. *Form and Intertextuality in Prophetic and Apocalyptic Literature*. Forschungen zum Alten Testament 45. Tübingen: Mohr Siebeck, 2005.

Vermeylen, Jacques. *Du prophète Isaïe à l'apocalyptique: Isaïe, IXXXV, miroir d'un demi-millénaire d'expérience religieuse es Israël*. Études bibliques. 2 vols. Paris: Gabalda, 1977 (vol. 1); 1978 (vol. 2).

Watts, John D. W. *Isaiah 1–33*. Word Biblical Commentary 24. Waco, TX/Dallas: Word / Nashville: Thomas Nelson, 1985.

——————. *Isaiah 34–66*. Word Biblical Commentary 25. Waco, TX/Dallas: Word / Nashville: Thomas Nelson, 1987.

Wedel, Ute. *Jesaja und Jeremia: Worte, Motive und Einsichten Jesajas in der Verkündigung Jeremias*. Biblisch-Theologische Studien 25. Neukirchen-Vluyn: Neukirchener Verlag, 1995.

Willey, Patricia. T. *Remember the Former Things: The Recollection of Previous Texts in Second Isaiah.* Society of Biblical Literature Dissertation Series 161. Atlanta: Scholars Press, 1997.

Williamson, Hugh G. M. *The Book Called Isaiah: Deutero-Isaiah's Role in Composition and Redaction.* Oxford: Clarendon, 1994.

_____. "Isaiah: Prophet of Weal or Woe?" Pp. 273–300 in *"Thus Speaks Ishtar of Arbela": Prophecy in Israel, Assyria, and Egypt in the Neo-Assyrian Period.* Edited by Robert P. Gordon and Hans M. Barstad. Winona Lake, IN: Eisenbrauns, 2013.

Zapff, Burkhard M. *Jesaja 40–55.* Neue Echter Bibel 36. Würzburg: Echter-Verlag, 2001.

Jeremiah

Bezzel, Hannes. *Die Konfessionen Jeremias: Eine redaktionsgeschichtliche Studie.* Beihefte zur Zeitschrift für die Alttestamentliche Wissenschaft 378. Berlin: de Gruyter, 2007.

Biddle, Mark E. A *Redaction History of Jeremiah 2:1–4:2.* Abhandlungen zur Theologie des Alten und Neuen Testaments 77. Zürich: Theologischer Verlag, 1990.

Duhm, Bernhard. *Das Buch Jeremia erklärt.* Kurzer Hand-Commentar zum Alten Testament XI. Tübingen and Leipzig: J.C.B. Mohr (Paul Siebeck) 1901.

Levin, Cristoph. *Die Verheißung des neuen Bundes: in ihrem theologiegeschichtlichen Zusammenhang ausgelegt.* Forschungen zur Religion und Literatur des Alten und Neuen Testaments 137. Göttingen: Vandenhoeck & Ruprecht, 1985.

Mowinckel, Sigmund. *Zur Komposition des Buches Jeremia.* Videnskapsselskapets Skrifter 2. Kristianan: Dybwad, 1914.

Pohlmann, Karl-Friedrich. *Studien zum Jeremiabuch: Ein Beitrag zur Frage nach der Entstehung des Jeremiabuches.* Forschungen zur Religion und Literatur des Alten und Neuen Testaments 118. Göttingen: Vandenhoeck & Ruprecht, 1978.

_____. *Die Ferne Gottes—Studien zum Jeremiabuch: Beiträge zu den "Konfessionen" im Jeremiabuch und ein Versuch zur Frage nach den Anfängen der Jeremiatradition.* Beihefte zur Zeitschrift für Alttestamentliche Wissenschaft 179. Berlin: de Gruyter, 1989.

Schmid, Konrad. *Buchgestalten des Jeremiabuches: Untersuchungen zur Redaktionsgeschichte von Jer 30–33 im Kontext des Buches.* Wissenschaftliche Monographien zum Alten und Neuen Testament 72. Neukirchen-Vluyn: Neukirchener Verlag, 1996.

Thiel, Winfried. *Die deuteronomistische Redaktion von Jeremia 1–25.* Wissenschaftliche Monographien zum Alten und Neuen Testament 41. Neukirchen-Vluyn: Neukirchener Verlag, 1973.

_____. *Die deuteronomistische Redaktion von Jeremia 26–45: Mit einer Gesamtteilung der deuteronomistischen Redaktion des Buches Jeremia.* Wissenschaftliche Monographien zum Alten und Neuen Testament 52. Neukirchen-Vluyn: Neukirchener Verlag 1981.

Ezekiel

Hiebel, Janina Maria. *Ezekiel's Vision Accounts as Interrelated Narratives: A Redaction-Critical and Theological Study*. Beihefte zur Zeitschrift für die Alttestamentliche Wissenschaft 475. Berlin: de Gruyter, 2015.

Hölscher, Gustav. *Hesekiel: Der Dichter und das Buch; eine literarkritische Untersuchung*. Beihefte zur Zeitschrift für die Alttestamentliche Wissenschaft 39. Giessen: Töpelmann, 1924.

Klein, Anja. *Schriftauslegung im Ezechielbuch: Redaktionsgeschichtliche Untersuchungen zu Ez 34–39*. Beihefte zur Zeitschrift für die Alttestamentliche Wissenschaft 391. Berlin: de Gruyter, 2008.

Krüger, Thomas. *Geschichtskonzepte im Ezechielbuch*. Beihefte zur Zeitschrift für die Alttestamentliche Wissenschaft 180. Berlin: de Gruyter, 1989.

Pohlmann, Karl-Friedrich. *Ezechielstudien: Zur Redaktionsgeschichte des Buches und zur Frage nach den ältesten Texten*. Beihefte zur Zeitschrift für Alttestamentliche Wissenschaft 202. Berlin: de Gruyter, 1992.

—————. *Das Buch des Propheten Hesekiel (Ezechiel) Kapitel 1–19*. Das Alte Testament Deutsch 22/1. Göttingen: Vandenhoeck & Ruprecht, 1996.

—————. *Der Prophet Hesekiel/Ezechiel Kapitel 20–48*. Das Altes Testament Deutsch 22/2. Göttingen: Vandenhoeck & Ruprecht, 2001.

—————. "Forschung am Ezechielbuch 1969–2004 (I–III)." *Theologische Rundschau* 71. (2006): 60–90, 164–91, 265–309.

—————. *Ezechiel: Der Stand der Theologischen Diskussion*. Darmstadt: Wissenschaftliche Buchgesellschaft, 2008.

Rudnig, Thilo A. *Heilig und Profan: Redaktionskritische Studien zu Ez 40–48*. Beihefte zur Zeitschrift für Alttestamentliche Wissenschaft 287. Berlin: de Gruyter, 2000.

—————. "Ezechiel 40–48." Pp. 527–631 in *Der Prophet Hesekiel/Ezechiel Kapitel 20–48 by Karl-Friedrich Pohlmann*. Das Altes Testament Deutsch 22/2. Göttingen: Vandenhoeck & Ruprecht, 2001.

Schöpflin, Karin. *Theologie als Biographie im Ezechielbuch: Ein Beitrag zur Konzeption alttestamentlicher Prophetie*. Forschungen zum Alten Testament 36. Tübingen: Mohr Siebeck, 2002.

Zimmerli, Walther. *Ezekiel*. Hermeneia. 2 vols. Philadelphia: Fortress, 1979, 1983.

5. The Twelve Prophets and Daniel

In the Book of the Twelve, four of the twelve books (Hosea, Amos, Micah, and Zephaniah) have historical superscriptions dating them according to the reigns of Israelite and Judahite kings. This and the parallels of these superscriptions to those in the two "Major" prophets Isaiah and Jeremiah suggest that a chronological order is intended. Thus, if we follow the order of the Masoretic canon, Hosea-Nahum (corresponding to Isaiah) represent the Assyrian period, then Habakkuk to Zephaniah (corresponding to Jeremiah) stand for the Babylonian period, and Haggai to

Malachi (corresponding to Ezekiel) reflect the time of the exile until the rebuilding of the temple. To this we may add a multiplicity of textual and thematic connections between the individual books of the Twelve, which in the manuscript tradition of Qumran are also transmitted as a unity (Lange 2009). On this basis, the question of the redactional composition of the Twelve has dominated the agenda of current research (Nogalski and Sweeney 2000; Redditt and Schart 2003; Wöhrle 2006: 1–27; 2008: 2–22; Schart 2008; Albertz et al. 2013).

How the composition of the Twelve originated and what it means are highly controversial questions. One group of scholars is convinced that it is possible to discover the sense of the present (Masoretic) collection, in which every detail has a purpose in the whole (e.g., House 1990). Others attempt to reconstruct the growth of the collection and divide the various indicators of redactional connection to different literary layers—starting from the historical prophets and ending up with the collection of the Twelve Prophets (Bosshard-Nepustil 1987; 1997; Steck 1991; Nogalski 1993a; 1993b; Jones 1995; Schart 1998; 2008; Wöhrle 2006; 2008). Occasionally, the individual motifs or thematic strands, such as the "day of Yʜᴡʜ," are singled out in order to explain the unity of the Twelve or to exemplify the development of the collection (Redditt and Schart 2003; on the "day of Yʜᴡʜ," Rendtorff 2001; Nogalski 2003; Barton 2004; Beck 2005; Roth 2005; Schwesig 2006). Others find both directions to be futile and are concerned only to examine the individual books on their own (Ben Zvi 1996; Perlitt 2004). Both the individual books as well as the collection (in MT and LXX) are examined by synchronic literary analysis with reference to diachronic insights (Sweeney 2000 vol. 1: xxxix).

There are reasons to suggest that the books of Hosea, Amos, Micah, and Zephaniah once represented a small collection to which the books of Joel, Obadiah, Jonah, Nahum, and Habakkuk were added secondarily. This hypothesis is first of all based on the similar superscriptions but also on numerous thematic and literary connections between the four books (Jeremias 1996; Schart 1998; the hypothesis has been harshly criticized, however, by Levin 2011). The partial collection of four books can be viewed as the nucleus of the Book of the Twelve. It is difficult to say when the four books were formed into a collection or what the collection was meant to express. However, the superscriptions that hold together the so-called "Book of the Four" are evidently late and presuppose the basic text (*Grundschrift*) of the Deuteronomistic History in Samuel and Kings. We cannot place it before the exile. Anything else depends upon the analysis of the books and the question of whether it is possible to discern one or more layers that had the goal of compiling the collection and thus may provide some information about its intention. In this respect, scholarship has admittedly not gotten beyond the starting line (Wöhrle 2006; Schart 2008).

Furthermore, it is quite probable that the books of Haggai and Zechariah (1–8) once formed a small unit of their own. They are held together by a common system of dating and various other features (Hallaschka 2009; Lux 2009: 3–26). The close textual links between the Books of Malachi and Haggai–Zechariah presumably suggest that Malachi was combined with them before their attachment to the Book of the Twelve. It may be that Malachi originated as an expansion (*Fortschreibung*) to this pair of books (Bosshard and Kratz 1990). A unit of two books is also worth pondering in the case of the books of Nahum and Habakkuk in light of their superscriptions and other commonalities (Kessler 2002).

In sum, the core of the Book of the Twelve was composed of at least two formerly independent smaller collections: the group of four prophets Hosea-Amos-Micah-Zephaniah at the beginning and the three prophets Haggai-Zechariah-Malachi at the end of the whole collection. Both parts of the collection were combined via the pair of Nahum and Habakkuk and subsequently supplemented through Joel, Obadiah, and Jonah. Undoubtedly, the cohesion of the collection and the literary connections between the books grew over time. Nevertheless, it is not always easy to determine on which level the literary layers and connections occur: the level of the individual books (with coincidental catchword connections to other books), the level of the partial collections and their precursors, or the level of the whole collection—that is, the Book of the Twelve.

To this we may add the evidence from the manuscript tradition, in which the order of the prophets is not always identical. Variation exists in both the Hebrew and Greek manuscripts. At very least, the two collections Hosea–Amos–Micah and Haggai–Zechariah–Malachi, as well as the intervening set of Nahum–Habakkuk–Zephaniah, appear to be relatively constant. Yet despite intensive efforts and impressive hypotheses, not least most recently from Wöhrle (2006; 2008), it appears to me that no clear criteria have been found yet that permit us to assign the literary layers in individual books to steps in the evolution of individual books, partial collections, or the Twelve as a whole. This is especially true for the attempt to extend the redactional cohesion of the Book of the Twelve outward to the entire corpus—that is, the *corpus propheticum* (Steck 1991; 2000; 2001; Bosshard-Nepustil 1997; Gärtner 2006). There is still much to be done here; not least, it is necessary to gain a better understanding of how the individual books themselves developed.

As with the three "Major" Prophets, so with the Twelve "Minor" Prophets we can order the books—based on their contents—according to the *terminus a quo* of their literary-historical beginnings: Hosea, Amos, Micah, Nahum, and Jonah presuppose at the very least the Assyrian period (late eighth and seventh centuries B.C.E.). Habakkuk and Zephaniah as well as large parts of Micah presuppose the Babylonian period (late seventh and sixth centuries B.C.E.), while Haggai, Zechariah, and Malachi presuppose the Persian period (late sixth and fifth to fourth centuries B.C.E.). It is difficult if not impossible to situate Joel and Obadiah within a relative chronology, but they—like Jonah—belong in the late Persian or Hellenistic period. The scholarship on the individual books has been thoroughly discussed by Wöhrle (2006; 2008), so I will restrict myself to a few comments.

The oldest traces of the prophetic tradition in the Book of the Twelve are presumably to be found in the books of Amos and Hosea and perhaps also in Micah 1. They emerge at about the same time as the oldest parts of First Isaiah. Several studies have shown that the material collected under the names of Hosea and Amos consists of oracles of two or more prophets from the end of the eighth century B.C.E. These prophets comment upon the events of the so-called Syro-Ephraimite war (734–732 B.C.E.) and the downfall of the kingdom of Israel in 722 B.C.E. (Vielhauer 2007; Wöhrle 2006: 59–137; Kratz 2011a: 287–309, 310–43; for a dissenting voice, see Hadjiev 2009). While Isaiah promises in God's name to save and protect the kingdom of Judah from its enemies in the north, Israel and Aram (Isa 8:1–4), the oracles of the prophets Hosea and Amos testify more to the horror at the internal and external collapse and fear in anticipation of the threatened defeat. These are presented primarily from the perspective of the kingdom of Israel, in the form of laments, woes, and polemical accusations. Such expressions of horror are given from a Judean perspective in the core of Micah 1—that is, the "towns poem" in Micah 1:10–15. This poem may reflect the situation during Jerusalem's siege by Sennacherib around 701 B.C.E. (Wöhrle 2006: 138–97; Corzilius forthcoming).

The *Books of Hosea and Amos* follow the pattern found in Isaiah, where the *post eventum* collection and literary reworking of older oracles took place within a new theological perspective. The foreign policy catastrophe leading to the downfall of the kingdom of Israel and then to the threat against the kingdom of Judah was interpreted as the work of the God YHWH, who was not well-disposed toward the two kingdoms. Apart from the oral or literary precursors of the collection, which are difficult to determine, the literary reworking of the older oracles within the framework of a developing prophetic book is the starting point for the idea of absolute judgment (Kratz 2011a: 49–70, 71–98).

As is the case with the Book of Jeremiah, this process repeats itself, but this time with the fate of Judah in view. The siege of Jerusalem by Sennacherib in 701 B.C.E. and Nebuchadnezzar's destruction of the kingdom of Judah in 597–587 B.C.E. are taken up once more in the books of Micah, Nahum, and Zephaniah. The old prophetic tradition in Hosea, Amos, and Isaiah provides the inspiration and serves as a model. As was also the case in the earlier books, the younger ones also contain older prophetic oracles that arise from the religious practice of Judah. These emerged from the usual framework of political theology and first received a new interpretation and the distinctive stamp of biblical prophecy through their literary integration into the biblical prophetic tradition.

As has already been observed, *Micah* 1:10–15 preserves an old "towns poem." The poem could stem from the situation of 701 B.C.E. but just as well from the time immediately before 597 B.C.E. It forms the literary core of the lament over the downfall of Samaria and Jerusalem, which originated in Micah 1–3 in several stages and was continued in a process of various *Fortschreibungen* with prophecies of salvation as well as further threats of doom in the exilic and postexilic period (Wöhrle 2006: 138–97; Corzilius forthcoming). The shift from Neo-Assyrian to Babylonian sovereignty over Palestine around 612 B.C.E. is reflected in the older oracles against Nineveh in the *Book of Nahum*. These were then supplemented with accusations and judgments against Israel and Judah in the style of the biblical prophets, which were directed against the wicked in general in Nah 1 (Köckert 2003; Hagedorn 2011; Kratz 2011a: 99–145; differently, Wöhrle 2008: 23–171). The core of the Book of Zephaniah is the oracle concerning the "day of YHWH," which reflects the situation around 597–587 B.C.E. After the destruction of Jerusalem, it becomes the starting point for a broad literary development that can also be seen beyond the *Book of Zephaniah*. In the scribal tradition of the prophetic books, the "day of wrath," which until 587 B.C.E. still implied the possibility of placating the deity and escaping his wrath, becomes the day of the final great judgment over Judah and Jerusalem, the neighboring lands, and the entire earth. Only the pious in Israel and among the nations will survive (Hagedorn 2011; somewhat differently, Wöhrle 2006: 198–228).

It is difficult to say whether an older prophetic oracle is also to be found behind the *Book of Habakkuk* (see Pfeiffer 2005: 135–66; Wöhrle 2008: 291–323). Only the Chaldean or cavalry oracle in Hab 1:6–11 and, perhaps, the original woe sayings in Hab 2:6–17 are possible candidates.

Should 1:6–11 contain an older oracle that expresses the expectation of the Chaldean or other cavalry force coming up (somewhat comparable to the complaint against the "enemy from the north" in Jer 4–6), then at the very least v. 5 and—with the divine "I"—v. 6 would have been aligned to their context and connected with the first complaint in Hab 1:2–4. Otherwise, Habakkuk is comparable to the books of *Joel and Obadiah*, which likewise communicate little about their historical context. These books may also be based on one or other older oracle from the Babylonian period or later times concerning a drought in Joel 1, an enemy advance in Joel 2, and Edom in Obad 1–14 (Bergler 1988; Wöhrle 2006: 391–431; 2008: 192–218; Hagedorn 2011). However, parallel to the development in other books, the older oracles have been overwritten according to the themes of the later prophetic tradition: the sinners and the righteous, the judgment of the nations, and the day of YHWH.

Finally, in the *Books of Haggai and Zechariah*, we can again identify with some certainty an older core (Hallaschka 2009; Kratz 2013: 79–92; for the discussion, see Wöhrle 2006: 285–385; Lux 2009). In Haggai, we have two oracles about the rebuilding of the temple in Hag 1:1, 4, 8 as well as 1:15b; 2:1, 3, 9b. They are dated precisely and were presumably preserved in an archive in the temple. They may go back to a historical prophet at the time of the rebuilding. Both oracles form the core of a small prophetic writing, which makes the temple building a symbol of the change from blessing to curse, and in the course of the book's literary history this change is connected to all sorts of conditions (in common with Zech 1–8). In Zechariah, a set of visions in Zech 1–6 marks the beginning of the literary development, which has grown internally, before further exegetical additions and clarifications aligned the entire cycle of visions in Zech 1–8 more and more with Haggai. It has become a consensus in scholarship that Zech 9–14 are indebted to more recent *Fortschreibungen* that create numerous connections with the rest of the prophetic tradition, in particular with Trito-Isaiah (Steck 1991; Gärtner 2006; Wöhrle 2008: 67–138).

As something of an appendix, I offer here a brief overview of research on the *Book of Daniel*, which was attributed to the prophetic writings not only in the Septuagint and in modern translations but also already at Qumran. Scholarship has been superbly treated by Baumgartner (1939), Koch (1980), Collins (1993), and Newsom (2014). Up to a certain point, there is also the (incomplete) annotated bibliography of Thompson (1993).

Hölscher (1919) and Noth (1969) have been crucial for subsequent scholarly analysis. Hölscher introduced a hypothesis of supplementation (*Aufstockungshypothese*), proposing three major stages: (a) Dan 1–6,

(b) Dan 7, (c) Dan 8–12; in addition, Noth, established the differentiation of Daniel 7. Further differentiation on this basis is appropriate for Daniel 2 (Kratz 1991; 2013: 187–226; Segal 2009) as well as Dan 8–12 (Berner 2006; Kratz 2013: 227–24, English version 2001). Many scholars have been satisfied with a division into stories from the pre-Maccabean period (Dan 1–6) and visions from the Maccabean period (Dan 7–12), and have taken the texts as they are. In this way, however, many subtle details and fine distinctions must be ignored or flattened and remain without adequate explanation. In terms of tradition-history, the apocryphal sections of Daniel in the Septuagint (Koch 2000) and from Qumran (Collins 1996) are relevant. They already testify very early to a broad reception of Daniel, but it is possible that they also partly preserve an earlier version of the material from Dan 4 and Dan 6 (Kratz 1991; 2002; 2011b; Collins 1993; 1998). A considerably divergent version is offered by the old Greek translation of Dan 4–6 that is frequently neglected and has not yet been satisfactorily explained (Albertz 1988; Meadowcroft 1995; Helms 2014).

The short overview of the origins of the prophetic books in this and the preceding section naturally leaves many open questions: what do we know about the historical prophets and the older oracles? Where were the oracles kept and who transmitted them? Why were these and not others picked up and integrated into a prophetic book? Who were the authors of the prophetic books, and did there exist a personal, sociological, or thematic (theological) connection between the old oracles and their literary reworking and *Fortschreibung*? How are the relative and absolute chronologies to be related to one another? What role did the prophet and, above all, the prophetic book play in Israelite and Judean communities in the preexilic and in the postmonarchic period?

The treatment of these and other questions must be reserved for individual investigation. I hope that a starting point and directions for the solution of all these questions nevertheless should be to some extent clear in the description offered here. The transition from old oracles, presumably from the eponymus prophet, to the biblical literature is crucial and is always accompanied by a new theological orientation. The transition is from a theology of prophetic revelation, in which all complaint and criticism concerning corruption and external danger remains indebted to the dominant societal system of king and cult, to the theology of the word of God that intervenes in history and uses the political powers in order to bring the dominant system to collapse. Consequently, in the prophetic tradition of the Hebrew Bible, new theological norms are articulated for kingdom, cult, and all other societal institutions and powers. These norms are advanced by the literary growth of the biblical tradition, not only in the prophets but also far beyond (Kratz 2005; 2008). These theological norms, which the biblical tradition has molded, continue their influence into the postbiblical history of interpretation as well as in the religious practice of Judaism and Christianity.

The Twelve Prophets

Albertz, Rainer, James D. Nogalski, and Jakob Wöhrle, ed. *Perspectives on the Formation of the Book of the Twelve: Methodological Foundations—Redactional Processes—Historical Insights.* Beihefte zur *Zeitschrift für die Alttestamentliche Wissenschaft* 433. Berlin: de Gruyter, 2012.

Barton, John. "The Day of Yahweh in the Minor Prophets." Pp. 68–79 in *Biblical and Near Eastern Essays: Studies in Honour of Kevin J. Cathcart.* Edited by Carmel McCarthy and John F. Healey. Journal for the Study of the Old Testament Supplement Series 375. London: T. & T. Clark, 2004.

Beck, Martin. *Der "Tag YHWHS" im Dodekapropheton: Studien im Spannungsfeld von Traditions- und Redaktionsgeschichte.* Beihefte zur Zeitschrift für Alttestamentliche Wissenschaft 356. Berlin: de Gruyter, 2005.

Ben Zvi, Ehud. "Twelve Prophetic Books or 'The Twelve': A Few Preliminary Considerations." Pp. 125–56 in *Forming Prophetic Literature: Essays on Isaiah and the Twelve in Honour of John D. W. Watts.* Edited by James W. Watts and Paul R. House. Journal for the Study of the Old Testament Supplement Series 235. Sheffield: Sheffield Academic Press, 1996.

Bergler, Siegfried. *Joel als Schriftinterpret.* Beiträge zur Erforschung des Alten Testaments und des Antiken Judentums 16. Frankfurt am Main: Lang, 1988.

Bosshard(-Nepustil), Erich. "Beobachtungen zum Zwölfprophetenbuch." *Biblische Notizen* 40 (1987): 30–62.

_____ . *Rezeptionen von Jesaja 1–39 im Zwölfprophetenbuch: Untersuchungen zur literarischen Verbindung von Prophetenbüchern in babylonischer und persischer Zeit.* Orbis Biblicus et Orientalis 154. Freiburg, Switzerland: Universitäts Verlag/Göttingen: Vandenhoeck & Ruprecht, 1997.

_____ , and Reinhard G. Kratz. "Maleachi im Zwölfprophetenbuch." *Biblische Notizen* 52 (1990): 30–32.

Corzilius, Björn. *Michas Rätsel: Eine Untersuchung zur Kompositionsgeschichte des Michabuches.* Ph.D. Göttingen, 2014. Beihefte zur Zeitschrift der Alttestamentlichen Wissenschaft. Berlin: de Gruyter, forthcoming.

Gärtner, Judith. *Jesaja 66 und Sacharja 14 als Summe der Prophetie: Eine traditions- und redaktionsgeschichtliche Untersuchung zum Abschluss des Jesaja- und des Zwölfprophetenbuches.* Wissenschaftliche Monographien zum Alten und Neuen Testament 114. Neukirchen-Vluyn: Neukirchener Verlag, 2006.

Hadjiev, Tchavdar S. *The Composition and Redaction of the Book of Amos.* Beihefte zur Zeitschrift für die Alttestamentliche Wissenschaft 393. Berlin: de Gruyter, 2009.

Hagedorn, Anselm C. *Die Anderen im Spiegel: Israels Auseinandersetzungen mit den Völkern in den Büchern Nahum, Zefanja, Obadja und Joel.* Beihefte zur Zeitschrift für die Alttestamentliche Wissenschaft 414. Berlin: de Gruyter, 2011.

Hallaschka, Martin. *Haggai und Sacharja 1–8: Eine redaktionsgeschichtliche Untersuchung.* Beihefte zur Zeitschrift für die Alttestamentliche Wissenschaft 411. Berlin: de Gruyter, 2011.

Herrmann, Siegfried. *Die prophetischen Heilserwartungen im Alten Testament: Ursprung und Gestaltwandel.* Beiträge zur Wissenschaft vom Alten und Neuen Testament 85. Stuttgart: Kohlhammer, 1965.

House, Paul R. *The Unity of the Twelve.* Journal for the Study of the Old Testament Supplement series 97. Sheffield, England: Almond, 1990.

Jeremias, Jörg. "Die Anfänge des Dodekapropheton: Hosea und Amos." Pp. 231–43 in *Hosea und Amos: Studien zu den Anfängen des Dodekapropheton.* Forschungen zum Alten Testament 13. Tübingen: J.C.B. Mohr (Paul Siebeck), 1996.

Jones, Barry A. *The Formation of the Book of the Twelve: A Study in Text and Canon.* Society of Biblical Literature Dissertation Series 149. Atlanta: Scholars Press, 1995.

Kessler, Rainer. "Nahum-Habakuk als Zweiprophetenschrift: Eine Skizze." Pp. 149–58 in *"Wort JHWHs, das geschah . . ." (Hos 1,1): Studien zum Zwölfprophetenbuch.* Edited by Erich Zenger. Herders Biblische Studien 35. Freiburg im Breisgau: Herder, 2002.

Köckert, Matthias. "Nahum/Nahumbuch." Columns 28–31 in vol. 6 of *Religion in Geschichte und Gegenwart.* 8 vols. 4th ed. Tübingen: Mohr Siebeck, 2003.

Kratz, Reinhard G. *The Composition of the Narrative Books of the Old Testament.* Trans. John Bowden. London: T. & T. Clark, 2005. (Trans. of *Die Komposition der erzählenden Bücher des Alten Testaments: Grundwissen der Bibelkritik.* Göttingen: Vandenhoeck & Ruprecht, 2000.)

_____. "The Growth of the Old Testament." Pp. 459–88 in *The Oxford Handbook of Biblical Studies.* Edited by John W. Rogerson and Judith M. Lieu. Oxford: Oxford University Press, 2006. 2nd ed. Oxford: Oxford University Press, 2008.

_____. *Prophetenstudien: Kleine Schriften II.* Forschungen zum Alten Testament 74. Tübingen: Mohr Siebeck, 2011. (= 2011a)

_____. *Das Judentum im Zeitalter des Zweiten Tempels: Kleine Schriften I.* Forschungen zum Alten Testament 42. Tübingen: Mohr Siebeck 2004; 2nd ed. Tübingen: Mohr Siebeck, 2013.

Lange, Armin. *Handbuch der Textfunde vom Toten Meer.* Tübingen: Mohr Siebeck, 2009.

Levin, Christoph. "Das 'Vierprophetenbuch': Ein exegetischer Nachruf." *Zeitschrift für die Alttestamentliche Wissenschaft* 123 (2011): 221–35.

Lux, Rüdiger. *Prophetie und Zweiter Tempel: Studien zu Haggai und Sacharja.* Forschungen zum Alten Testament 65. Tübingen: Mohr Siebeck, 2009.

Nogalski, James D. *Literary Precursors to the Book of the Twelve*. Beihefte zur Zeitschrift für die Alttestamentliche Wissenschaft 217. Berlin: de Gruyter, 1993. (= 1993a)

_____ . *Redactional Processes in the Book of the Twelve*. Beihefte zur Zeitschrift für die Alttestamentliche Wissenschaft 218. Berlin: de Gruyter, 1993. (= 1993b)

_____ . "The Day(s) of Yhwh in the Book of the Twelve." Pp. 192–213 in *Thematic Threads in the Book of the Twelve*. Edited by Paul L. Reddit and Aaron Schart. Beihefte zur Zeitschrift für die Alttestamentliche Wissenschaft 325. Berlin: de Gruyter, 2003.

_____ , and Marvin A. Sweeney. *Reading and Hearing the Book of the Twelve*. Society of Biblical Literature Symposium Series 15. Atlanta: Society of Biblical Literature, 2000.

Perlitt, Lothar. *Die Propheten Nahum, Habakuk, Zephania*. Das Alte Testament Deutsch 25/1. Göttingen: Vandenhoeck & Ruprecht, 2004.

Pfeiffer, Henrik. *Jahwes Kommen von Süden: Jdc 5, Hab 3, Dtn 33 und Ps 68 in ihrem literatur- und theologiegeschichtlichen Umfeld*. Forschungen zur Religion und Literatur des Alten und Neuen Testaments 211. Göttingen: Vandenhoeck & Ruprecht, 2005.

Redditt, Paul L., and Aaron Schart, eds. *Thematic Threads in the Book of the Twelve*. Beihefte zur Zeitschrift für die Alttestamentliche Wissenschaft 325. Berlin: de Gruyter, 2003.

Rendtorff, Rolf. "Alas for the Day! The 'Day of the Lord' in the Book of the Twelve." Pp. 253–64 in *Der Text in seiner Endgestalt. Schritte auf dem Weg zu einer Theologie des Alten Testaments*. Neukirchen-Vluyn: Neukirchener Verlag, 2001. German: Pp. 1–11 in *"Wort JHWHs, das geschah . . ." (Hos 1,1): Studien zum Zwölfprophetenbuch*. Edited by Erich Zenger. Herders Biblische Studien 35. Freiburg im Breisgau: Herder, 2002.

Roth, Martin. *Israel und die Völker im Zwölfprophetenbuch: Eine Untersuchung zu den Büchern Joel, Jona, Micha und Nahum*. Forschungen zur Religion und Literatur des Alten und Neuen Testaments 210. Göttingen: Vandenhoeck & Ruprecht, 2005.

Schart, Aaron. *Die Entstehung des Zwölfprophetenbuchs: Neubearbeitungen von Amos im Rahmen schriftenübergreifender Redaktionsprozesse*. Beihefte zur Zeitschrift für die Alttestamentliche Wissenschaft 260. Berlin: de Gruyter, 1998.

_____ . "Das Zwölfprophetenbuch als redaktionelle Großeinheit." *Theologische Literaturzeitung* 133 (2008): 227–46.

Schwesig, Paul-Gerhard. *Die Rolle der Tag-JHWHs-Dichtungen im Dodekapropheton*. Beihefte zur Zeitschrift für die Alttestamentliche Wissenschaft 366. Berlin: de Gruyter, 2006.

Steck, Odil Hannes. *Der Abschluß der Prophetie im Alten Testament: Ein Versuch zur Frage der Vorgeschichte des Kanons*. Biblisch-Theologische Studien 17. Neukirchen-Vluyn: Neukirchener Verlag, 1991.

_____ . *The Prophetic Books and Their Theological Witness*. Trans. James D. Nogalski. St. Louis: Chalice, 2000. (Trans. from *Die Prophetenbücher und ihr theologisches Zeugnis: Wege der Nachfrage und Fährten zur Antwort.* Tübingen: J.C.B. Mohr [Paul Siebeck], 1996.)

_____ . *Gott in der Zeit entdecken: Die Prophetenbücher des Alten Testaments als Vorbild für Theologie und Kirche.* Biblisch-Theologische Studien 42. Neukirchen-Vluyn: Neukirchener Verlag, 2001.

Sweeney, Marvin A. *The Twelve Prophets.* 2 vols. Berit Olam: Studies in Hebrew Narrative & Poetry. Collegeville, MN: Liturgical, 2000.

Vielhauer, Roman. *Das Werden des Buches Hosea: Eine redaktionsgeschichtliche Untersuchung.* Beihefte zur Zeitschrift für die Alttestamentliche Wissenschaft 349. Berlin: de Gruyter, 2007.

Westermann, Claus. *Prophetic Oracles of Salvation in the Old Testament.* Trans. Keith Crim. Louisville: Westminster/John Knox, 1991. (Trans. of *Prophetische Heilsworte im Alten Testament.* Forschungen zur Religion und Literatur des Alten Testaments 145. Göttingen: Vandenhoeck & Ruprecht, 1987.)

Wöhrle, Jakob. *Die frühen Sammlungen des Zwölfprophetenbuches: Entstehung und Komposition.* Beihefte zur Zeitschrift für die Alttestamentliche Wissenschaft 360. Berlin: de Gruyter, 2006.

_____ . *Der Abschluss des Zwölfprophetenbuches: Buchübergreifende Redaktionsprozesse in den späten Sammlungen.* Beihefte zur Zeitschrift für die Alttestamentliche Wissenschaft 389. Berlin: de Gruyter, 2008.

Daniel

Albertz, Rainer. *Der Gott des Daniel: Untersuchungen zu Daniel 4–6 in der Septuagintafassung sowie zu Komposition und Theologie des aramäischen Danielbuches.* Stuttgarter Bibelstudien 131. Stuttgart: Katholisches Bibelwerk, 1988.

Baumgartner, Walter. "Ein Vierteljahrhundert Daniel-Forschung." *Theologische Rundschau* 11 (1939): 59–83, 125–44, and 201–28.

Berner, Christoph. *Jahre, Jahrwochen und Jubiläen: Heptadische Geschichtskonzeptionen im Antiken Judentum.* Beihefte zur Zeitschrift für die Alttestamentliche Wissenschaft 363. Berlin: de Gruyter, 2006.

Collins, John J. *Daniel: A Commentary on the Book of Daniel.* Hermeneia: A Critical and Historical Commentary on the Bible. Minneapolis: Fortress, 1993.

_____ . "4QPrayer of Nabonid ar (4Q424), 4Qpseudo-Daniel a–c (4Q243–245)". Pp. 83–93, 95–164 + Pl. VI, VII–X in *Qumran Cave 4.XVII.* Discoveries in the Judaean Desert XXII. Oxford: Clarendon, 1996.

_____ . "New Light on the Book of Daniel from the Dead Sea Scrolls." Pp. 180–96 in *Perspectives in the Study of the Old Testament and Early Judaism.* Edited by Florentino García Martínez and Ed Noort. Supplements to Vetus Testamentum 73. Leiden: Brill, 1998.

_____ , and Peter Flint, eds. *The Book of Daniel: Composition and Reception.* Supplements to Vetus Testamentum 83/1–2. Leiden: Brill, 2001.

Helms, Dominik. *Konfliktfelder der Diaspora und die Löwengrube: Zur Eigenart der Erzählung von Daniel in der Löwengrube in der Hebräischen Bibel und der Septuaginta*. Beihefte zur Zeitschrift für die Alttestamentliche Wissenschaft 446. Berlin: de Gruyter, 2014.

Hölscher, Gustav. "Die Entstehung des Buches Daniel." *Theologische Studien und Kritiken* 92 (1919): 113–38.

Koch, Klaus. *Das Buch Daniel*. Erträge der Forschung 144. Darmstadt: Wissenschaftliche Buchgesellschaft, 1980.

_____ , and Martin Rösel. *Polyglottensynopse zum Buch Daniel*. Neukirchen-Vluyn: Neukirchener Verlag, 2000.

Kratz, Reinhard G. *Translatio imperii: Untersuchungen zu den aramäischen Danielerzählungen und ihrem theologiegeschichtlichen Umfeld*. Wissenschaftliche Monographien zum Alten und Neuen Testament 63. Neukirchen-Vluyn: Neukirchener Verlag, 1991.

_____ . "The Visions of Daniel." Pp. 91–113 in *The Book of Daniel: Composition and Reception*. Edited by John J. Collins and Peter Flint. Supplements to Vetus Testamentum 83/1. Leiden: Brill, 2001.

_____ . "From Nabonidus to Cyrus." Pp. 143–56 in *Ideologies as Intercultural Phenomena: Proceedings of the Third Annual Symposium of the Assyrian and Babylonian Intellectual Heritage Project Held in Chicago, USA, October 27–31, 2000*. Melammu Symposia III. Edited by Antonio Panaino and Giovanni Pettinato. Milan: Mimesis, 2002.

_____ . "Nabonid in Qumran." Pp. 253–70 in Babylon: Wissenskultur in Orient und Okzident. Edited by Eva Cancik-Kirschbaum et al. Berlin: de Gruyter, 2011. (= 2011b)

_____ . *Das Judentum im Zeitalter des Zweiten Tempels: Kleine Schriften I*. Forschungen zum Alten Testament 42. Tübingen: Mohr Siebeck 2004; 2nd ed. Tübingen: Mohr Siebeck, 2013.

Meadowcroft, T. J. *Aramaic Daniel and Greek Daniel: A Literary Comparison*. Journal for the Study of the Old Testament Supplement 198. Sheffield: Sheffield Academic Press, 1995.

Newsom, Carol A., with Brennan W. Breed. *Daniel*. The Old Testament Library. Louisville: Westminster John Knox, 2014.

Noth, Martin. "Zur Komposition des Buches Daniel." *Gesammelte Studien zum Alten Testament* II (1969): 11–28.

Segal, Michael. "From Joseph to Daniel: The Literary Development of the Narrative in Daniel 2." *Vetus Testamentum* 59 (2009): 123–49.

Thompson, Henry O. *The Book of Daniel: An Annotated Bibliography*. New York/London: Garland Publishing, 1993.

Woude, Adam S. van der, ed. *The Book of Daniel: In the Light of New Findings*. Bibliotheca Ephemeridum Theologicarum Lovaniensium 106. Leuven: Leuven University Press, 1993.

6. Perspectives for Further Research

When we take stock of the current situation of research on the prophets, we have to start from the following premise: an identity between prophet and prophetic book does not exist. This is the case whether one gives priority to the prophet or to the prophetic book. Likewise, neither the biblical prophet nor the content of the prophetic book can simply be correlated with historical reality. Finally, the prophetic book does not form a unity—whether literary, conceptual, dramatic, or whatever. Within the book we have to differentiate first between the ancient Near Eastern phenomenon of prophecy and the individual biblical traditions. Second, we have to differentiate between older and younger strands of textual and literary tradition in individual books. On this basis current questions about the prophets have arisen that were already addressed in the previous chapters of this book.

*   *   *

(*a*) One of these questions is the relationship between the words of the prophet and the prophetic book. Prophets and prophetesses of the ancient Near East enjoyed confidential communion with the gods and transmitted their messages. These messages were handed down orally or were written down either individually (in letters, inscriptions, or on other materials) or in small collections (Neo-Assyrian prophetic tablets) such that we know them only by archaeological chance. As far as we can see, neither the prophets of the ancient Near East nor their Judean counterparts known from the Lachish letters wrote books.

Against this background, the prophetic books of the Bible and even more the collection of prophetic books pose a conundrum. Scholarship has not yet been successful in determining and explaining the *genre* of the prophetic book. The prophetic book unites oracles addressing specific situations, prophecy masquerading as the words of the prophet but written down at a later stage and composed with the prophetic book in view, as well as narratives about the prophets. The prophetic book, then, presents itself as an entity of lasting significance and validity. However, when all is said and done, we still do not know what we have in front of us when we look at the prophetic books. We do not know what the purpose of the books was, who read them, and how they were used. Above all, we do not know who is responsible for their composition: the prophet himself, his "pupils," or some other anonymous tradents or scribes.

Only the *pesharim* from Qumran, the oldest commentaries on the prophetic books, provide a concrete use of the books from the first century B.C.E. onward. Here, the books are quoted line by line or in sections and then interpreted for the current time and especially in relation to the situation of the Qumran community. All of this reminds us of the book of Ben Sira and the ideal scribe who not only contemplates the Torah but also explores the wisdom of all the ancestors. Thus, he studies the prophecies, the speeches of eminent men as well as the hidden meanings of proverbs and the enigmas found in parables (Sir 39:1ff.). Now, where did such scribes live, where did they study the scrolls, and to whom did they teach their insights? We encounter scribes in the Dead Sea Scrolls. Is it possible that prophetic books were originally composed for study in learned and pious circles like the Qumran community? Are they—rather like proverbial collections—a kind of established part of one's general education or an orientation for insiders such as theologians and pious men?

*   *   *

(b) A further issue is raised by the juxtaposition of prophetic speech and narratives about the prophets in the prophetic books and the remaining biblical tradition. The prophetic books are mostly made up of prophetic speech, but they also contain narratives about the prophets: reports about symbolic actions (Isa 8:1–4), short stories (Amos 7; Isa 7 or Jer 20; 27–28), and even complete narrative cycles (Isa 36–39; Jer 36–45). Conversely, we find in the historical books, especially in the Book of Kings, narratives about prophets but only a few oracles or speeches. If one considers this evidence from a religio-historical perspective, one realizes that—in terms of phenomenology—the narratives in the prophetic and historical books of the Hebrew Bible are much closer to other forms of ancient Near Eastern prophecy than the speeches in the books of the prophets. The biblical prophecies have in common with their ancient Near Eastern counterparts the form of speech but not the content. Conversely, the literary analysis shows that the speeches are often much older and more original than the narratives.

This state of affairs poses great difficulties for the interpretation of the prophets. As a rule, scholars follow the lead of the biblical portrayals and label the prophecy we encounter in the prophetic narratives (of the historical as well as the prophetic books) as "pre-classical." The prophecy of the speeches and oracles in the prophetic books, on the other hand, is described as being "classical" prophecy. In light of the religio-historical comparison as well as the traditio-historical issues that are involved, however, this classification is misleading. What biblical scholarship calls "pre-classical" corresponds on a phenomenological level to the "classical" prophecy of the ancient Near East, while the "classical" prophecy of the Hebrew Bible seems to be the exception to the rule in the ancient Near East. Clearly, we have to reckon with a complex development. It seems that the biblical prophets (in the prophetic speeches) started to depart from the phenomenon of "classic" ancient Near Eastern prophecy in terms of both content and form. Later tradition, however, returned phenomenologically (at least in the narratives) to the old ancient Near Eastern models. At the same time, however, it kept its distance and denounced mantic and magical practices that were inherently part of the phenomenon of ancient Near Eastern prophecy.

To what extent the speeches and narratives date from the historical prophet or are only attributed to him by later tradition is another story. The complex religio-historical and traditio-historical evidence, however, should prevent the exegete from a hasty correlation of one with the other. There is no easy way to construct from such blending a biography of the prophet or the contours of his message.

*   *   *

(*c*) The scholarly agenda continues to be interested in not only the strange juxtaposition of speeches and narratives but also the literary relationship of the oracles and speeches collected in the prophetic books. Form criticism has taught us that the books of the prophets are made up of smaller textual units that very often are introduced as prophetic speeches or words of God. Thus, it can be safely assumed that individual oracles or prophetic sayings form the core of the books. On the other hand, scholarship agrees that we find some sayings, most notably the announcements of salvation (*Heilsweissagungen*), that can also be identified form-critically but do not have an oral prehistory and cannot be traced back to the eponymous prophet. Rather, these sayings were authored by later, anonymous scribes using the name of the prophet and were added to his book. These later oracles, too, insist on being understood as a divine message received by the prophet of the book through God in a mysterious way.

It is the task of scholarship on the prophets to reconstruct the route from the original, oral, and sometimes even written oracles of a prophet to the present prophetic book. Since within this book all the oracles are regarded as the precise words of the eponymous prophet and everything we know about the prophet comes from the book handed down to us in his name, it is difficult to differentiate between original and later, as well as between oral and literary oracles. For this purpose we simply do not have the criteria. Therefore, it is advisable to concentrate the investigation on the literary form of the prophetic book and to begin by differentiating between older and younger texts using literary dependencies and theological tendencies. Each individual case should then be checked for signs of an oral or literary prehistory and whether the text originated in the prophetic praxis or is of a purely literary character. Finally, we have to take into account that an older, formerly independent oracle does not necessarily have to come from the prophet who gave the book its name but may equally derive from another source.

*   *   *

(*d*) Next to the literary-critical analysis, the religio-historical comparison can also be helpful in answering the question of how the prophetic message was transformed into a prophetic book. This, too, is a pressing task of current scholarship. The ancient Near Eastern parallels from Mari, Assyria, and occasionally from the northwest Semitic region show that the communication, recording, and transmission of prophetic sayings was a complex process that took place at certain times and occasions as well as in particular social and political settings. The sources provide us not only with insight into the phenomenon of ancient Near Eastern prophecy and its various manifestations, participants, and contents but also into the transmission of prophetic messages, which very often resulted in changes to the original wording. The prophets themselves, who received a divine message and were instructed to hand it down, were very often illiterate. To record their message they had to use a professional scribe (cf. Jer 36). As a result, the divine disclosure went through several hands before it was quoted (in abbreviated form) as part of a letter, collected on clay tablets and deposited in the royal archive or placed as an inscription on the inner wall of a house. The changes made to a divine message during this process can hardly be determined. Only in few cases are we able to trace these changes in the sources. Whether an oracle was transmitted in oral or written form, the process of interpretation began here.

The potential and the limitations of a religio-historical comparison will have to be carefully considered in future research if we are to arrive at a picture of the prophetic books' origins that is as accurate as possible. This is all the more so if we expand our cultural horizons to include ancient Greece and Rome. Similarities and differences confirm the impression gained from a literary-historical analysis that biblical writings do indeed contain remnants of a prophecy related to the ancient Near Eastern examples. These prophecies originated in a similar milieu and were, at the beginning, handed down in a similar manner.

It is evident, however, that the biblical books follow their own path as far as content and form is concerned. Unlike the ancient Near Eastern parallels, the prophetic books of the Bible develop into a literary genre of their own that was handed down over the centuries and constantly reworked at a literary level. As to their content, they differ from both their ancient Near Eastern parallels and their own historical Israelite-Judean roots. The interpretation and actualization of the original oracles in the course of their transcription and transmission means that they no longer serve to protect or restore the prophet's world but instead seek to overcome this world by an alternative world ruled by God. It is the task of scholarship to distinguish between these two forms of prophecy recorded in the biblical tradition and to offer a historically plausible explanation for their specific traits.

*   *   *

(e) One of these specific traits, and perhaps the most important one, is that the biblical prophets are by their very nature prophets of doom and that they attribute to God the doom they see coming. The unconditional prophecies of judgment are the starting point of the tradition in the prophetic books and are presupposed by the later prophecies of salvation as well as by the prophetic narratives. True, the notion that a deity desires doom and brings it about has parallels in the world of the ancient Near East. Here, too, the disaster suffered by a community can be understood as the result of the wrath of the gods. Interestingly enough, in the ancient Near Eastern texts, such an explanation only happens after the occurrence of the disaster. Its purpose is either to placate the gods and ask them to remove the misery or to anticipate better times and the overcoming of disaster. The biblical books differ here. Doom and salvation always appear in the announcement of the prophet and are yet to come—either in reality or only in the literary fiction.

This issue makes it clear that a religio-historical comparison cannot be done in a sweeping manner or simply phenomenologically, as is often the case. Instead, one has to apply literary and traditio-historical differentiation to the ancient Near Eastern texts as well. In any case, the ancient Near Eastern notion of the "wrath of god" is not typical for ancient Near Eastern prophecy. Nevertheless, it belongs to the common heritage from which biblical prophecy developed. Therefore, one has to clarify what function the ancient Near Eastern concept has within biblical prophecy. While it is indisputable that the biblical announcements of salvation articulate a (still) pending expectation, the ancient Near Eastern parallels pose the question of whether the understanding of doom as God's wrath in the prophetic books goes back to actual pronouncements by the historical prophets or to later interpretations within the scribal tradition. The majority of scholars tend to assume that the oracles of doom in the biblical tradition are genuine prophetic words without offering a plausible religio-historical or historical explanation. Comparison with ancient Near Eastern prophecy demonstrates that the prophets' criticism of their own people, and even their announcement of doom, was usually intended to warn in the name of the deity and not to declare the doom as inevitable. This fact supports the view that biblical pronouncements of doom belong to the later scribal tradition using the form of prophecy.

The important dates that have to be taken into account for this explanation are the catastrophes of 722–720 B.C.E. (the demise of the northern kingdom) and 597/587 B.C.E. (the fall of the southern kingdom). Historically, these events did not leave too many traces because the majority of the survivors who remained in the land overcame the military defeat quickly. On the literary level, however, both events were deeply embedded in the memory of the biblical tradition. As a result, we can safely assume that both dates were the reason why the prophets of the biblical books announced a disaster that belonged to the past to acquaint future generations with the will of God and to warn them of the consequences of ignoring his will. Future scholarship on the prophets will have to consider this possibility seriously or propose an alternative that includes a nuanced religio-historical comparison, as well as considering historical plausibility.

*   *   *

(f) The question of the tradents of the biblical prophetic tradition and their historical context has often been discussed but is still unresolved. The question is so difficult to answer because the biblical tradition has parted from the historical phenomenon of ancient Near Eastern prophecy and—as far as we can see—also from its own roots in Israel and Judah and assumed an independent existence. Historically, the phenomenon of prophecy in Israel and Judah never stopped but continued to exist from Assyrian to Hellenistic-Roman times. This much is clear from individual finds like the ostraca from Lachish and from occasional clues in Jewish and pagan sources. In biblical and related literature (such as the texts from Qumran), however, contemporary prophets or prophetesses are generally stereotyped as "false prophets." For the authors and tradents of this literature the word of God can only be found in the biblical writings. As a result biblical literature becomes the subject of scribal and inspired interpretation. In this way the separation between active prophets and the biblical prophetic tradition of Israel and Judah deepens.

So, who were the tradents of the biblical prophetic tradition, and what was their historical setting? As far as we can see from the sources in the ancient Near East, the recording of prophetic oracles usually took place in close proximity to the royal court or the temple—that is, official institutions—and was carried out by professional scribes. We can assume that the same was true for Israel and Judah. Nevertheless, this may not have been the case for the prophetic books of the Bible, which are mostly opposed to these institutions. The authors responsible for them also came from scribal schools or families where they had received extensive training and had access to archives, but they seem to have left their profession and to have begun participating in the alternative world of prophetic writings and their interpretation.

Scholarship traditionally has had difficulties with classifying the phenomenon of literary prophecy. The biblical fiction of the lonely voice in the wilderness, ignored and despised by king and people, that turns against its own people and institutions (kings, priests, prophets) cannot be taken at face value and projected into history. The biblical presentation was developed further in the popular notion of a prophetic school that faithfully recorded the message of its master and handed it down to later generations. This theory creates more problems than it actually solves. Similar things have to be said about the oft-cited scribal schools with their oral and literary curriculum, since it cannot be shown (and is in fact rather questionable) whether the biblical tradition was ever part of the curriculum of the scribal schools in ancient Israel or Judah.

All explanations work with data from the biblical tradition itself or with cultural-historical analogies from the ancient Near East and, more recently, from Greece. Unfortunately, they disregard the idiosyncrasies of the biblical tradition that do not fit the historical and institutional context. The crucial question, therefore, is: in what circles and institutions did the transition from the prophecy common in the ancient Near East and known from Israel and Judah to biblical prophecy take place? To answer this question, one probably has to spin the same amount of historical fantasy that we find in the common hypotheses of the writing prophet and his "pupils," or the curriculum of the scribal school, or the diverse interest groups of Israelite society—about which we know virtually nothing. With the community of Qumran documented in the Dead Sea Scrolls, we have at least one historical example of an institution that lived outside the common institutions (temple, kingship, or provincial administration) but within the biblical tradition. Perhaps this example can constitute a point of orientation for a historical immagination of the earlier periods. The diverse attestation, use, and dissemination of the prophetic books in Palestine and the Diaspora as well as the diverse Jewish communities and parties have to be taken into account as well.

*   *   *

(*g*) This leads to a last question that should be on the agenda of current research on the prophets: the textual transmission of the biblical prophetic books and their literary and theological reception history. As is well known, the text of the prophetic books of the Bible is transmitted in more than one version. Several of these versions differ considerably from the Masoretic Text. Here we have to compare the ancient versions, especially the Septuagint and the manuscripts from the Dead Sea. The differences are not only significant for textual criticism, because they often demonstrate the fluid boundary between literary and textual history. Consequently, the method of textual criticism no longer simply serves the reconstruction of an (alleged) original or, better, an oldest accessible text, but it also serves the study of the history of interpretation. This history begins with the origin of the text and continues with its transmission. The use of prophetic texts in quotations or exegetical works such as the apocryphal prophetic writings or the *pesharim* from Qumran continues this process more or less seamlessly.

Usually, the transmission of the text and the ancient reception of the prophetic books are treated separately, and this has led to the development of highly specialized branches of scholarship. In light of the professionalization of individual branches of scholarship, there is nothing wrong with this. Such a development, however, has resulted in a lack of interaction between the different branches and, when it does occur, there is a tendency to work with outdated hypotheses from the other scholarly areas. It will be the task of future scholarship to unite the different branches once again and to relate them to each other. Thus, the literary-critical scholar who investigates the development of a biblical book can learn from texual criticism and reception history what a lively, scribal handling of texts looks like and in what direction the tradition tends. The text-critical scholar or the specialist in Dead Sea Scrolls, in turn, can learn from the literary critic at which point within the origin or interpretation of a prophetic book the transmission, translation, or reception begins.

All this requires that we consider the literary history of a prophetic book, as well as its textual tradition and reception in quotations, apocryphal writings, or commentaries, to be part of the same history of interpretation—a history that is based on a comparable hermeneutic and that works with the same or similar methods. If one shares this assumption, it can only be the goal of scholarship to trace the patterns of inner- and extra-biblical interpretation from the beginnings of the prophetic books to the different final versions of the Bible, to trace the shift from textual transmission to ancient Jewish and Christian reception, and thus to reconstruct the genesis and development of a most important part of Jewish (and Christian) tradition.

Chronology

18th century	Old Babylonian Period. *Prophecy from Mari.*
ca. 1000	Emergence of Israel and Judah and their neighboring states. Saul, David, Solomon. *The Egyptian Wenamun encounters an ecstatic at the harbor of Sidon.*
927–907	Jeroboam I establishes the dynastic and cultic independence of the northern kingdom (Israel).
9th/8th century	Assyrian military campaigns in the West. The Syro-Palestinian states offer tribute. Israel and Judah lie between Assyria and Egypt.
880–845	Omride dynasty in Israel. The anti-Assyrian coalition is defeated at the battle of Qarqar (853). *Elisha and Elijah.*
845–747	Jehu dynasty in Israel. Jehu, under pressure from Aram-Damascus, prostrates himself before Shalmaneser III and pays tribute to him.
ca. 800	Zakkur of Hamath defeats an (anti-Assyrian) Aramaic coalition led by Bar-Hadad, son of Hazael, of Damascus. *Seers and Soothsayers predict the victory.*
8th century	*Bil'am of Tell Deir 'Alla.*
747–727	Tiglath-pileser III, king of Assyria, gains ascendancy over Syria–Palestine.
734–732	Aram-Damascus and Israel attack Judah: The "Syro-Ephraimite war." Israel becomes an Assyrian vassal state; Ahaz of Judah bows to Tiglath-pileser III and pays tribute. *Prophets Isaiah, Hosea, and Amos.*
727–722	Shalmaneser V, king of Assyria, conquers Israel and besieges Samaria.
722–705	Sargon II, king of Assyria, conquers Samaria (722); Israel becomes an Assyrian province. End of the northern kingdom followed by anti-Assyrian uprisings in Syria–Palestine. *Beginning of the tradition in Isaiah, Hosea, and Amos.*
705–681	Sennacherib, king of Assyria, conquers Judah and in 701 besieges Jerusalem ruled by Hezekiah. Judah becomes an Assyrian vassal state. *Prophet Micah (1:10–15).*

7th century	*Neo-Assyrian Prophecies for Esarhaddon and Ashurbanipal.*
696–640	Period of peace for Judah under Manasseh, followed by his son Amon.
639–609	King Josiah of Judah. Disengagement from weakening Assyrian (and Egyptian) foreign rule.
612	Fall of Nineveh; end of the Neo-Assyrian Empire. *Prophet Nahum.*
609	Josiah moves against Pharaoh Necho II and is killed at Megiddo. His son Jehoahaz becomes his successor but—at the behest of Egypt—is replaced by Jehoiakim (Eliakim).
605	Battle of Carchemish. Nebuchadnezzar II, king of Babylon, defeats Necho II and gains ascendancy over Syria–Palestine. Anti-Babylonian uprisings and negotiations with Egypt follow. *Prophets Jeremiah, Zephaniah, and the anonymous prophet of Lachish Ostracon No. 3.*
597	Nebuchadnezzar II conquers Jerusalem. King Jehoiachin is deported to Babylon and replaced by Zedekiah (Mattaniah).
587	Nebuchadnezzar II conquers Jerusalem for the second time. The city is leveled to the ground and the temple plundered and destroyed, the population deported. End of the kingdom of Judah. *Beginning of the tradition in Jeremiah, Zephaniah, and Micah.*
6th–3rd century	Israel and Judah between "Babel" and Egypt in Neo-Babylonian, Persian, and Hellenistic times. *Formation and Development of Isaiah, Jeremiah, Ezekiel and the Twelve Prophets.*
539	Cyrus II, king of Persia, conquers Babylon and gains ascendancy over Syria–Palestine. *Beginning of the tradition in Deutero-Isaiah.*
520–515	Rebuilding of the temple in Jerusalem under Darius I. Judah becomes a Persian province. *Prophets Haggai and Zechariah, beginning of the tradition in Haggai, Zechariah, and Malachi.*
465–425	Artaxerxes I dispatches Nehemiah to Judah to restore the walls of Jerusalem. *Prophets in Jerusalem (Neh 6)*
336–323	Alexander the Great begins his world domination (Battle of Issus in 333). Beginning of the Hellenistic Period. Diadochi (Ptolemies and Seleucids) struggle for supremacy over Syria–Palestine. *Trito-Isaiah, Deutero-Zechariah (chap. 9–14), and Aramaic Daniel.*

301	Battle at Ipsus. Palestine is ruled by the Ptolemies (Egypt).
198	Battle of Paneas. Palestine is ruled by the Seleucids ("Assur," "Babel").
2nd century	Translation of the prophetic books into Greek (Septuagint).
	The Book of Ben Sira (in Hebrew ca. 190; after 132 in Greek) attests to the *prophetic corpus and "Torah and Prophets" as parts of the canon.*
	Foundation of the *community of Qumran.* Manuscripts of almost all books of the Hebrew canon. Only the Isaiah Scroll is completely preserved.
169–167	Antiochus IV initiates a cult reform in Jerusalem.
166–164	Maccabean revolt. Reversal of the cult reform. Purification and rededication of the temple. *Visions of Daniel.*
after 160	Hasmoneans and Hasmonean kingship. Writing of the Qumran community *rules (1QS, CD);* from 100 onward a growing number of *exegetical works (pesharim).*
63	Pompey conquers Jerusalem. Beginning of Roman rule in Syria–Palestine.
66–74 C.E.	First Jewish revolt. The settlement at Khirbet Qumran is destroyed.
70	Titus conquers Jerusalem and destroys the Second Temple.
since 100	The Septuagint becomes the Bible of Christianity. Fixing of the Hebrew canon.
132–134	Second Jewish revolt (Bar Kokhba).

Index of Authors

Index of Scripture

New Testament

Apocrypha and Pseudepigrapha

Index of Other Ancient Sources

Dead Sea Scrolls (Qumran)

Classical, Jewish, and Christian Authors